MARC BEUSTER

THE HIDDEN EAGLE

THE EAGLE SAGA - SONS OF ROME - BOOK II

Copyright © 2025 by Marc Beuster

All rights reserved. No part of this publication may be reproduced, stored or transmitted in any form or by any means, electronic, mechanical, photocopying, recording, scanning, or otherwise without written permission from the publisher. It is illegal to copy this book, post it to a website, or distribute it by any other means without permission.

This novel is entirely a work of fiction. The names, characters and incidents portrayed in it are the work of the author's imagination. Any resemblance to actual persons, living or dead, events or localities is entirely coincidental.

Designations used by companies to distinguish their products are often claimed as trademarks. All brand names and product names used in this book and on its cover are trade names, service marks, trademarks and registered trademarks of their respective owners. The publishers and the book are not associated with any product or vendor mentioned in this book. None of the companies referenced within the book have endorsed the book.

Impressum / Contact:

Marc Beuster — Erlenweg 4 – 24598 Boostedt — Germany

Email: Marc.Beuster@icloud.com

First edition

Contents

Foreword v
Acknowledgments vi
Prologue vii
I. Fog Over Britannia 1
II. The Price of Discipline 6
III. Sparks of Rebellion 15
IV. Masks of Ambition 23
V. Between Two Fronts 33
VI. Scouts in the Fog 41
VII. Foreign Allies 48
VIII. Path Through the Marsh 56
IX. Signs of Fire 65
X. The Ambush 73
XI. Blood in the Fern 81
XII. Flight Through the Woods 88
XIII. In Chains 97
XIV. The Blood Priest 103
XV. In the King's Presence 110
XVI. An Old Debt 118
XVII. Paths of the Night 126
XVIII. Separate Ways 132
XIX. Before the Storm 143
XX. The King's Wrath 153
XXI. Walls and Memories 162

XXII. Moves in the Shadows	172
XXIII. The Price of Haste	180
XXIV. Waiting and Longing	186
XXV. Shadows of Doubt	197
XXVI. The Call of Ancestors	204
XXVII. The Assault	212
XXVIII. The Blood Price	219
XXIX. Blades in the Rain	224
XXX. The Breaking Point	230
XXXI. Between Mistrust and Unity	235
XXXII. In Uneasy Anticipation	241
XXXIII. Night and Fog	249
XXXIV. The Aftermath	257
XXXV. Caratacus's Gamble	262
XXXVI. Locked Out	266
XXXVII. Hours of Decision	273
XXXVIII. The Eagle Against the Wolf	279
XXXIX. The Eagle on the Hill	285
XL. The Might of Rome	290
XLI. Council of Victors and Shadows of Doubt	302
XXXXII. Waiting	308
XLIII. Homecoming	313
XLIV. The Shadows of the Past	318
XLV. Brothers in Spirit	326
About the Author	333
Also by Marc Beuster	334

Foreword

I am an avid fan of historical stories where past and fantasy merge into gripping adventures. This passion led me, **a new author**, to embark on a personal journey, one that finds its expression in this first book. This work marks my entry into the world of writing. It is also intended to be the start of a series of novels where ancient times meet new, imagined adventures.

My dedication to historical tales was the driving force behind writing this book. I hope, dear readers, to draw you into its spell, just as the works of other authors once captivated me. May this story transport you to distant times and bring you joy.

I invite you to immerse yourselves in this world with me – a world where fact and fiction are wondrously interwoven.

As a new author, your feedback means the world to me. If you enjoyed this journey, I would be deeply grateful if you considered leaving a review or star rating on Amazon—it truly helps other readers find the book.

Yours,
Marc Beuster

Acknowledgments

Prologue

Rome, 43 AD.

The air in the small chamber deep within the Palatine hung heavy and still. Only the soft rustle of parchment and the distant, muffled echo of the capital's bustling life broke the silence. Tiberius Claudius Narcissus, freedman and, through his closeness to Emperor Claudius, one of the most powerful men in Rome, bent over a collection of secret reports. His face, usually a mask of impenetrable calm, showed a flicker of focused tension. His dark eyes scanned line after line, analyzing every word, carefully weighing each piece of information.

Ever since returning from Britannia, the name had haunted him: Gaius Julius Maximus. Young, disciplined, educated, and brave. *Too* brave. He had saved the Emperor, fighting his way through hordes of Britons with his cohort. Claudius had found it dramatic, almost theatrical. Narcissus, however, observed. Something about the boy was wrong—or rather, too perfect.

The official records were thin. Origins unclear, father unknown, mother deceased. A few lines in Roman script, nothing more. No sources, no witnesses. Just a name, entered in conspicuously clean ink. He dispatched his agents—those who knew how to open archives without leaving a trace.

The trail led to an old town house near Capua, destroyed

in the last fire. Coincidence? Intentional? Then to a country estate once belonging to a certain Livia Domitia. She possessed a flawless pedigree but had vanished strangely during the years of Tiberius's seclusion on Capri. Finally, they found an old, faded entry in a private register of *Alimenta* payments: Julius Maximus.

No father was named, but an amount had been deposited usually reserved only for children of high birth. The entry bore a second, barely visible seal—the mark of one of the old administrators of the imperial household. He nodded and unrolled another report, an intercepted letter whose seal matched the administrator's. This man had also managed the estate on Capri, and the letter was addressed to an old-school senator in Rome. The content was trivial, daily business, except for one casual mention:

"...the young Maximus, in his manner, bears a striking resemblance to old Prosonius, may the gods be merciful to his soul... It's rumored his mother was not entirely untouched by imperial blood, a forgotten dalliance of Tiberius, perhaps? But those are likely just latrine rumors..."

The truth did not impose itself but seeped through like ink on papyrus. Maximus was not an unknown, but a mistake that had survived. A shadow, grown in secret.

Narcissus froze. A name from the past, linked to rumors of an illegitimate daughter of Tiberius. He had always dismissed these old stories as nonsense, gossip among the Roman elite. But here it was, in black and white, even if dismissed as a rumor. Maximus... grandson of Emperor Tiberius?

A slow, cold smile spread across Narcissus's lips. This changed everything. A possible heir with imperial blood, serving secretly in a distant province? An uncontrollable variable. A potential threat to the stability he and Claudius were striving so hard to maintain. Or... a weapon?

He carefully rolled up the parchment. His thoughts raced, forging plans, weighing options. Vespasian surely knew, that old fox. Was he withholding this information? Protecting the boy? Or using him for his own ends?

Narcissus stood and walked to the window. He looked out at Rome by night, the vast, pulsating heart of the Empire. Power was a dangerous game, and information was the most valuable piece on the board.

"Maximus, Tribune of the Second Legion... grandson of Tiberius," Narcissus murmured the words softly, testing their sound. A secret of this magnitude could shake empires.

He locked the parchment away in a heavy chest. Then he stepped to the window again. The rain had intensified. In the distance, the city blinked—vast, sated, and sleepy. Narcissus gazed out, wondering what destiny the gods held for Maximus.

I. Fog Over Britannia

Several months had passed since the bloody battle on the Medway. The wounds of the Second Legion Augusta healed slowly. It was a painful process, leaving scars on body and soul. Autumn cast a cool, damp veil over the conquered lands south of the Tamesis. Its clammy embrace seemed to seep into the legionaries' very bones. Morning fog swirled from the dense, ancient forests and across the rolling hills, upon which newly built Roman forts and outposts perched like sentinels in a hostile world.

Maximus stood on the timber rampart of a small outpost. It lay several days' march west, somewhere between Camulodunum and Rutupiae—the port town that also served as the main base for the Second Legion Augusta. The damp air bit at his lungs. Each breath was a struggle against the pervasive dampness. The scar on his neck pulled uncomfortably tight, reminding him of the spear thrust that had missed killing him by a hair's breadth. The wound was a constant, itching reminder of his mortality. He was officially fit for duty again, but his full-strength and easy vitality had yet to return. A deep exhaustion clung to him like the mud on his boots, an exhaustion that was more than just physical. Maximus rubbed his eyes, trying to banish the images that haunted his restless nights.

He was young, a Tribune, but war aged a man quickly. It gnawed at the soul until a man barely recognized himself.

Beside him stood Brutus, his sturdy frame like an old, weather-beaten rock in the misty dawn. The hardships had not left him untouched, either. The Centurion surveyed the surroundings with the unwavering vigilance of a man who had spent many years on the bloody frontiers of the Empire. His expression was grim, almost gaunt. In the pale light, the scars on his face—testament to countless battles—seemed deeper, darker than usual. There was a certain emptiness in his eyes; he had learned to hide the pain behind a wall of Stoic calm.

"Still quiet," Brutus finally observed, his voice a low rumble. "Too quiet for my liking."

Maximus nodded, pulling the collar of his cloak tighter. "Caratacus is like a ghost. He strikes and vanishes back into the forests. Plautius hunts him in the north, but here in the south… it's a different kind of war. One that wears us down." He thought of the constant small raids on supply columns, the patrols that vanished without a trace, the faces of the young recruits who flinched at every snap of a twig. The victories at the Medway and Camulodunum had come at a high price, a blood toll that had thinned the ranks and marked the survivors. The peace here was an illusion, a deceptive veil as thin as the morning fog.

"Ambushes," Brutus grunted contemptuously. "Cowardly tactics. They avoid open battle because they know they're no match for us there." His voice held the frustration of a veteran soldier who preferred direct combat, the clear clash of steel on steel.

I. FOG OVER BRITANNIA

"But they're effective," Maximus countered thoughtfully, though the words came hard. He felt Brutus's gaze on him, the look of a mentor perhaps still testing the young Tribune. "They know this land. Every path, every marsh, every dense forest is their ally. We secure the roads and the rivers, but the land in between still belongs to them. We are strangers here, Brutus. Invaders."

They were currently securing this very outpost—a small, almost forlorn collection of rough timber buildings and palisades guarding a vital supply route. It was arduous, grinding work in a land that did not welcome them. The men were tired, their faces gray beneath a patina of grime and exhaustion. Losses had torn gaps that hadn't yet been filled; every cohort was understrength, every task seemed to demand more effort.

"How are the men?" Maximus asked. His gaze swept over the few sentries huddled on the palisades against the cold. He felt the weight of responsibility settle heavily upon him— responsibility for their lives, their morale.

"They're holding on," Brutus replied, without much conviction. "They're legionaries. But morale…" He sighed deeply, a sound like the grinding of stones. "They need a victory, Sir. A real, tangible victory. Something to show them their sacrifices weren't in vain." His gaze grew distant. "The deaths of their comrades weigh heavily on them. On all of us."

Maximus placed a hand on his friend and mentor's shoulder. The gesture felt familiar; the initial distance between the young Tribune and the veteran Centurion had long since given way to a deep camaraderie, forged in the hellfire of battle. "I know, Brutus. Their sacrifices were not in vain. We honor them by doing our duty." He tried to inject a confidence into his voice that he didn't always feel himself.

Brutus nodded slowly, but the worry lines on his forehead remained, deep furrows in his weathered face. "'Duty,'" he repeated the word softly, almost bitterly. "Sometimes I wonder who we truly serve."

Maximus understood the unspoken question only too well. The arrival of Emperor Claudius in Camulodunum, his absurd, inflated 'Triumph,' and the disturbing rumors of political purges and intrigue back in Rome gnawed at the loyalty of many veteran soldiers. They risked their lives for an ideal betrayed by many of those in power.

Added to this was Maximus's own dangerous secret: he still hadn't confided the truth about his origins to Brutus, his closest confidant. This secret weighed on him like a second suit of armor, cold and heavy. The fear of the consequences should it be revealed was greater than his fear of the enemy. Would Brutus despise him? Would he see him as a threat?

"We serve Rome, Brutus," Maximus said quietly, but with a firmness, he had to force. "And we serve each other." That last part was the only truth he could truly cling to.

Before Brutus could reply, Optio Decimus approached. His usually cheerful face had grown serious and dutiful; Maximus could see the weariness in his eyes, too.

"Sir! Report from the eastern patrol. They've found fresh tracks—a large group, possibly warriors, moving west."

Maximus and Brutus exchanged a brief, meaningful glance. The underlying tension, the talk of morale and doubt—all of it was swept away by the sudden, tangible threat.

"Double the sentries! Brutus, have the men stand to. We must be ready," Maximus commanded, his voice suddenly clear and authoritative again. The Tribune had overcome the doubting young man.

The dawn slowly yielded to a gray, dreary morning, but the threat lurking in the fog only seemed to grow denser, colder.

II. The Price of Discipline

Under the gray sky, the outpost buzzed like a disturbed hornets' nest. News of the sighted Celtic group—heavily laden and moving with purpose—had spread like wildfire, reaching the sodden ranks of the garrison.

Initial weariness gave way to feverish activity. Weariness had been a tenacious companion during the endless watches and patrols in this inhospitable land. Legionaries hurried through the sodden mud that had turned the parade ground and the paths between tents and roughly built barracks into a miry trap. Their hobnailed boots left deep, sucking prints, the clang of metal mixing with the squelch of boots pulled from the mire.

Armor was strapped tight, straps pulled until they bit into leather. The rhythmic rasp of *gladii* on whetstones sounded sharp and ominous in the damp air. Dull thuds echoed as heavy *pila* were handled, each spear holding a silent promise of deadly precision. Cold smoke from hastily rekindled fires mingled with the pungent aroma of wet leather, oiled metal, and the sour reek of human sweat under wool and iron. This was the scent of the legion on the verge of battle, a mix of fear and determination.

II. THE PRICE OF DISCIPLINE

At the center of this controlled chaos, Brutus stood like a steadfast rock in a turbulent sea. His mere presence, the sheer force of his physicality, seemed to have a calming effect on the men of his century and beyond. His expression was as unforgiving as the gray granite of the Apennines. Methodically, he moved through the ranks, a walking embodiment of military perfection. His experienced gaze, honed by decades on the Empire's bloody frontiers, checked every strap, every buckle, the correct fit of every helmet on tense faces. He spoke little; the time for long speeches was over. His curt commands—"Tighter, soldier! That strap won't last three steps!" or "Your *scutum* hangs too low—are you offering the enemy your chest?"—and his corrective gestures were precise and unmistakable. He knew his men, not just their names and ranks, but their fears, their hopes, their breaking points. He knew that in the coming confrontation, whether an ambush or the prelude to something larger, any carelessness could mean the difference between life and death.

"Decimus!" he called out to one of his Optios. The stocky Gaul with the weather-beaten face was trying to help a young recruit secure his complicated *Lorica Segmentata*, but the lad's hands trembled with nerves. "Ensure the *pila* points are clean and sharp! I don't want to see a weapon glance off an enemy's shield uselessly because of rust or dirt!"

"Yes, Centurion!" Decimus replied with a curt nod, without pausing his work on the trembling recruit. "Sagittarius, hold still, damn you! Or I'll strap you in backwards!"

Maximus observed the scene from the slightly raised platform before the small *praetorium*, the command tent that was barely more than a large hut. He had just given the final instructions to the ten cavalrymen of the reconnaissance patrol. These swift, experienced men, drawn from Vespasian's own guard, had been detailed for such tasks. The fog, still clinging stubbornly in the valleys, now swallowed them. Maximus bent back over the rough map of the surrounding area, spread out on a makeshift table of raw planks. His fingers traced the marked paths and watercourses, his mind trying to anticipate the Celts' possible routes and intentions: Warriors with carts. That was unusual. Smugglers? Raiders on their way back? Or something more serious, a vanguard for a siege? Were they trying to build a bridge over one of the smaller rivers further west to move their forces more quickly?

Maximus watched Brutus's efficiency, his natural, almost instinctive authority, and the way the men reacted to him—a complex blend of profound respect, camaraderie, and a healthy dose of fear of his legendary temper. It was the authority of the battlefield, born of shared dangers and countless crises survived. Despite his own high rank as Tribune, his classical education, and his growing experience, Maximus still had to learn this raw, immediate form of command. His own command was based on rank and strategic thinking. Brutus's came from the gut, from the heart of the legion. He felt the weight of responsibility on his shoulders, not just for the men under his direct command, but for the entire outpost, for this small, exposed spearhead of Rome in hostile territory.

Suddenly, a loud, angry shout shattered the tense concentration, followed by a dull thud and the ugly sound of metal striking bone. The noise came from the Fourth Century's area, a unit heavily depleted by recent battles and only lately filled out with replacements from various parts of Gaul. Their cohesion was still fragile, discipline less ingrained than in the veteran centuries. Alarmed, Maximus looked up, his hand instinctively going to the hilt of his *gladius*. Brutus froze mid-motion, as if stung by a scorpion. His head snapped around, blue eyes narrowing to dangerous slits.

In the midst of the camp, an ugly knot of men had formed. Fists flew, curses in various dialects merging into an angry roar. Two legionaries grappled in the ankle-deep mud, their armor hindering them more than protecting. One was Cotta, a lean, wiry veteran with a scarred face and weary eyes; the other Valerius, a younger, burlier recruit from Aquitania. Other soldiers stood around. Some made half-hearted attempts to separate the fighters, but most seemed to watch the spectacle with a mixture of amusement and vicious curiosity. A few even shouted encouragement.

"By Jupiter's reeking beard, what is this pigsty?" Brutus growled, his voice a dangerous rumble that held more menace than any shout. He didn't hesitate. Like a boar crashing through undergrowth, he forged a path through the gawking soldiers, who stepped aside quickly in awe and fear. No one wanted to be unnecessarily close to the Centurion's wrath.

"Make way! Break it up, you maggots!" his voice thundered over the din, a force of nature that made the air tremble and carried unmistakable authority. The sheer power of the command made the fighters pause, their faces contorted with exertion and fury. Brutus roughly grabbed the two brawlers by their shoulder plates. Filthy, panting, and bleeding, they stood there as he ripped them apart with raw strength as if they were disobedient children, setting them side-by-side and surveying them from head to toe. Cotta, the veteran, had surely served under Germanicus and was known for his toughness, but also for a growing bitterness after countless campaigns. Valerius, the young recruit, had a fiery gaze and a defiantly jutting jaw that spoke of youthful impetuosity.

"What in the goddamned hells is this, Cotta, Valerius?" Brutus barked, his face inches from the veteran's. The smell of sweat and mud hung between them. "We're facing a possible attack, maybe within the hour, and you're brawling like washerwomen in the slave market over the last rotten cabbage? Have you lost your minds?"

Cotta spat a mixture of blood and mud onto the ground, his eyes still flashing with anger. "This snot-nosed brat, Centurion! This Gallic pup from Aquitania!" He pointed a trembling finger at Valerius. "He called me a coward! In front of all our comrades! Said I was afraid of a few Celts in the fog! Me, who fought Suebi and Cherusci when this milk-drinker was still on his mother's tit! He has no idea what awaits us here, how fast this can end!"

Young Valerius, whose lip was swollen and bleeding, his breath coming fast, retorted just as angrily, though with a hint of uncertainty in the face of Brutus's presence: "He said we're all running blindly to our doom! That the officers—that *you*—are throwing our lives away needlessly! That we stand no chance against the hordes out there! He was undermining morale, Centurion! Poisoning the new men's ears, telling horror stories of lost battles!"

A dangerous murmur went through the surrounding men of the Fourth Century, who now shifted uneasily. The accusations hung heavy in the air. Fear and doubt, fed by Cotta's words and the uncertainty of the situation, festered like poisonous weeds beneath the surface of military discipline, threatening now to erupt and consume the unit's cohesion. Exactly what they could least afford at this critical moment.

II. THE PRICE OF DISCIPLINE

Brutus sensed the situation tipping.

His gaze turned icy, his voice losing all warmth. He released the two men, but his stance radiated extreme, barely controlled tension. "Fear?" His voice was dangerously quiet again, but each word cut like a knife through the tense silence. "Every man here has the right to be afraid. Anyone who isn't afraid, facing what might await us, is either a liar or a fool. We'd all be fools not to be afraid." He looked around, his gaze locking onto each man in turn. "But!" His voice rose again. "No man in this legion, by Jupiter, *no man* has the right to show his fear through cowardice, through mutiny, or by undermining the morale of his comrades! Keep your fear to yourself, or share it with the gods, but don't you vomit it at your brothers' feet!"

He took a step back, his chest rising and falling heavily. He surveyed the assembled men of the Fourth Century, his eyes seeming to pierce each one. "Listen to me, all of you! You are not some rabble thrown together! You are soldiers of the Second Legion, Augusta! You carry the Eagle on your standard!" He gestured towards the Legion's symbol. "We've fought Germans who tear out trees with their bare hands and stand twice your height, Valerius! We've crossed deserts where the sun bleaches your bones and climbed mountains where the ice wind rips the flesh from your cheeks! We have bled, sweated, and conquered for Rome! We are Romans! We are the wall against which the barbarians break!"

He paused dramatically, letting the words echo in the silence. Only the patter of rain and the distant hammering from the forge could be heard. The mood began to shift. Heads lifted, shoulders straightened.

His gaze fell again on the two brawlers, who now stood with

heads bowed. "Cotta," he said, his voice calmer now but still stern. "You're a veteran. You've seen more battles than this boy has hairs on his balls. You should know the taste of fear, but you should also know when to hold your tongue. Falling for a greenhorn's stupid provocations is unworthy of your experience. You should be an example, not a troublemaker." He turned to Valerius. "And you, recruit! Your courage is commendable, but it's misguided and undisciplined. If you ever again, by all the gods of Gaul, question the orders of your superiors or the courage of your comrades—or lay a hand on a comrade—I will have you tied to the nearest tree and flogged until you cannot stand, and your own mother wouldn't recognize you! Is that perfectly and unequivocally clear?"

Both men mumbled a barely audible "Yes, Centurion," their earlier anger replaced by shame and fear of the threatened punishment.

"I didn't hear you!" Brutus suddenly bellowed again. The pent-up tension and fury over this needless disruption erupted in a single, deafening roar that startled even the horses at the far end of the camp.

"YES, CENTURION!" shouted the two men and a large portion of the onlookers, as if with one voice.

"Good." Brutus's expression relaxed fractionally, but his eyes remained hard. "Now pick up your damned gear and fall in! And mark my words, both of you: the next Celt who gets too close feels your anger, not your comrade! You will fight side-by-side, and if one falls, the other picks him up! Understood?"

"Yes, Centurion!"

He turned abruptly, without another word. "Rufus!" he

II. THE PRICE OF DISCIPLINE

called to the Optio in charge of the Fourth Century, who saluted with relief. "I want these two heroes in the front rank when we move out. Right next to each other. And after the battle, no matter the outcome, they report to me for latrine duty—for a full week! Let them discuss their differences there!"

"Sir!" the Optio replied, visibly glad the situation had been brought under control without further bloodshed.

Several hours after the incident, Brutus walked back to Maximus, who had watched the entire scene with a mixture of concern and quiet approval. He hadn't intervened, knowing this was Brutus's territory, his way of maintaining the iron discipline that was the legion's foundation. He had to admit, though the methods were harsh, almost brutal, they were undoubtedly effective. The budding unrest, the poison of doubt and fear, had been stamped out before it could spread. Order was restored.

"Well handled, Brutus," Maximus said quietly, as the Centurion stood beside him on the platform.

Brutus merely shrugged his broad shoulders, his gaze scanning the now disciplined ranks of his own century forming up again. "Discipline is the backbone, Sir." His voice was calmer now. "If it breaks, everything breaks. Especially out here, so far from Rome." He inconspicuously rubbed his knuckles, still slightly sore from gripping the soldiers' armor. "But sometimes," he added after a pause, almost wistfully, "I wish it were simpler… that the men would just… obey without the need for shouting."

"Nothing is simple here, Brutus," Maximus replied, his gaze meeting the older man's. "That's why we're here. To do the hard things." He glanced at the map on the table, then back towards the horizon. "The riders should be back soon. Then we'll know what the rest of today holds."

Just as he spoke the words, the shrill, clear sound of a signal horn cut through the damp morning air—the triple blast from the watchtower at the west gate, the agreed signal for the scouts' return. Every head in the camp turned towards the sound as if on command. Even the smiths' hammers fell silent for a moment. Maximus and Brutus exchanged a brief, meaningful look. The internal disorder was settled. Now, their full attention turned back to the threat waiting beyond the protective palisades, shrouded in fog. The real fight might be imminent. The legionaries' faces were focused again, ranks closed, weapons ready.

III. Sparks of Rebellion

The cold, damp grip of the morning fog seemed to envelop the small outpost. Ten cavalrymen of the reconnaissance patrol trotted through the hastily opened west gate, their horses steaming in the cool air, mouths lightly flecked with foam. Mud splashed high from their hooves. The riders' faces were tense, their eyes watchful, their damp leather and mail armor speckled with mud and pine needles. Decurio Marcus Aelius led them, an experienced cavalryman from Vespasian's own guard, his angular face beneath his helmet etched with grim concentration.

Maximus and Brutus had already descended from the *praetorium*'s platform to meet them. Now they stood near the gate, ready to receive the report. Around them, the legionaries had briefly paused their work. Only the snorting of the horses and the soft jingle of the riders' equipment broke the silence. All eyes were fixed on the returning scouts.

Decurio Aelius swung himself from the saddle with practiced ease, landing lightly on the muddy ground. He stepped before Maximus and Brutus, saluting with a hand to his helmet. "Sir, we have returned," he said, his voice rough but steady.

"Report, Decurio," Maximus ordered, his voice calm, though tension was evident in his stance. He stepped closer, his gaze fixed on the cavalryman.

Aelius took a deep breath. "We picked up the trail, Sir. It leads clearly west, along the old Celtic trade path that winds through the forests. The signs are unmistakable: heavy carts, drawn by oxen, accompanied by a considerable number of warriors on foot."

"How considerable?" Brutus asked, his voice a low rumble.

The Decurio hesitated a moment, wiping a bead of sweat mixed with rainwater from his forehead. "Hard to say precisely, Centurion, without seeing them directly. We followed orders and didn't ride too close. But the width of the trail, the number of footprints… we estimate at least three to four hundred men, maybe more. They're moving slowly, but purposefully."

Maximus exchanged a quick glance with Brutus. Three to four hundred warriors and carts. This was no mere raiding party. It was an organized force. "Did you see what they were transporting? Weapons? Siege equipment?"

"No, Sir," Aelius replied. "We couldn't identify the cargo. The carts were covered with tarpaulins. But they were sunk deep; the load must be heavy. It could be supplies, but… it could be other things." The unspoken possibility of dismantled siege engines or heavy weaponry hung in the air.

"Could you determine their destination?" Maximus pressed, his mind racing.

"They're following the path west, Sir. If they stay on that route, it leads directly towards the larger fort near Durovernum Cantiacorum, about two days' march from here."

III. SPARKS OF REBELLION

The Decurio paused. "Alternatively, they could turn south, deeper into our secured territory, threatening our supply lines. Perhaps even trying to reach Rutupiae, though that would be a long march."

Rutupiae. The main supply port. An attack there would be catastrophic. Maximus felt a cold knot form in his stomach. Was this Caratacus's plan? A diversion in the north while a second force attempted to cut their lifeline? He pushed the thought aside. Speculation wouldn't help now.

"Any sign of other groups? Scouts?" Brutus wanted to know.

"We saw tracks of lone riders moving off the main path," Aelius reported. "Likely their own reconnaissance. They seem cautious, perhaps aware we're in the area."

"Well done, Decurio," Maximus said appreciatively. "You've done your duty. See that your men and horses are cared for. Hold yourselves ready."

"Yes, Sir!" Aelius saluted again, turned, and led his exhausted men and horses towards the makeshift stables.

The Decurio's words still echoed in the damp morning air as Maximus and Brutus absorbed the report's implications. Three to four hundred Celts, ready for battle, were traveling with heavy carts on a path that took them dangerously close to the Roman supply line or the weakly garrisoned fort at Durovernum. This wasn't a random band of looters; it was a calculated maneuver, a plan designed to strike a painful blow against the Roman presence in the south.

Brutus spoke immediately. "They must be stopped." His voice rumbled deeply, his fist clenching around the hilt of his *gladius*. "We cannot allow them to reach Durovernum or threaten our supply routes. That puts a knife to our throat."

Maximus nodded in agreement, his strategic mind already working at high speed. He stepped back to the makeshift map table he had left moments before. His finger traced the marked path, searching for suitable ambush locations. "You're right, Brutus. Here," he tapped a marked spot, "the ford near the old oak wood. The path narrows there, the forest crowds close on both sides, the bank is marshy. Perfect for bogging down their carts in the mud and then hitting them from the flanks."

"A classic ambush," Brutus agreed with grim satisfaction. "Give me the Second Century, Sir. We'll ride out to meet them, lie in wait. As soon as their vanguard crosses the ford and the carts are in the bottleneck, we strike. We block the path, catch them in a pincer." His eyes flashed at the prospect of teaching the enemy a sharp lesson.

"Varro and Felix with the First and Third could then support us from the rear, cut off their retreat," Maximus added, already mentally mapping out the necessary troop movements. "The Fourth and Fifth secure the post here…"

But before he could elaborate further, the sound of a single, rapidly galloping horse tore him from his thoughts. A rider charged through the still-open west gate, almost ignoring the startled guards. He wore the insignia of an official messenger from the legion command. His cloak was soaked and crusted with mud from his journey; his horse wheezed, flecked with foam. The man leaped from the saddle before the animal had fully stopped, nearly stumbling in the deep mud but regaining his balance. He hurried towards Maximus and Brutus, clutching a sealed parchment scroll tightly in his hand.

"Tribune Maximus, Sir! Urgent dispatch from Legate Vespasian!" the messenger panted, holding the scroll out to

III. SPARKS OF REBELLION

Maximus, his chest heaving.

A sudden, inexplicable foreboding, cold and unpleasant, crept over Maximus. He took the scroll, noting Vespasian's intact but hastily applied seal. With steady hands, despite his inner turmoil, he broke it. He unrolled the parchment, his eyes scanning the terse lines written in the Legate's familiar, precise military hand.

> To Tribune Gaius Julius Maximus, Commander, Outpost Secundus.
>
> Secret message arrived from Rome. Your immediate presence required in Rutupiae. Important strategic meeting brooks no delay.
>
> Order: Transfer command of the outpost to the senior remaining Centurion. Depart immediately for Rutupiae with your personal escort and Centurion Brutus.
>
> Further instructions upon arrival.
>
> Utmost haste required.
>
> Signed, Titus Flavius Vespasianus, Legatus.

Maximus read the message twice, then a third time, as if unable to grasp its content. *Immediate presence required? Important strategic meeting?* What could be more important than the imminent threat of four hundred Celts with heavy carts marching towards their lifeline? The order made no mention of the local danger. Vespasian wouldn't have received his reports yet, of course. *Secret message from Rome...* That sounded ominous.

He looked up, meeting Brutus's questioning, impatient gaze. Wordlessly, he handed the parchment to the Centurion.

Brutus scanned the lines, his eyebrows drawing together into a thick bar, his expression darkening progressively. A low growl escaped his throat as he finished. He handed the scroll back, his gaze hard, almost accusatory.

"Immediately to Rutupiae," Brutus said tonelessly, each word seeming difficult to utter. "With you and your escort. And what about the damned Celts who are about to tear us a new asshole out here? What about the threat to Durovernum? What about our damned duty *here*? Are we just supposed to ignore them? Leave Varro and the others here alone while we rush off to the Legate for some 'important meeting'?" The bitterness and disbelief in his voice were unmistakable.

The question hung between them like a heavy, wet blanket. Maximus felt the eyes of the surrounding officers and soldiers, who sensed the tension even if they didn't know the order's content. This was the moment of truth, caught between conflicting priorities, between the immediate, tangible danger and a vague but urgent command from the highest authority.

Obedience. That was the first virtue of a Roman soldier. An order was an order, especially one from a Legate like Vespasian, a man to whom he owed not only loyalty but personal gratitude. Vespasian had mentored him, protected him, trusted him. To disobey this order would be more than insubordination; it would be a betrayal of trust.

But Brutus was right. The danger here was real, immediate. The Celts with the carts posed a serious threat. Simply letting them pass would be negligent, potentially catastrophic. His duty as commander of this post, his responsibility for the men here and the security of this sector, weighed heavily.

"The order is clear, Brutus," Maximus said slowly, forcing himself to remain calm though his insides were churning.

"We are to leave for Rutupiae at once. Vespasian wouldn't have issued this command unless it was absolutely necessary. The situation must be more serious than we realize. Perhaps Caratacus isn't as far north as we think. Perhaps Rutupiae itself is in danger."

"Or perhaps the Legate sits too far from the action!" Brutus retorted, his anger barely suppressed. "Perhaps he sees only his maps and his couriers, not the damned mud and blood here! We have an immediate threat, Sir! One we can eliminate *now*! If we leave, we give them free rein! What's more important—an unclear 'meeting' or the defense of our position and our men?"

"It is not an 'unclear meeting,' Brutus, it is a direct order from the Legate!" Maximus countered sharply, the authority of his rank now clear in his voice. "We are soldiers of Rome. We obey orders. That is what separates us from the barbarians!" He saw the flicker of hurt in Brutus's eyes, knew he had just crossed a line, but he couldn't back down. The hierarchy had to be maintained, especially now.

Brutus visibly swallowed, his jaw working. He pressed his lips together, as if holding back a flood of further angry words. After a long, tense moment, he gave a stiff nod. "As you command, Sir." His voice was now devoid of emotion, professional, but the warmth had vanished. A rift had opened between them, thin as a hair, but palpable.

Maximus took a deep breath, trying to suppress his own disappointment and doubt. He hated having to rebuke Brutus so directly, but the chain of command was sacred. "Good," he said, striving for a businesslike tone again. "We leave at once. Centurion Varro!"

The stocky Centurion of the First Century stepped forward.

"Sir?"

"You will assume command of the post in my absence. The threat from the Celtic group to the west remains. Maintain the highest alert! Reinforce the palisades at the east gate. Send out patrols, but don't let them range too far. Hold this position at all costs until we return or further orders arrive."

"Yes, Sir Tribune!" Varro replied, his expression serious and determined.

"Centurion Felix," Maximus addressed the next officer. "Your century and the Fourth also remain here. Support Varro in the defense."

"Understood, Sir!"

"Brutus," Maximus said, his tone softening slightly, "select twenty of your best men as an escort. Plus Vespasian's ten guard cavalrymen. We travel light, only essentials. We must be swift."

"Sir," Brutus replied curtly, already turning away to select his men.

Maximus watched him go, a bitter taste in his mouth. He had made his decision, obeyed the order. But the feeling of doing the right thing refused to materialize. Instead, he felt a gnawing uncertainty and the quiet fear that he had just made a grave mistake. He cast one last look at the map, at the path leading west, where the Celts and their carts continued their journey unhindered. Then he turned and walked towards his tent to prepare for the urgent ride to Rutupiae, his heart heavy as lead.

IV. Masks of Ambition

An icy silence marked the ride to Rutupiae, broken only by the steady hoofbeats of the small escort on the damp, well-trodden path and the incessant drizzle from the Britannic sky. Maximus rode silently beside Brutus, the words of Vespasian's urgent order still burning in his memory. Worry about the outpost left behind and the unresolved threat of the Celts with their carts sat like a heavy stone in his stomach. He had obeyed, placing duty above immediate tactical necessity, but the feeling of having done the right thing remained elusive. Instead, doubt gnawed at him, fueled by the obvious, though disciplined suppressed, disapproval in Brutus's posture.

The Centurion rode with a face carved from stone, his gaze fixed rigidly on the path ahead. Since their exchange at the outpost, he had barely spoken, issuing only the most necessary military commands to the escort. Maximus felt the gulf between them, a distance created by his decision. He understood Brutus's anger, his frustration. Brutus was a man of direct action, a fighter who wanted to face a tangible danger and combat it, rather than follow a vague order whose urgency escaped him. Maximus shared those instincts. Yet, his rank, his responsibility, and perhaps the subtle, ingrained caution of his patrician upbringing had led him to decide differently. He had to trust Vespasian, believe in the larger strategy, even when his gut told him otherwise.

When the outlines of Rutupiae finally emerged from the haze, some of the tension eased among the riders. The coastal fortress was an impressive sight, even under the gray sky. Unlike the small, isolated outpost they had left, Rutupiae pulsed as a center of Roman power in southern Britannia. Massive earth ramparts, reinforced with palisades and watchtowers, enclosed a sprawling area. Behind them rose the roofs of permanent buildings—barracks, storehouses, workshops, the legate's *praetorium*. In the sheltered harbor basin lay not only cumbersome supply ships but also sleeker Liburnians, warships whose masts rose like a bare forest against the sky. The smell of saltwater, tar, and fish mingled with the familiar camp odors of smoke, leather, and latrines. Hundreds of soldiers moved purposefully along the paths, unloading ships, repairing equipment, or drilling on the central square. It was a picture of orderly military activity, a stark contrast to the nervous tension of the small outpost. Here, one felt the concentrated might of Rome.

The guards at the main gate recognized Maximus and Brutus immediately and opened it without hesitation. The two officers rode through, their small escort following. They attracted attention; many legionaries knew the young Tribune and the legendary Centurion from the battles on the Medway and at Camulodunum. Respectful, yet curious, glances followed them.

They dismounted before the *praetorium*. The surprisingly large and solid timber building was guarded by Vespasian's personal guard—a clear sign of the Legate's status and perhaps

IV. MASKS OF AMBITION

the tense situation. Vespasian's adjutant, a young, eager Optio, approached them.

"Tribune Maximus, Centurion Brutus, Legate Vespasian awaits you."

Maximus nodded. "Thank you, Optio. Announce us."

They were admitted without delay. The interior of the *praetorium* was larger and better appointed than the tent Maximus was used to. Several tables were covered with maps and scrolls; standards and military decorations hung on the walls. Vespasian stood in the center of the room, conversing with Tribune Flaccus and another man Maximus didn't immediately recognize.

Vespasian looked up as they entered. His expression was serious, his gaze appraising but not unfriendly. "Ah, Maximus, Brutus. You were swift. Excellent." He gestured towards the other two men. "You already know Tribune Flaccus, and this is Prince Adminius, son of Cunobelinus, who assists us on behalf of General Plautius."

Maximus and Brutus gave curt salutes. Flaccus returned the greeting with a thin smile that didn't reach his eyes. Adminius inclined his head slightly, his posture that of a man aware of his importance but who considered courtesy a useful tool.

"Sit," Vespasian said, indicating two free stools. "There is much to discuss."

Maximus and Brutus took their seats, their armor creaking softly. The atmosphere in the room was tense, a mixture of military formality and underlying political currents.

"I summoned you here urgently, Maximus," Vespasian began without preamble, "because a situation has arisen that takes highest priority and requires your particular skills." He chose his words carefully. "Prince Adminius, as General

Plautius has already indicated, is key to a potential division among the Celtic tribes. He has offered to cooperate with us to bring some of the southern chieftains over to Rome's side. Tribune Flaccus will accompany him and handle the diplomatic aspects."

He paused, his eyes meeting Maximus's. "And you, Tribune Maximus, will accompany and support Tribune Flaccus on this mission. I require your strategic foresight and military experience to ensure the operation's security. You know the Celts' tactics; you have proven yourself in the field. Ensure our diplomats are safe, assess the military situation on the ground, and take necessary precautions. You are responsible for the military execution and security of this mission."

Maximus was surprised. He had expected to remain in Rutupiae, perhaps as a reserve or quiet observer. Now he was to directly accompany Flaccus. On one hand, he was relieved not to be sitting idle in camp. On the other, it meant close cooperation with Flaccus, the man he instinctively distrusted, and with Adminius, the traitor to his people. And what about the outpost?

"Legate," Maximus began cautiously, "I am honored by your trust. But what about the threat near Secundus? The report about the large Celtic group with the carts…"

Vespasian cut him off with a brief wave of his hand, his gaze turning stern. "I have received the report, Tribune. A local matter, likely plunderers or a minor clan on the move. Annoying, yes, but strategically irrelevant in the larger picture. Centurion Varro is a capable man; I am certain he will monitor the group and report if they pose a direct threat to the post or the main route. Your priority, *our* priority, now lies with this alliance mission. It is crucial to secure Plautius's rear in the north. We cannot afford to delay this opportunity over every local skirmish."

Maximus felt Brutus's gaze upon him, sensed the unspoken disapproval, the disappointment. The Centurion would have confronted the Celts, eliminated the immediate danger. But Maximus was the Tribune. He had to obey the Legate, even if it contradicted his instincts. "As you command, Legate," he said finally, his voice firm, though a residue of doubt remained.

"Good." Vespasian seemed to ignore, or deliberately overlook, the subtle tension between his two officers. "Brutus, you will accompany Tribune Maximus. Your experience is indispensable."

"Yes, Legate," Brutus replied curtly, his expression unmoving.

"You depart tomorrow at sunrise," Vespasian continued, turning back to Flaccus and Adminius. "Your route initially takes you west, towards the Atrebates. King Cogidubnus is considered pro-Roman, but even he must be persuaded. Be convincing, offer protection and trade, but make it clear: Rome forgets neither friends nor enemies."

"We will succeed, Legate," Flaccus assured him again.

Adminius added with his slippery smile, "Cogidubnus is a man who recognizes his advantage. He will understand. I am more concerned about the Durotriges. They are not quite so civilized or predictable."

Further details were discussed, routes finalized, potential courier rendezvous points agreed upon. Maximus participated attentively, ensuring the military aspects—march order, security, reconnaissance—were clearly defined. He noted every nuance in Flaccus's and Adminius's words, searching for hidden clues, for contradictions, but found nothing tangible.

As they left the *praetorium*, they almost collided with Centurion Valerius Longinus, commander of the cohort assigned to escort Flaccus and Adminius. Vespasian stepped out of the tent as well.

"Centurion Longinus," Vespasian said. "Tribune Maximus and Centurion Brutus will join your mission. Tribune Flaccus holds diplomatic command, Tribune Maximus the military command. You report to both, but in urgent military matters, Tribune Maximus has the final word. And you continue to report directly to me."

Longinus, a lean man with watchful eyes, saluted. "Understood, Legate." His gaze briefly flickered over Flaccus, then Maximus, showing no emotion.

Maximus and Brutus exchanged a quick glance. Vespasian had made his arrangements. Longinus was his man on the ground.

They all exchanged military salutes and headed back towards their respective quarters. Outside, the rain had intensified again, now falling in thick sheets from the sky. Dusk was settling, bathing the camp in a gloomy light. Torches were lit, their flickering glow reflecting in the puddles.

"He underestimates the danger out there," Brutus said immediately once they were out of earshot. "Varro is good, but against four hundred men…"

"I know," Maximus interrupted him. "Varro has precise instructions: observe, under no circumstances engage, withdraw south immediately if the Celts attack. And I will ask Scipio to increase his cavalry patrols in that sector." He sighed. "We can do no more for now, Brutus. We have to trust Vespasian knows what he's doing."

IV. MASKS OF AMBITION

"Trust?" Brutus snorted. "I trust my *gladius* and the men beside me. Politicians and generals, I trust only as far as I can throw them." He looked seriously at Maximus. "Be careful with Flaccus. And even more careful with this Adminius. Snakes aren't always recognizable at first glance."

"I'll watch out, Brutus," Maximus assured him. "You too."

They parted before the tent allocated to Maximus as Tribune—somewhat larger and drier than the centurions' quarters, but still far from any comfort. Brutus continued towards the barracks of his own century, his figure quickly disappearing into the dim torchlight and falling rain. Maximus stood for a moment longer, gazing in the direction they had come from, his thoughts with Varro and the men at Outpost Secundus. He uttered a low curse and entered his tent.

* * *

A few tents away, in the quarters assigned to Senior Tribune Servius Flaccus, a different atmosphere prevailed. No simple oil lamp burned here; instead, several fine bronze candelabras cast a bright, warm light on surprisingly comfortable furnishings. A thick rug covered the packed-earth floor, a small table of polished wood held a carafe of wine and two silver goblets, and neatly folded, dry clothes lay on a collapsible camp chair. Flaccus had made himself as comfortable as circumstances allowed.

He stood before a small, polished bronze mirror held by one of his personal slaves, critically examining his reflection. He adjusted his perfectly fitted tunic, smoothed an imaginary crease. The journey had been arduous, the camp primitive, but he refused to show even a hint of negligence. His appearance was part of his armor, a symbol of his status and control.

"Enough, Lepidus," he finally said to the slave. "You may go. Ensure my wine is tempered, and wake me an hour before sunrise."

"Yes, master." The slave bowed deeply and withdrew silently.

Alone in his tent, Flaccus let the mask drop for a moment. A flicker of anger and frustration crossed his face. Vespasian, Maximus, Brutus—these upstarts, these rough soldiers! They understood nothing of the real games being played. They saw only the battlefield, the immediate danger. They didn't grasp that the true struggle took place in Rome, in the corridors of power, whispered into the ears of the Emperor and his advisors. And he, Flaccus, was stranded in this godforsaken swamp while others reaped the laurels in Rome.

But then he straightened again. He wasn't here for nothing. Plautius had given him a task. Cooperating with Adminius was a chance to gather information, gain influence, make himself indispensable. And then there was the matter of Maximus...

He went to his heavy travel chest, opened it, and retrieved a small, inconspicuous wax tablet. He had received it before his departure from the north, delivered by a discreet messenger who had come and gone under cover of night. It came directly from Narcissus.

With practiced fingers, he broke the complex seal and, in the bright light of the candelabras, deciphered the coded message once more:

IV. MASKS OF AMBITION

Tribune Maximus. Possible grandson Tiberius. Illegitimate. Mother Prosonia. Danger to stability. Observe. Act discreetly. Claudius must not learn. Narcissus.

Grandson of Tiberius! The mere thought sent a cold shiver down Flaccus's spine. A potential rival with imperial blood, right here, under the command of his rival Vespasian. Narcissus was right. This was a danger, an incalculable variable that could destroy everything men like him worked for. Maximus had to disappear. Discreetly, permanently.

But how? Vespasian seemed to protect the boy. Brutus was loyal to him like a guard dog. A direct "accident" was too risky. It had to be subtler. He needed a scapegoat, an opportunity where Maximus's death would look like a tragic but unavoidable loss in the fight against the barbarians.

He thought of Adminius. The Celt was ambitious, unscrupulous, and likely just as eager to eliminate potential rivals as Flaccus himself. Adminius knew the Celtic tribes, their paths, their methods. Could he use the prince to lure Maximus into a trap? A trap from which there was no escape?

A slow, cold smile crept onto Flaccus's lips. Yes, that was the way. He would use Adminius. He would use the "diplomatic mission" to get rid of Maximus. He would report the "tragic loss" to Vespasian while ensuring all traces led away from him, Flaccus. It was a dangerous game, and the stakes were high. But if he succeeded, he would not only eliminate a threat but also make himself indispensable to Narcissus. And who knew where that might lead?

He carefully hid the wax tablet again in the false bottom of his chest. He poured himself a goblet of the expensive

Falernian wine he had brought from Rome and toasted his reflection. The mask of the ambitious, loyal Tribune was firmly back in place, impenetrable and cold. Tomorrow, he would depart with Adminius. Tomorrow, the game would begin. And he, Servius Flaccus, was ready to make his move.

V. Between Two Fronts

Dawn grayed over Rutupiae, offering none of the gentle promise of a new day. Instead, night yielded reluctantly to a sky the color of wet lead. A fine drizzle persisted, its invisible dampness seeping into clothes and bone. The legionaries' faces looked gray and weary. Heavy, salt-laced air from the nearby sea mingled with the ubiquitous smells of damp earth, smoke, and latrines.

Despite the inhospitable conditions, focused activity bustled in the area of the Third Cohort. Centurion Longinus and the centurions of the detached units supervised the final preparations for departure. Soldiers checked their armor one last time, loaded pack animals, and distributed march rations: hard, nutritious *bucellatum* (hardtack) and salted meat. The men spoke little, their movements efficient, almost mechanical. Beneath the surface of discipline lay a palpable tension. They were embarking on a journey into the unknown, many distrusting the mission's purpose—diplomacy with the native barbarians seemed madness.

Maximus and Brutus stood slightly apart, observing the activity. Maximus had barely slept, his thoughts constantly returning to the Celtic cohort near Secundus and the men stationed there.

He glanced at Brutus. The Centurion stood with his arms crossed over his massive chest, his gaze fixed on the men. He, too, looked tired, the lines etched deeper than usual into his face. The disagreement over Vespasian's order had placed a noticeable chill between them. Maximus missed the uncomplicated camaraderie, the blind trust that had bound them in battle. Now a shadow lay between them—the shadow of command, of rank, and perhaps of unspoken secrets.

"They're almost ready, Sir," Brutus said, without taking his eyes off the men. His tone was correct, military, but the familiar warmth was absent.

"Good," Maximus replied just as curtly. "Ensure the rearguard is especially vigilant. I don't trust this peace one bit."

"Yes, Sir." Brutus gave a short nod.

At that moment, Tribune Flaccus and Prince Adminius approached, accompanied by Longinus and several cavalrymen. Flaccus appeared immaculate as always, his red cloak seemingly repelling the rain entirely. He put on a professional smile. Adminius, in more practical travel attire, still looked out of place, an exotic bird among crows, though his expression was unreadable.

"All prepared for departure, Tribune Maximus?" Flaccus asked, his voice affable but lacking genuine warmth. "The men seem… eager." A faint mockery tinged the word "eager."

"They are ready to do their duty, Tribune Flaccus," Maximus answered coolly. "As are we all." He ignored the provocation. "Centurion Longinus has established the march order. Prince Adminius and you will ride with your personal guard in the center of the column, well protected. Centurion Brutus and I will lead the vanguard."

Flaccus raised an eyebrow. "An unusual arrangement,

V. BETWEEN TWO FRONTS

Tribune. Typically, the senior officer rides at the head."

"The safety of our... diplomatic guests takes precedence," Maximus countered smoothly, his gaze meeting Flaccus's. "Besides, I know Centurion Brutus's capabilities at the point. We have operated successfully this way before." He left no room for argument.

Flaccus's lips thinned, but he nodded. "As you wish, Tribune. The Prince's safety is indeed paramount." He turned to Adminius with exaggerated friendliness. "No worries, Prince. You are in the best of hands."

Adminius offered his slippery smile. "I do not doubt it, Tribune. The efficiency of the Roman legion is legendary."

And its ability to use traitors, thought Brutus bitterly, having watched the scene with a dark expression.

The order to move out was given. Horns sounded, commands echoed through the camp. Slowly, the column began to move: roughly four hundred legionaries of the Third Cohort, the mounted escort, and the small group surrounding Adminius. The sound of thousands of hobnailed boots in the mud, the clank of weapons and armor, the snorting of horses, and the cursing of men formed the symphony of the march. They left the security of Rutupiae and plunged into hostile, unknown territory.

The first day was grueling, the terrain and weather taking their toll. The path led them westward, away from the coast, into dense, dripping forests, treacherous swamps, and muddy hills. Although the fog lifted by mid-morning, the sky remained overcast, punctuated by brief, cold showers. The track was barely more than a worn path, often ankle-deep in mud that clung to their boots, making every step an effort. Pack animals slipped and stumbled, their loads constantly needing readjustment.

Maximus rode with Brutus at the head of the column. They spoke little. Maximus focused on the path, the surroundings, and the reports from the scouts, who returned periodically without enemy contact. He tried to ignore the tension knotting his neck, the constant expectation of an arrow from the thicket, a sudden ambush. He thought of Varro and Outpost Secundus. Was there any news? Were the Celts attacking? He didn't know. The distance felt immense, the uncertainty an additional burden.

Around noon, Optio Decimus suddenly rode up from the rear, his face serious. He halted beside Brutus. "Centurion," he said tersely, "scouts report fresh tracks off the path. Not many, perhaps one or two men, but they seem to be following us, parallel to our course. Keeping their distance, hiding well."

Brutus nodded, his expression darkening further. "Observers. They want to know where we're going and how strong we are." He turned to Maximus. "I don't like this, Sir."

"Neither do I," Maximus replied. "It suggests we're being watched, perhaps even by Caratacus's people. Decimus," he addressed the Optio, "double the flank scouts. Absolute caution. No unnecessary risks, but I want to know who's following us."

"Yes, Tribune!" Decimus saluted briefly and fell back to relay the orders. The short interruption had charged the already tense atmosphere even further.

Beside Maximus, Brutus seemed even more withdrawn. His gaze was vigilant, his hand rarely far from the hilt of his *gladius*. Once, as they traversed a particularly dense stretch of forest where light barely penetrated the canopy and tree trunks rose like silent sentinels, he muttered, "An ideal place

V. BETWEEN TWO FRONTS

for an ambush."

"The scouts reported nothing," Maximus replied, though he felt the same tension.

"Scouts can be missed, or killed," Brutus growled. "I don't like it when I can't see the enemy. And I like it even less when I don't know who the real enemy is." His gaze flickered almost imperceptibly back towards the center of the column, where Flaccus and Adminius rode.

Maximus nodded silently. He understood.

Further back in the column, Flaccus and Adminius rode side-by-side, seemingly unaffected by the rigors of the march. They conversed quietly, their heads inclined towards each other. No one could hear their words, but their familiarity seemed ominous. Maximus saw Flaccus laugh occasionally, saw Adminius gesture. They looked like two men pursuing a common interest, speaking a common language that wasn't military. Centurion Longinus rode unobtrusively nearby, his face expressionless, but his eyes missed nothing.

Late in the afternoon, as the sun vanished behind the clouds and shadows lengthened, they reached a small clearing by a stream. Longinus had identified it as suitable for the night's camp. The spot was relatively open but offered natural protection from the stream and a steep slope.

Immediately, the orderly routine of setting up camp began. Sentries were posted, patrols sent out, and the perimeter secured. Men gathered wood for fires and dug shallow latrine trenches. They erected small leather tents (*papiliones*), each housing eight men. Despite their fatigue, the legionaries worked quickly and efficiently, like a well-oiled machine.

As the fires burned and the smell of cooking *puls* mingled with the smoke, the officers gathered. Maximus and Brutus shared a simple meal by their century's fire. Flaccus and Adminius retreated to Flaccus's more spacious tent, where slaves presumably served them wine and better fare.

"See?" Brutus grumbled, gesturing with a piece of hardtack towards Flaccus's tent. "They think they're better than everyone else, even out here in the muck."

"Let them be, Brutus," Maximus said wearily, "as long as they do their part." He himself felt the sting of inequality, the gulf between the common soldiers and the privileged officers from patrician families. Maximus stood somewhere in between. His rank gave him privilege, but his origins and his experiences in the *ludus* and on the front lines placed him closer to the common men than Flaccus ever could be.

Later that evening, when most men were either asleep or murmuring quietly by the fires, Adminius emerged from Flaccus's tent. He slowly walked towards the fire where Maximus and Brutus still sat.

"A cool night, Tribune, Centurion," he said with his charming smile. "May I join you for a moment?"

Maximus and Brutus exchanged a brief, unreadable glance. The chill between them was still palpable. "Please, Prince," Maximus said politely, but with deliberate neutrality.

Adminius sat on an overturned bucket. "I admire the discipline of your men, even after such a strenuous march."

"Discipline is our strength," Brutus answered curtly, without looking at Adminius.

"Indeed," Adminius said. "But sometimes I wonder if it is enough against the... passion of my people." He sighed dramatically. "My brother Caratacus... he is a fool, blinded by pride. But he can ignite the hearts of warriors."

"Passion doesn't win wars, Prince," Maximus said coolly.

"Strategy and endurance do."

"Perhaps you are right, Tribune." Adminius's eyes glittered in the firelight, fixing on Maximus. "But never underestimate the strength of a man fighting for his homeland." He leaned forward slightly, his voice becoming more confidential. "Tell me, Tribune, you seem younger than most men of your rank; your rise has been swift. How does a man like you end up in a place like this? What drives you?" The question sounded casual, but the focus was clearly on Maximus now, the curiosity sharper, almost probing.

Maximus sensed the calculation behind the question, also felt Brutus's sudden, silent attention beside him. He forced a calm tone. "I am a soldier, Prince. I do my duty where Rome needs me. My rank is the result of fulfilling that duty, and perhaps some luck in battle." He deliberately sidestepped the personal part of the question.

Adminius smiled again, a smile that seemed insincere. He appeared to notice the evasion. "Fulfilling duty—a Roman virtue." He stood gracefully. "Forgive my curiosity. It is rare to meet Romans who seem… different. Perhaps it is merely your youth." He gave them a brief nod. "A good night, gentlemen." He turned and walked back towards Flaccus's tent with springy steps.

"'Different'?" Brutus muttered suspiciously once Adminius was out of earshot. His gaze met Maximus's. "What did he mean by that? And why is he asking you such questions?" The coolness was still in his voice, but now worry and curiosity mingled with it.

Maximus shrugged, staring into the fire, but the uneasy feeling intensified. "I don't know, Brutus. But he's too curious."

Later, Maximus inspected the sentries. He stood for a long time at the edge of the camp, gazing into the impenetrable darkness of the Britannic forest. The night was filled with eerie sounds: branches snapping, a wolf howling in the distance, the wind rustling through the trees. Sometimes, the rustling sounded like whispers.

Was something out there? Was he being watched? Or was fear just playing tricks on him? Maximus only knew that this mission with Flaccus and Adminius felt more dangerous than it appeared. The real enemy might not wear woad and war paint, but a Roman uniform and a false smile.

VI. Scouts in the Fog

The westward march was a grinding ordeal, a daily struggle against Britannia's relentless nature and the leaden fatigue that seeped into the soldiers' limbs. They left the relative security of the more heavily Roman-controlled coastal region around Rutupiae, pushing deeper inland into territory only vaguely marked on the legion's maps. It was a patchwork of dense, ancient forests, treacherous bogs, and gently rolling hills under a perpetually overcast sky.

Fog was their constant companion. It crept from the river valleys and hollows each morning, shrouding the landscape in an impenetrable gray, muffling all sounds and shrinking the world to the narrow confines of the visible path. Even when the midday sun attempted to break through, it rarely offered more than a pale, diffuse light. In the afternoon, the fog returned or transitioned into a cold, fine drizzle that soaked everything. The tracks were narrow, often little more than game trails winding through dense undergrowth or leading through ankle-deep mud. Tree roots hidden beneath wet leaves became tripping hazards. Every stream they had to ford presented an obstacle of cold water and slippery stones.

Maximus continued to ride at the head of the column, his

senses sharp, his eyes constantly scanning the surroundings. He forced himself to suppress his inner turmoil—the worries about his origins and the growing skepticism towards Flaccus and Adminius. His task was clear: the military security of this diplomatic expedition. He focused on the terrain, the marching formation, the reports from the scouts who slipped ahead like shadows and reappeared just as silently. They reported no enemy activity, only occasional signs of hunters or small groups of farmers, who immediately retreated into the woods at their approach. There was no trace of the followers from the previous day. The land was inhabited, but its people avoided contact with the heavily armed Romans.

Beside him rode Brutus, his face an unmoving mask. Maximus knew him well enough by now to recognize the tension in the way he held the reins, how his gaze constantly shifted from one side of the path to the other. Brutus hated this kind of march through unknown territory. He was a man of the open battlefield, of the honest fight, shield to shield. This creeping through the fog, the constant uncertainty of whether a spear lurked behind the next tree, went against his nature. The disagreement in Rutupiae still hung between them like an invisible wall. They spoke only when necessary: brief military coordinations, curt commands. The easy camaraderie and jokes they once shared had yielded to tense professionalism. Maximus missed it, but he also knew that the burden of command and the hardships of war inevitably created such fractures. Loyalty was often severely tested in the field.

"The ground here is treacherous," Brutus grumbled one afternoon as they traversed a particularly boggy section of forest, the horses sinking deep. "One wrong step, and a man

VI. SCOUTS IN THE FOG

sinks to his waist. Not good for a fast formation."

"We move cautiously," Maximus replied. "The scouts secure the way ahead. But you're right; this is no terrain for heavy infantry like ours." Maximus glanced back. The main column struggled laboriously through the mire, the men cursing softly, their faces smeared with exertion and mud.

Further back, in the relative safety of the column's center, rode Flaccus and Adminius. The march's hardships seemed to affect them less. Flaccus sat upright on his magnificent horse, his cloak protecting him from the drizzle, his expression mostly impassive, occasionally pursing his lips when a splash of mud hit his polished boots. He conversed quietly with Adminius, who rode beside him.

Adminius played the role of the knowledgeable guide perfectly. He pointed out landmarks, explained the names of streams, and recounted anecdotes about the local tribes: their customs, their feuds, their leaders. He did so with a mixture of charm and apparent openness that only fueled Maximus's and Brutus's mistrust.

"The Prince knows a great deal," Brutus remarked sarcastically once, during a halt while Adminius entertained Flaccus with a lively description of a Druidic ritual. "Almost too much for a man supposedly in exile for years."

"He was a king's son, Brutus," Maximus countered. "He'll have his sources. He wants to make himself useful."

"Or he wants to lead us astray," Brutus growled. "Don't forget whose brother he is."

Maximus remained silent. He couldn't dismiss Brutus's suspicion because he shared it. He watched Adminius closely, listened to his stories, alert for contradictions, hesitations, false notes. He found nothing concrete, but the feeling that the Celt was playing a double game wouldn't leave him. Particularly unsettling was the apparently growing familiarity between Adminius and Flaccus. They seemed to have found a common language, a level of understanding that appeared to extend beyond the official mission. What did they discuss so eagerly when they thought themselves unobserved? Maximus discreetly instructed Centurion Longinus to keep a closer eye on the pair, though Longinus, being only a Centurion, could not directly eavesdrop on the Tribune's conversations.

On the third day of the march, a minor incident occurred that further heightened the underlying tension. The scouts riding ahead returned in great haste.

"Sir!" reported Decurio Aelius, his face pale beneath the grime. "We found a village, a few miles ahead. It's… it's been burned, completely destroyed. No survivors, just… bodies. Celts—men, women, children."

An icy silence fell over the head of the column. "Romans?" Brutus asked immediately, his voice harsh.

"No, Centurion. No sign of Roman weapons. It looks like… tribal warfare. Brutal, merciless. The way the bodies were mutilated…" The Decurio swallowed hard. "We've seen things like this among the Germans."

Maximus exchanged a troubled look with Brutus. A massacre, here, so close to their route. "Which tribe could have done this?" he asked.

"Hard to say, Sir. It's in the borderlands between the Atrebates and the Durotriges. Both are known for not being gentle," Aelius replied.

At that moment, Flaccus and Adminius arrived from the rear, alerted by the sudden halt. "What has happened, Tribune Maximus?" Flaccus inquired, his expression concerned, but

VI. SCOUTS IN THE FOG

his eyes remained cold.

Maximus briefly reported the discovery. Adminius's face became unreadable for a moment, then he said in a serious voice, "The Durotriges. That is their signature. They are fierce warriors, hate outsiders, and often raid their neighbors. Cogidubnus of the Atrebates will be appalled. This could influence our negotiations."

"Influence them? How?" Maximus asked sharply.

"Cogidubnus might hesitate to ally with Rome if he sees we cannot even control the tribes in our immediate vicinity," Adminius explained. "Or," his gaze turned calculating, "he might see this as an opportunity, proof that he urgently needs Rome's protection. It depends on how we present it to him."

"We will bypass the village," Maximus decided. "We have no time for investigations, and I don't want to burden my men with that sight. Alter course slightly north, Decurio. Find a way around the valley."

"But Tribune," Flaccus interjected, "shouldn't we show presence, help any survivors, hunt down those responsible? That would be a sign of Roman strength and justice."

"We have our orders, Flaccus," Maximus replied coolly, his gaze fixed firmly on the patrician. "Our mission is to reach the Atrebates and forge an alliance. We will not be distracted by every local conflict. The safety of our troops takes precedence." He saw the disappointment, or perhaps feigned anger, in Flaccus's eyes, but he held firm. He would not let Flaccus provoke him into rash action.

Flaccus gave a slight shrug. "As you wish, Tribune. You hold the military command." But his tone held a subtle barb.

They continued their march, taking a detour through even denser forest. The mood in the column was now more somber.

News of the massacre had spread quickly, serving as a grim reminder of the land's brutality and the fragility of the peace they promised to bring. Maximus felt his men's stares, their unspoken questions, their doubts. Was he leading them down the right path? Was this entire campaign justified at all? Was Rome truly bringing order and civilization, or was it just another wave of brutal, efficient conquerors seeking to subjugate tribes? In the fog of his thoughts, the lines blurred, the landscape around him dissolving into the gray Britannic weather.

Late on the afternoon of the fourth day, they finally reached the edges of the Atrebates' territory. The forest thinned, giving way to more open pastureland and the first small, thatched farmsteads. Smoke rose peacefully from chimneys. The scouts reported no signs of hostility, only curious but cautious glances from the locals.

They made camp on a strategically advantageous hill, offering a good view over the valley where the main settlement of the Atrebates was said to lie. The routine of setting up camp began again, but this time a different kind of tension filled the air: the anticipation of the upcoming diplomatic encounter.

As night fell and the fires were lit, Adminius approached Maximus and Brutus at their fire. "Tomorrow, we meet Cogidubnus," he said, his voice confident. "I have already sent messengers ahead to announce our arrival. He will receive us."

"Are you certain he is friendly?" Brutus asked suspiciously.

Adminius smiled. "Cogidubnus is a realist, Centurion. He knows the wind has changed. He will grasp the hand Rome extends—if it is filled with gold."

Maximus studied the Celt in the flickering firelight. He

saw the ambition in his eyes, the calculation behind the smile. But he also saw something else—a deep uncertainty, perhaps even fear. Adminius was playing a high-stakes game, betting everything on one card. His survival depended on making himself useful to Rome.

"We will see what morning brings," Maximus said finally. He gazed into the darkness, where somewhere out there the king of the Atrebates waited. And he thought of the riders in the fog, the burned village, Flaccus's cold smile. The omens were not good. The journey through the fog had brought them to their first destination, but the most dangerous part of the path might still lie ahead.

VII. Foreign Allies

The new day began not with fog, but with unexpected, almost blinding sunlight fighting its way through the cloud cover, bathing the damp landscape in a soft gold. It seemed as if the gods themselves wished to grace the impending diplomatic encounter with a favorable omen. Maximus, however, did not trust the deceptive peace. The tension in the Roman camp on the hill was almost palpable. Today they would meet King Cogidubnus, leader of the Atrebates, whose decision could significantly influence the balance of power in southern Britannia.

Maximus had spent the night studying the scant information Rome possessed on Cogidubnus. He was considered clever and pragmatic, more politician than warrior, appreciating the value of trade and stability. Traditionally, he maintained a certain closeness to Rome, or at least a cautious neutrality. But times had changed. The Roman invasion was no longer a distant threat but a harsh reality. Would Cogidubnus grasp Rome's outstretched hand, or reject it out of fear of Caratacus or his pride?

Shortly after sunrise, he met Brutus at the edge of the camp, where the men of the Second Century already stood, ready to escort the diplomatic delegation. Brutus's expression was still

VII. FOREIGN ALLIES

closed off, but the open hostility of the previous day seemed to have given way to resigned vigilance.

"The men are ready, Sir," Brutus reported curtly. "The escort for Flaccus and Adminius is also formed up."

"Good," Maximus said. "Longinus leads the escort, as discussed. We follow with the century within sight, but at enough distance not to appear threatening. We are the military presence offering protection, but we don't want to jeopardize the negotiations with an excessive show of force."

"A fine line," Brutus muttered, "especially with those two snakes leading the way."

"We keep our eyes open," Maximus replied. "Watch for Longinus's signals and anything unusual."

Brutus nodded. "You can count on that, Sir."

Shortly thereafter, the delegation set off. Flaccus and Adminius rode at the head, flanked by Centurion Longinus and ten cavalrymen. Flaccus today wore lighter but still elegant armor over his purple tunic; his helmet gleamed in the morning sun. Adminius had also changed, now wearing a mix of Roman and Celtic attire, a gesture presumably meant to underscore his role as mediator. His smile today seemed particularly winning, almost too friendly.

Maximus and Brutus followed with the Second Century, about eighty men strong, in disciplined marching formation. They maintained a distance of roughly two hundred paces—enough not to be part of the immediate diplomatic group, but close enough to intervene quickly if necessary.

The path led them down from their hill into the valley, through fertile pastureland where shaggy cattle grazed, and past small, well-kept farmsteads. The inhabitants—mostly women, children, and older men—came out of their huts, watching the Romans with a mixture of curiosity and fear. There were no open hostilities, but no friendly gestures either. They were intruders in this land, and they felt it with every step.

After about an hour, they reached the main settlement of the Atrebates, situated on a slight rise in the center of the valley. It wasn't a fortified town like Camulodunum, but rather a large, sprawling settlement of timber houses with thatched roofs, surrounded by a simple earth rampart and palisade fence. A larger building stood out in the center, presumably the king's hall. Smoke rose from numerous hearths, and the busy activity of people and animals filled the air.

A delegation of Atrebate warriors already awaited them at the main gate. They were dressed and armed differently than the Catuvellauni Maximus had fought so far. Their shields were smaller, often round, their clothing more colorful, many wearing intricately worked bronze jewelry. Their faces were unpainted, but their gazes were just as watchful and suspicious as the Romans'. They were led by a tall man with a gray-streaked beard, holding a long spear.

Flaccus and Adminius halted; Longinus and the escort formed a protective semicircle around them. Maximus had his century halt as well, the men automatically forming a defensive line, shields ready.

Adminius stepped forward and addressed the warrior leader in Celtic. A short, apparently formal exchange followed. Then the warrior nodded and motioned for the Roman delegation to follow him.

"They receive us," Flaccus said to Longinus with feigned relief. "All according to plan."

The small group around Flaccus and Adminius rode

through the gate into the settlement. Maximus hesitated a moment, then signaled Brutus. "We follow slowly. Keep the men ready, but avoid any provocation."

"Understood, Sir."

Maximus and Brutus rode through the gate with their century. The interior of the settlement was a labyrinth of narrow lanes, wooden houses, and animal pens. It smelled of smoke, livestock, and damp earth. The inhabitants crowded the sides, watching the heavily armed Romans with open mouths; children hid behind their mothers' skirts. The atmosphere was tense, but not openly hostile.

They were led to the large hall in the center of the settlement. It was a long, low building of dark timber, the roof adorned with intricate carvings. Before it stood another group of warriors, clearly the king's personal guard. Flaccus, Adminius, and Longinus dismounted and were led into the hall by the gray-haired warrior who had met them at the gate. The ten men of their escort remained outside, forming a watchful circle around the horses.

Maximus had his century take up position as well, slightly aside from the hall's entrance. They were now inside the walls, surrounded by potential enemies. It was a tactically unfavorable position, and Maximus didn't like it.

"Stay alert," he instructed Brutus. "Watch the roofs, the alleys. If something happens, we need to be able to withdraw quickly."

Brutus merely nodded, his hand never leaving the hilt of his sword.

The minutes stretched into an eternity. No sounds emerged from the hall, no indication of how the negotiations were proceeding. Maximus felt the tension grow among his men. They stood silently, their faces impassive beneath their helmets, but their eyes darted nervously, registering every movement of the surrounding Atrebates.

Suddenly, the heavy wooden door of the hall was thrown open. Adminius emerged, his face beaming with triumph. Behind him followed Flaccus, though his expression seemed less enthusiastic. And then King Cogidubnus himself appeared.

He was a middle-aged man, smaller than expected, but possessing an aura of natural authority. He wore a magnificent cloak of dyed wool and a golden torc around his neck. His hair was carefully styled, his beard trimmed. His gaze was sharp, intelligent, and inscrutable as he surveyed the Roman soldiers. Beside him stood the gray-haired warrior from the gate, evidently his closest advisor.

"Tribune Maximus, Centurion Brutus," Flaccus called out. "King Cogidubnus has agreed to become a friend and ally of Rome!"

A low murmur went through the legionaries' ranks. This was good news, a significant diplomatic success.

Cogidubnus stepped forward, raising a hand. He spoke in Latin, his voice surprisingly clear and strong, though with a distinct accent. "Romans, you come in a time of great uncertainty. My people suffer from the raids of the Durotriges. Their savagery knows no bounds; their warriors are wolves who tear at our flocks and threaten our villages. You offer protection. For that, I am grateful. Alone, we cannot withstand this threat." He paused, his gaze sweeping over the disciplined ranks of the legionaries, lingering briefly on Brutus, then Maximus. "Rome is mighty. A reality we must face. An alliance with Rome can bring my people prosperity and security. Trade routes open, new knowledge, new tools come to our land. But," his voice hardened, "Rome also demands a price: loyalty, submission." He looked searchingly at Flaccus. "A friendship based on respect, or that of a master to his vassal?"

"Rome demands friendship and cooperation, King Cogidubnus," Flaccus replied smoothly. "We respect your authority and your traditions. We ask only that you recognize Rome as the supreme protecting power and support us in our fight against common enemies—against those who disturb the peace of Britannia, like Caratacus and his savage followers."

Cogidubnus nodded slowly. "Caratacus's path is one of war and destruction. An honorable path, perhaps, in the eyes of some, but it leads to ruin, not only for him but also for those who follow him. I choose a different path, the path of survival, the path of reason." He looked directly at Maximus. "I have heard of you, Tribune, of your fight on the Medway. You are a young man, but you bear the marks of war."

Maximus was surprised by the direct address. "I do my duty, King Cogidubnus, for Rome and for peace."

"Peace," the king repeated thoughtfully. "A precious commodity. But a peace enforced under Rome's boot is fragile." He turned back to Flaccus and Adminius. "I will accept your alliance. I will swear loyalty to Rome. But I expect Rome to keep its promises, to truly protect my people from the Durotriges! We need more than words; we need shields on our border, your legions as guarantors. Bring trade and prosperity, teach us your building arts, your administration—not just tax collectors and arrogant commanders." His gaze flickered briefly towards Flaccus.

"Rome always keeps its word, King," Flaccus assured him, perhaps a fraction too quickly.

Adminius added, "This is the beginning of a new era for the Atrebates, Majesty, an era of peace and progress under the eagle's protection."

Cogidubnus offered a thin smile, one full of skepticism. "We shall see, Prince Adminius. Words are cheap; deeds will decide. We shall see." He raised his hand in a gesture of conclusion. "My advisors will negotiate the details of the agreement with you, Tribune Flaccus. For today, you are my guests. Let us dine and drink together."

A feast was prepared. Roasted meat, bread, mead, and strong Celtic beer were served. The Roman officers—Maximus, Brutus, Flaccus, Longinus—were invited to the king's table, with Adminius seated as guest of honor beside Cogidubnus. The common legionaries remained outside but also received generous rations of food and drink.

The atmosphere was strained politeness. There was drinking, talking, laughter, but mistrust lurked beneath the surface. Maximus observed the interactions closely. Cogidubnus was clever, cautious, weighing every word. His warriors were disciplined, but their gazes on the Romans remained watchful. Flaccus played his role as charming diplomat, while Adminius acted as a skillful mediator, switching between cultures and languages. Brutus remained mostly silent, eating and drinking little, his eyes missing nothing. Longinus was equally taciturn, a quiet observer.

Maximus himself spoke only when directly addressed. He felt Cogidubnus's eyes on him, sensed the king's curiosity, perhaps even respect. He thought of the massacre in the neighboring valley. Had Cogidubnus known about it? Was it the Durotriges? Or was he truly just a victim of circumstances, now seeking protection from Rome? He couldn't tell.

VII. FOREIGN ALLIES

Later in the evening, when the mead had flowed freely and the mood seemed somewhat more relaxed, Cogidubnus withdrew with Flaccus and Adminius for separate talks to hammer out the alliance details. Maximus and Brutus remained with the king's advisors.

"Your king is a wise man," Maximus said to the gray-haired warrior who had received them.

The man nodded slowly. "He does what he must for his people. Rome is a flood that cannot be stopped. One can only try to build a dam or swim with it." His gaze was old and weary.

"And you believe the alliance is the right path?" Brutus asked directly.

The warrior sighed. "It is *a* path. Whether it is right, the gods will decide. But the path of war, chosen by Caratacus, leads only to ruin." He looked searchingly at Brutus. "You are a warrior, Centurion. You have seen much. Do you not know when a fight is lost?"

Before Brutus could answer, Flaccus and Adminius returned, their faces showing satisfaction. "The agreement is sealed!" Flaccus announced triumphantly. "The Atrebates are now allies of Rome!"

Polite applause echoed through the hall. Maximus and Brutus exchanged a look. The first step was taken. But the road was still long, and the shadows over Britannia had not yet receded.

VIII. Path Through the Marsh

The departure from the Atrebates and their cautious King Cogidubnus was marked by a stiff, formal courtesy that barely concealed the underlying tension. The alliance was sealed, an important diplomatic success on paper. Yet, Maximus sensed the foundation of this pact was fragile. Cogidubnus had sworn loyalty to Rome, but his eyes spoke a different truth. He was playing for time, hedging his bets: a king caught between the Roman flood and the Britannic rock of Caratacus.

Leaving the relatively open, cultivated valleys of the Atrebates behind, the Roman cohort changed course again, heading west towards the territory of the Durotriges, where further talks were planned. The landscape shifted dramatically. It was as if they had crossed an invisible border, stepping from a known, albeit foreign, world into a realm of ancient, untamed nature. The land flattened but grew more treacherous. Dense, dark forests, overgrown with ivy and thorny brush, alternated with vast marshes and swamps, their surfaces covered by a deceptive green carpet of moss and rushes that hid black, bottomless mud beneath.

The air grew heavier, damper, filled with the musty odor of stagnant water and rotting vegetation. The sky seemed to

VIII. PATH THROUGH THE MARSH

hang lower, a permanent, dense gray from which fell either a relentless cold drizzle or sudden, violent downpours that reduced visibility to a few paces and made the march an agony. Fog became a constant companion, swirling between trees, creeping over the bogs, often enveloping the column for hours in a milky, disorienting twilight. The sounds changed too. The familiar clank of armor and tramp of boots sounded muffled, swallowed by the soft ground and damp air. Instead, there was the constant gurgle and suck of water, the eerie calls of unknown birds, the rustle of something unseen in the dense undergrowth. It was a land that felt hostile, seeming to devour the intruders.

The march turned into a nightmare. Narrow paths, often mere animal tracks, frequently vanished into the swamp or ended abruptly in impenetrable thickets. Men slipped on slick roots, sinking knee-deep in mire, their heavy armor dragging them down. The pack animals grew restless, frightened by the uncanny surroundings. They stumbled, often getting stuck, their loads salvaged only with immense effort and the loud curses of their handlers. More than once, an animal that broke a leg had to be put down, its burden painstakingly redistributed among the remaining beasts, slowing the advance to a tenacious crawl.

Maximus felt his men's morale sink with every arduous step. Their faces were gray with exhaustion, their clothing and armor permanently soaked and caked with mud. Grumbling grew louder; discipline began to fray at the edges. Even the most experienced veterans glanced around nervously, hands clutching the hilts of their swords. They were far from any support, deep in hostile territory, surrounded by a natural world that seemed an adversary in itself.

He continued to ride at the point, trying to project confidence and determination, though he himself was filled with growing concern. The scouts he constantly sent ahead reported no direct enemy contact but repeatedly found unsettling signs: fresh footprints of small groups seeming to cross their route, remnants of recently abandoned campfires, strange markings on trees whose meaning they didn't know. It was clear they were being watched, that the inhabitants of this marshland tracked their every move.

Beside him, Brutus had grown even quieter, his expression a stone mask. The coolness between him and Maximus, born from the disagreements at Secundus and Rutupiae, had not dissipated. Only the occasional twitch of a muscle in his jaw betrayed his inner tension. He spoke only to point out potential dangers or give curt orders for security. Every difficulty on this march seemed to confirm his unspoken criticism of Maximus's decision to follow Vespasian's order.

On the second day in the marshland, the scouts had their first direct, though fleeting, encounter. They came upon a small group of hunters or warriors—the distinction was difficult—clad in animal hides and armed with spears and simple bows. The men were small and sinewy, their faces camouflaged with mud and plant dyes, moving almost silently through the undergrowth. Barely spotted, they vanished like wisps of fog among the trees before the Romans could react, leaving behind no trace but a sense of unease and the certainty of not being alone.

On the afternoon of the same day, they found the source of these warriors. After a particularly grueling trek through knee-deep bog, they reached slightly drier high ground where a small, fortified settlement stood. It was different from

VIII. PATH THROUGH THE MARSH

the main Atrebate settlement. The palisades were lower but thicker, built of massive, rough-hewn logs-driven deep into the marshy ground. Behind them, only a few low, round huts of wattle and daub were visible, their roofs covered with turf, blending almost invisibly into the landscape. No smoke rose from any hut. It looked deserted, but Maximus sensed it wasn't.

He halted the column and sent scouts forward to reconnoiter. They returned quickly. "The gate is barricaded, Sir," reported Decurio Aelius. "No movement visible, but we assume they're inside. Watching us."

Maximus surveyed the settlement. It looked impregnable, a small fortress in the middle of the swamp. A direct assault would be costly and likely futile. He turned to Flaccus and Adminius, who had ridden up. "Prince Adminius, do you know this tribe?"

Adminius regarded the settlement with a frown. "I believe this is the territory of the... Marsh Warriors, as they call themselves. A small, isolated clan known for fiercely defending their territory. They are excellent hunters and masters of ambush. Their leader is a man named Bryn. Old, cunning, suspicious of all strangers." He hesitated briefly, then added, "I had the... pleasure of meeting him briefly years ago at a tribal council of the Catuvellauni. A man who holds his cards close to his chest."

"Can we negotiate with them?" Flaccus asked.

Adminius shook his head. "Unlikely. Bryn hates the Romans, but he also hates the larger tribes like the Catuvellauni or the Durotriges. He just wants to be left alone. He will refuse an alliance, I am sure of it."

"We cannot simply ignore them," Maximus said thoughtfully. "They control this area. If they are hostile, they could significantly hinder our further march, attack our rearguard."

"What do you propose, Tribune?" Flaccus inquired, a hint of irony in his voice. "Shall we smoke these swamp rats out?"

Maximus ignored the absurd suggestion. "No. We attempt contact. Peacefully, but firmly. I will go forward with a small delegation. Brutus, you command the main body and hold them ready." He turned to Adminius. "Prince, you will accompany me and act as translator. Let us show them we do not come only as conquerors."

Adminius seemed less than enthusiastic but nodded in agreement. Flaccus interjected, "I shall accompany you as well, Tribune. The diplomatic aspects…"

"No, Flaccus," Maximus interrupted firmly. "You remain here with the main group. I need only the Prince and a small honor guard. We don't want to appear threatening." He didn't want Flaccus along, distrusting him and unwilling to bring him into a potentially dangerous situation where he might make rash decisions.

Flaccus's lips thinned, but he didn't argue. Maximus selected ten of his most reliable legionaries, left the heavy *pila* behind, and slowly approached the settlement's gate, the white banner of his small group clearly visible. Adminius rode beside him.

They stopped about fifty paces from the gate. For a long time, nothing happened. Then a figure appeared on the low rampart behind the palisades. It was a gaunt, elderly man, clad in animal hides, his face deeply lined and painted with old mud-based colors. His eyes were small, sharp, and full of suspicion. He carried a long spear and watched the Romans silently. This had to be Bryn.

VIII. PATH THROUGH THE MARSH

Adminius called out something to him in Celtic, his voice surprisingly respectful. Bryn didn't answer immediately. He studied Maximus, then Adminius, then the legionaries behind them. Finally, he spoke, his voice quiet but carrying far in the still air, like the rustling of dry leaves.

Adminius translated: "He asks what the Roman wolves seek in his swamp."

"Tell him we come in peace," Maximus replied calmly. "We are on our way west to speak with other tribes. We seek no quarrel with his people. We ask only for free passage through his land."

Adminius translated again. Bryn listened, his expression unchanging. He spoke again, longer this time.

"He says," Adminius translated, "this is the land of his ancestors. Roman wolves have no business here. Our path leads through his swamp. Turn back, or his warriors will sink our bones in this marsh." The message was clear, a blatant threat.

"Tell him Rome desires no war with his people," Maximus retorted, his voice remaining calm but firm. "We are many. We are strong. A fight would only mean needless bloodshed, for both sides. Let us pass in peace, and we will leave you in peace."

Adminius relayed the words. Bryn laughed softly, a dry, humorless sound. He spat on the ground and vanished wordlessly from the rampart.

"And that's it?" Maximus asked incredulously.

"That's it," Adminius confirmed. "He refused us. He won't let us pass. He will fight."

Maximus looked towards the palisade. It was low but sturdy. Behind it waited unseen warriors, masters of this terrain.

An attack would be a bloody undertaking with an uncertain outcome and a high cost in time. He thought of Vespasian's order, of the mission.

"We cannot risk a battle here," he decided. "We must find another way." He gave the signal to withdraw.

As they returned to the main group, Flaccus met them with a smug smile. "Well, Tribune? Did the swamp rats show you the door?"

"They refuse passage," Maximus said curtly, ignoring the jibe. Brutus, who had watched the scene, shot Flaccus a dark look but said nothing. "We must find a detour."

"A detour? Through this damned swamp?" Flaccus asked incredulously. "That will cost us days!"

"Better than sacrificing our men in a pointless assault," Maximus replied coolly, his patience with Flaccus wearing thin.

"We have no time for detours!" Flaccus insisted. "We must reach the Durotriges!"

"We will reach them, Tribune," Maximus said firmly. "But we will do it our way, with minimal losses. Find a path north, Decurio," he ordered Aelius. "We bypass this settlement widely."

Reluctantly, Flaccus had to comply. The rest of the day and the entire next day became an even more grueling march through terrain that seemed even more impassable than the original path. They had to skirt treacherous bogs whose surfaces hid danger beneath deceptive green, hack their way with swords through thorny brush that grew like a living wall, and cross rushing streams where the water reached their chests and the current threatened to sweep men and animals away. The men were at the end of their strength,

VIII. PATH THROUGH THE MARSH

cursing, stumbling, their spirits hitting rock bottom. Friction between Maximus and Flaccus increased, barely contained by military hierarchy. Brutus remained distant, his silence often louder than Flaccus's open complaints, offering Maximus no overt support. Adminius seemed almost to enjoy the situation, watching the Romans with a faint, inscrutable smile.

On the evening of the sixth day, when they finally reached firmer ground again and set up a temporary camp, everyone was exhausted and irritable. The diplomatic mission had stalled, tensions within the leadership were openly apparent, and the eerie presence of the marsh warriors still weighed upon them. The marshland had exacted its toll, not just physically but morally. Front lines had hardened, not only against the Celts but within their own ranks.

As the sentries were posted and the first meager meals were cooked over smoking fires, Maximus, Brutus, and Decimus sat together for a rare moment of respite, slightly apart from the others. The tension of the day still hung heavy upon them.

Decimus poked at the fire with a twig, a deep sigh escaping him. "Hard days, Sir. This land… it eats you up." He looked at his calloused hands. "But the pay is good. When this campaign's over, hopefully I'll have enough saved to buy my wife that little vineyard she always wanted. Back in Gaul, near Lugdunum. And my daughter…" A soft smile touched his serious face. "She'll have a decent dowry. Makes it all worthwhile."

Maximus listened intently, nodding. "A good goal, Decimus. Something worth fighting for." He felt the simple humanity behind the Optio's words, a contrast to the cold calculations of men like Flaccus or the burden of his own hidden origins.

Brutus grunted in agreement but continued to stare into

the fire, the distance to Maximus still palpable.

Decimus seemed to sense the mood and tried to bridge the chill. "Still…" he smiled more broadly now, a memory seeming to cheer him, "…sometimes there are good adventures too, right? Remember back in Camulodunum, when we threw on those rags like we were Celts and brought down that damned Catuvellauni watchtower?" He chuckled softly. "By the gods, that was an adventure! I'll still be telling my grandchildren about that one when I'm old and gray." He looked expectantly from Brutus to Maximus.

Maximus smiled at the memory. "Yes, it was. Risky to the point of madness, but it worked." He shared a brief glance with Brutus, a reminder of a time when their camaraderie was untroubled.

Brutus's expression softened almost imperceptibly. A short nod, a reluctant twitch at the corner of his mouth. "Lots of noise and dirt," he muttered.

The small reaction seemed enough for Decimus. He sighed again, this time more contentedly. "Well, let's hope we get out of this mess safely too, so we have more stories to tell." He looked at Maximus and Brutus, his expression serious again, the professional Optio returning, but the warmth and familiarity he'd shown still lingered.

Maximus nodded. "We will, Decimus. We will." But as he gazed into the dancing flames, he felt the chill of uncertainty and the heavy burden of responsibility more keenly than ever.

IX. Signs of Fire

Departure from the temporary camp in the borderlands of the Atrebates occurred under a merciless sky. The pale gold of the morning sun that had accompanied the alliance with Cogidubnus gave way to a persistent, leaden gray. A cold, fine rain began again as they resumed their westward march, deeper into the territory marked on their crude maps as the land of the Durotriges.

The landscape changed noticeably. Rougher, more inhospitable terrain replaced the gentle hills and relatively open pastures of the Atrebates. Rocky outcrops broke through the dense forest canopy, often crowned by the ominous silhouettes of ancient hillforts. These silent witnesses to past wars perched above narrow valleys, their crumbling ramparts seeming to eye the Roman intruders with cold hostility. The forests grew denser and darker, choked with more undergrowth and thorny bushes that snagged at clothing and skin. While there were fewer swamps, the paths remained treacherous, often mere ribbons of scree on steep slopes or worn game trails winding through impenetrable thickets.

Maximus felt the change not only in the terrain but also in the atmosphere. Here, there were no more curious or fearful glances from scattered farmers. The few homesteads they passed seemed deserted, hearths cold, doors barred. Sometimes the scouts found fresh tracks, showing the inhabitants had fled only shortly before their arrival. Once, they discovered a small village by the path, but it wasn't just abandoned—it was a smoking ruin. Thatched roofs were burned away, timber walls charred, and the bitter smell of ash hung heavy in the air. There were no bodies, no signs of a fight, only the silent, brutal message of destruction. A trail of flames, either guiding their way or warning them.

"They know we're coming," Brutus stated grimly as they left the smoking ruins behind. "They're burning their own land to deny us supplies, or to show us what awaits."

"It's the scorched earth tactic," Maximus nodded darkly. "That means they're prepared to go to extremes. They won't give an easy fight." He looked around, his eyes scanning the hilltops and dense woods. The feeling of being watched was almost tangible here, no longer a nervous imagining, but the cold certainty of being in enemy territory.

The attacks began on the afternoon of the first day in the Durotriges' lands. They didn't come as an open battle, but as Maximus and Brutus had feared: swift, brutal pinpricks.

Brutus was leading the vanguard through a narrow gorge, rocky walls rising steeply on both sides, when suddenly a hail of stones and spears rained down. These weren't precise Roman *pila*, but crude yet deadly missiles: sharp-edged rocks and simple, fire-hardened wooden spears, striking the legionaries with surprising accuracy.

"*Scuta* up! Hold formation!" Brutus bellowed, deflecting a falling boulder with his shield. The impact shuddered up his arm, but the thick wood and leather held. Around him, men groaned. Shields splintered. A spear struck a legionary in the calf, and he went down screaming. A rock hit another on the helmet, and he collapsed unconscious. Chaos threatened as men instinctively sought cover, the tight formation breaking.

"Stand fast, you dogs!" Brutus's voice thundered through the gorge, louder even than the crash of impacting stones. "Eyes up! Archers, loose! Cover the slopes!"

The few archers assigned to the cohort reacted instantly. Dropping their large shields, they nocked arrows and sent volleys towards the cliffs above. Their arrows rarely found visible targets, but the covering fire at least forced the attackers to duck down; the rockfall lessened.

"Recover the wounded! Withdraw to the main body! Move!" Brutus commanded. The legionaries now responded with discipline, forming a shield wall facing upwards while some men retrieved the wounded, slowly retreating step by step from the kill zone. The attack had lasted only minutes, but it had achieved its effect: two dead, five wounded, and a significant blow to morale. The Celts had shown their mastery of the terrain and their willingness to use it as a weapon.

As the vanguard rejoined the main column, Flaccus rode towards them, his expression a mask of feigned concern. "What happened, Centurion? Difficulties?"

"A small welcoming committee from the locals, Tribune," Brutus retorted bitingly, helping lift a wounded man onto a makeshift stretcher. "Nothing the Second Legion can't handle." He shot Flaccus a dark look.

Flaccus ignored the glare. "We must be more cautious," he said, lecturingly. "This land is more treacherous than it appears." He turned to Maximus. "Tribune, perhaps we should slow the pace, send out more scouts?"

"We already have scouts out, Tribune Flaccus," Maximus replied coolly. "And we cannot afford to crawl. We must press on. But," he glanced at Brutus, "we will strengthen flank security, and the men will maintain a tighter formation from now on, even in seemingly open ground."

Brutus nodded in agreement. It was a small compromise, but it showed Maximus took the danger seriously.

"Why don't we turn back? It seems the Durotriges aren't friendly towards us," Maximus asked, looking towards Flaccus and the Prince. The two exchanged a quick glance, and Adminius answered, "The Durotriges are a warlike tribe; if we flee now, it appears weak. However, if we resolutely push forward and show strength, that could form a good basis for negotiations."

"Maybe then we should just burn their villages along the way and take their people as slaves. After all, they're killing our boys too, and if they want strength, then…"

"Enough!" Maximus cut Brutus off. "We handle the military matters. If these two say we continue, then we continue, Centurion." Maximus's look and annoyed tone left no room for argument.

"Yes, Sir," Brutus grumbled, saluted, and walked away to relay the command.

The march resumed, tension mounting. Every shadow seemed to hold a threat; every rustle in the undergrowth made men flinch. The night brought no relief. Double sentries guarded the fortified camp, fires kept small. Still, disturbances occurred. Arrows hissed silently from the darkness, thudding harmlessly into the earth rampart or dangerously close to the tents. Once, a small group of Celts tried to sneak up on the tethered horses but were spotted by alert legionaries and driven off after a brief scuffle, leaving one Roman slightly wounded. Sleep was fitful, interrupted by alarm calls and the constant fear of attack.

The Durotriges' war of attrition was working. By the next morning, the men's faces were paler, the circles under their eyes deeper. The constant threat, lack of sleep, and arduous march drained strength and morale.

Tensions flared again at the improvised council of war around the meager breakfast fire.

"We're losing too much time!" Flaccus urged impatiently. "These pinpricks are annoying, and they're just slowing us down. We must move faster!"

"The alliance with the Atrebates won't do us much good if we get ground down by the Durotriges on the way!" Brutus countered sharply. "These 'pinpricks' are costing us men! We need to proceed more slowly, secure every meter, perhaps even establish a fortified strong point and operate from there."

"Establish a strong point?" Flaccus laughed scornfully. "And how long shall we sit here in the swamp, Centurion? Weeks? Months? Until winter traps us? That's cowardice, not caution!"

"Are you calling me a coward, Tribune?" Brutus growled menacingly, his hand balling into a fist.

"Enough!" Maximus cut them both off sharply, his voice slicing through the tense atmosphere. "Arguments get us nowhere!" He looked from one to the other. "Brutus is right, the danger is real, and we must be cautious. But Flaccus is also right; we have a mission and cannot afford unnecessary delays." He thought for a moment, then made a decision. "We will slightly increase the pace, but double the flank security and the vanguard. We march in compact formation. No man leaves the ranks without orders. At the slightest sign of a major ambush, we withdraw immediately and form a defensive circle. We will not be drawn into a fight on their terms."

It was another compromise that satisfied no one completely, but it was a clear order. Flaccus nodded reluctantly; Brutus's expression remained dark, but he gave a curt salute.

At that moment, Adminius, who had remained silent during the argument, stepped forward. "Tribune, Centurion," he said in his smooth, persuasive voice. "I may know a way that could help us. Slightly off the main route, there is an old Druid path. It is hard to find and little known, even among my own people. It leads more directly west, avoiding the most dangerous narrows and swamps. I… I could scout it for you."

Maximus and Brutus eyed him suspiciously. A secret path? Offered by Adminius?

"How do you know this path, Prince?" Brutus asked directly.

"Old stories from my father," Adminius replied. "And… observations during my travels, before… before things changed." He smiled sadly. "I wish to make myself useful. If this path is safe, it could save us valuable time and protect us from further attacks."

"And if it's a trap?" Brutus asked bluntly.

Adminius's smile vanished. "Centurion, I have tied my fate to Rome. Your victory is my victory. Your defeat would also be my ruin. Why would I betray you?" His eyes seemed sincere, almost pleading.

Maximus hesitated. It sounded too good to be true. But the alternative was another grueling march through hostile territory under constant attack. The "Druid path" was a risk, but perhaps a calculated one?

IX. SIGNS OF FIRE

"What do you think, Tribune Flaccus?" Maximus asked, buying time and gauging Flaccus's reaction.

Flaccus seemed to consider it briefly, then nodded slowly. "The Prince offers a better way, and time is a critical factor. His knowledge could be valuable." He looked encouragingly at Adminius. "A bold suggestion, Prince. But also dangerous."

"I am prepared to take the risk," Adminius said firmly. "Give me a small escort, just a few riders. I will scout the path and return before nightfall to report."

Maximus exchanged a long look with Brutus. The Centurion gave an almost imperceptible shake of his head. *Don't trust him,* his eyes said.

But Maximus was torn. The potential time saved, the possibility of avoiding further losses—it was tempting. And Vespasian had instructed him to use Adminius's knowledge.

"Very well, Prince," Maximus said finally, against his better judgment. "Choose five of your riders. Be extremely cautious. Return before sunset. If you are not back by then, we will assume the worst has happened and resume our original march."

"Thank you for your trust, Tribune," Adminius said with a beaming smile that Maximus felt was false. "You will not regret it." He saluted in a strangely clumsy manner and hurried off to select his riders.

Flaccus clapped Maximus on the shoulder. "A wise decision, Tribune. Sometimes one must take calculated risks." His smile was impenetrable.

As Adminius and his small group rode off shortly thereafter at dawn, disappearing quickly into the forest, Brutus watched them with undisguised suspicion. "He's not coming back," he muttered, so low only Maximus could hear.

"How do you know?" Maximus asked, though he harbored the same fear.

"I feel it," Brutus said. "That man has betrayal in his eyes. He's not leading us to a safe path; he's leading us deeper into the trap."

Maximus fell silent. He looked towards where Adminius had vanished, then at the long column of his tired but resolute men. The trail of flames they followed—whether lit by Celtic destruction or the intrigues of their supposed allies—was leading them ever deeper towards an uncertain fate. Maximus sincerely hoped Brutus was wrong.

X. The Ambush

The hours after Adminius's departure crawled by with agonizing slowness. The Roman cohort remained in their temporary camp on the high ground, an island of tense expectation amidst the hostile marshland. The drizzle had returned, falling silently and incessantly, transforming the ground into a deep, sticky mire and muffling all sounds to a dull murmur. Men sat or stood in small groups around the smoking, reluctantly burning fires, cleaning their weapons, checking their gear, or staring silently into the gray, impenetrable wall of forest and fog that surrounded them. Every snap of a twig, every unfamiliar bird call made them flinch.

Maximus felt his men's nervousness as if it were his own. He paced the hastily erected defensive lines, exchanging encouraging words with the sentries on the crudely reinforced earthworks and checking the archers' positions. He tried to appear busy, projecting his usual calm authority, but inwardly he was a turmoil of doubt and worry. Had it been right to trust Adminius? Had the pressure of the mission, the hope of saving time, overridden his better judgment? The hours crept by, and with each one, his fear grew that he had made a fatal mistake. Was the "Druid path" real or just a fiction, a lie to lure them off the main route or buy time? What if something had actually happened to Adminius? What if he was now leading the Celts, perhaps even the Durotriges, directly to their camp?

He sought out Brutus and found the Centurion with the men of his own century, stoically supervising the repair of damaged equipment. Brutus looked up as Maximus approached, his expression unreadable, but a deep seriousness in his eyes mirrored Maximus's concerns.

"Still no word from the scouts we sent after Adminius?" Maximus asked quietly. Shortly after Adminius left, he had dispatched two of his most reliable mounted scouts with orders to follow the small group discreetly and turn back immediately at the slightest sign of danger or betrayal.

Brutus shook his head. "Nothing. They haven't returned. That could mean many things." His tone was heavy.

"Or nothing good," Maximus muttered. He glanced at the sun, barely visible as a pale disk through the thick cloud cover. It was already low in the western sky. The deadline he had set for Adminius—return before sunset—was drawing relentlessly closer. The tension inside Maximus became almost unbearable.

"We shouldn't have let him go," Brutus growled, voicing Maximus's own doubts and regrets aloud. "It was a mistake to believe a single word from that traitor."

Maximus rubbed his temples; his head throbbed. "Perhaps. Probably even." He abandoned his earlier defense of the decision; reality was catching up. "But it's too late for regrets, Brutus. We made a choice; now we live—or die—with the consequences." His expression was grim. "My gut screamed betrayal, just like yours. But hope... the damned hope of

X. THE AMBUSH

shortening this march, of getting the men out of this swamp… it was stronger." He sighed, a mix of exhaustion and self-reproach. "I listened to the wrong advice, or the right advice for the wrong reasons."

"Five good Roman cavalrymen are worth more than that entire Celtic prince," Brutus retorted bitterly.

Maximus fell silent. He had no counterargument. The truth of Brutus's words hit him hard.

The sun continued its crawl across the sky, shadows lengthened, the rain fell unabated. The mood in the camp grew heavier. Everyone instinctively looked west, listening for the sound of hooves that never came. Centurion Longinus kept unobtrusively near Flaccus's tent, observing the Tribune, who seemed detached, talking with his slaves or studying maps. Flaccus appeared outwardly calm, almost bored, but Maximus thought he detected suppressed tension in his posture. Was Flaccus waiting too? Did he know more than he let on?

Sunset came and went, with no sign of Adminius or the two scouts sent after him. Darkness fell quickly over the marshland, broken only by the flickering light of campfires and a few torches on the ramparts. The rain intensified again, drumming on tent roofs and the sentries' helmets. The deadline had passed. The trap, if it was one, had either sprung, or Adminius had failed and was lost.

Maximus met with Brutus and Longinus in the small *praetorium*. The air was thick with the smell of wet wool and tension.

"He's not coming back," Brutus stated. It wasn't a question. "I knew it." His voice was full of bitterness, but also a grim satisfaction.

"We can wait no longer," Maximus said decisively, his voice now free of doubt, only cold and resolute. "Adminius had his chance. Either something happened to him, or he betrayed us. Either way, we must act."

"What do you propose, Tribune?" Longinus asked.

"We break camp at first light tomorrow," Maximus decided. "But not via the supposed Druid path. We return to the main route and continue our march west as originally planned, but with double caution. We assume we were meant to be led into a trap."

"A wise decision, Sir," Brutus said with a hint of relief, the coolness yielding to professional agreement. "We stay on known ground, however hostile it may be."

"Yes, Sir," Longinus said curtly. "I will inform the men."

"One question remains," Brutus interjected, looking pointedly at Flaccus, who had entered unbidden. "What about Tribune Flaccus? He was supposed to lead this diplomatic mission. Without Adminius, it is... difficult."

Flaccus stepped closer, his face showing feigned regret. "The loss of the Prince is tragic. A severe blow to our plans." He sighed. "But the mission must continue. Perhaps we can convince the other tribes even without Adminius, or find another way." His gaze was fixed on Maximus, almost challenging.

"We continue the march west, Tribune Flaccus," Maximus said coolly, the decision final. "On the main route. The cohort's safety is the top priority."

Flaccus nodded slowly. "Of course, Maximus. Safety first. But we must not lose sight of the goal." He sounded reasonable, almost cooperative. Too cooperative, Maximus thought, but he let it rest for the moment.

X. THE AMBUSH

The night passed restlessly. Reinforced sentries, constant patrols, yet nothing happened. It was the calm before the storm, an ominous quiet more frightening than open attacks.

At first light, before the fog had fully lifted, the cohort was ready to march. They left the temporary camp and returned to the main path. The men were tense but disciplined. They knew something was coming. They sensed the trap, even if they couldn't see it.

They marched for about an hour on the main path, which now wound again through dense forest. Visibility was poor, the ground slippery. Maximus and Brutus rode at the point, their eyes ceaselessly scanning the treelines.

Then it happened. Not with a loud war cry, but with an eerie whirring sound, followed by dull thuds. Arrows. Dozens, hundreds of arrows rained down from the trees onto the surprised column. They came from both sides, from the treetops, from the dense undergrowth.

"*Scuta* up! Shield wall!" Brutus roared instinctively, yanking his horse around, trying to find cover.

Legionaries cried out, hit by arrows that pierced armor or found unprotected spots. Horses shied, reared, throwing their riders. The orderly marching column dissolved into sheer chaos in seconds.

"Form up! Hold the line!" Maximus shouted over the din, drawing his *gladius*, trying to rally the men around him. He saw legionaries fall, saw Optios trying to hold their centuries together, saw Centurion Longinus attempting to form a defensive circle around Flaccus, who sat pale but strangely calm on his horse. *Did he know about this? Was he expecting it?*

The arrow storm subsided, only to be replaced by something worse. From the forest on both sides of the path, Celtic warriors erupted. Not disciplined ranks, but wild figures, painted and clad in hides—Durotriges, mixed with Bryn's marsh warriors, as Maximus and Brutus instantly recognized. They charged the disorganized Romans with axes, spears, and simple swords, their yells like those of predators sensing prey.

It was no longer an ambush; it was a slaughter. The Romans were trapped, pinned on the narrow, muddy path, unable to deploy their superior formations and discipline. They fought man-to-man now, desperately, for survival.

Maximus and Brutus fought side-by-side at the front, trying to hold the initial onslaught, buying time for the men behind them to rally. Maximus's sword flashed, parrying an axe blow, thrusting, connecting. A Celt collapsed, groaning. Brutus roared with fury and exertion, his *gladius* felling attacker after attacker, but there were too many. They came from all sides, leaping from trees, emerging from the undergrowth.

"Fall back!" Maximus yelled to Brutus. "We need to regroup! Form a circle!"

"Fall back where?" Brutus roared back, deflecting a spear thrust. "We're surrounded!"

He was right. The Celts had completely enveloped them. The path was blocked, the forest too dense for an orderly retreat.

Maximus looked around desperately. He saw Flaccus, still mounted, surrounded by Longinus and a handful of legionaries trying to maintain a small defensive ring. But they were being pushed back, away from the main fighting line. *We're being cut off from the cohort,* the thought flashed through Maximus's mind. *Were they trying to isolate us here?*

Then he saw a particularly large group of Celts, led by a warrior wearing a wolf pelt over his shoulders—it was Bryn—

X. THE AMBUSH

charging specifically towards his and Brutus's position. They ignored the fighting on the flanks; their objective was clear: eliminate the Roman command.

"Brutus! They're coming for us!" Maximus shouted.

Brutus saw it too. He let out a savage curse. "Good! Let them come! Let's kick their hairy barbarian asses!" He raised his sword.

The Celts crashed into their small, shrinking circle of legionaries. The fight became even more brutal, more desperate. Maximus felt a heavy blow against his shield that sent him stumbling back. He saw Brutus attacked by two warriors simultaneously, saw him parry, strike back, but slowly give ground. He saw his men falling, one after another, overwhelmed by sheer numbers.

"Maximus!" he heard Brutus's desperate cry. He spun around and saw the Centurion go down, a Celtic arrow protruding from his shoulder.

A cry of raw fury tore from Maximus's throat. He forgot tactics, caution, rank. He launched himself like a berserker at the Celts surrounding Brutus, his *gladius* a whirling storm of death. He slashed, stabbed, kicked, fighting with the frenzy of a gladiator with nothing left to lose. He reached Brutus, hauled him up, covered him with his shield.

"We have to get out of here, Brutus!" he gasped.

Brutus grinned bloodily. "Where to… my friend?"

At that moment, they heard horns. Roman horns. But they weren't coming from the direction they had marched from, but from further back, from the direction Flaccus had been pushed towards. A signal to retreat or rally?

Then they saw it. Flaccus, Longinus, and the rest of the cohort—or what was left of it—were indeed withdrawing.

Not fighting their way clear to help Maximus and Brutus, but pulling back in an orderly, yet unstoppable, retreat from the battlefield, leaving the head of the column to its fate.

The betrayal was obvious, brutal, final.

Maximus stared in disbelief at the retreating backs of his comrades. Flaccus had done it. He had lured them into the trap and was now leaving them here to die.

A triumphant roar went up from the Celts as they saw the main Roman force withdraw. They turned their full attention now to the remaining, isolated Romans around Maximus and Brutus.

"Damn him, the son of a whore from the Suburra," Brutus choked out, leaning heavily on Maximus.

"We're on our own," Maximus said tonelessly, looking into the hate-filled faces of the charging Celts. Around them stood perhaps twenty, thirty legionaries of his original century and Brutus's. Cut off, surrounded, deep in hostile marshland. The trap had sprung.

XI. Blood in the Fern

The world shrank around Maximus and Brutus, reduced to mud, blood, the metallic clang of weapons, and the bloodcurdling screams of the dying and the attackers. Flaccus's retreat with the rest of the cohort was betrayal. It was a death sentence for the few dozen legionaries now cut off and surrounded in the heart of the hostile marshland. The initial shock over Flaccus's act gave way to cold, desperate resolve. There was no way back, no retreat possible. There was only the fight, to the last man, to the last breath.

"Shield wall! Form circle!" Brutus bellowed, though the arrow still jutted painfully from his shoulder. Adrenaline and a veteran's survival instinct masked the pain. He snapped off the shaft, ignored the welling blood, and raised his *scutum*. Beside him stood Maximus, his face a mask of grime, sweat, and enemy blood, *gladius* held firm. The two men's eyes met for a fraction of a second—a silent understanding, a final salute between brothers-in-arms.

The remaining legionaries—perhaps thirty in number, the rest already lying dead or wounded in the bloody mire—reacted instinctively to Brutus's command. They pressed together, shoulder to shoulder, forming a tight circle, their large rectangular shields facing outwards, short, deadly *gladii* at the ready. It was a hedgehog formation, the last refuge of hopelessly outnumbered infantry.

The Celts, led by the gaunt Bryn and other fierce Durotrigan warriors, hesitated for a moment, surprised by the Romans' sudden discipline, perhaps impressed by their defiance of death. But then they charged, a chaotic, roaring mob, fueled by imminent victory and hatred for the invaders. They crashed like a wave against the small Roman shield circle.

The impact was brutal. Shields slammed together, wood splintered, metal screamed on metal. Spears stabbed over and under shield rims. Axes struck shields with thunderous blows. Long Celtic swords probed for gaps in the Roman wall. The Romans held. They thrust with their *gladii* through the narrow openings between shields, aiming for unprotected legs, arms, faces. It was chaotic, bloody close-quarters combat.

Maximus fought in a frenzy. He parried a wild blow, thrust, and met flesh. A Celt screamed and collapsed before him, only to be instantly replaced by another. He felt a stab of pain in his left arm as a spear pierced his shield, grazing his forearm. He ignored it, thrust again, his breath coming in ragged gasps. He saw Brutus beside him, fighting with the strength of a wounded bear despite his injury, his face contorted into a grimacing mask, each blow a death sentence.

But the odds were overwhelming. For every Celt that fell, two more seemed to take his place. The Roman circle shrank, tightened, the men slowly giving ground, stumbling over the bodies of their fallen comrades. They were exhausted, many wounded, their strength fading.

"They're breaking through! Right side!" a legionary yelled

XI. BLOOD IN THE FERN

before being cut down by an axe blow.

Maximus spun, saw several Celts exploiting a gap in the shield wall, pouring into the circle. He threw himself towards them, Brutus following, panting. They managed to cut down the intruders, but it cost precious strength and time.

The situation was hopeless. Maximus knew it. Brutus knew it. The men knew it. They would die here, in the mud of this godforsaken swamp, betrayed by their own people. But they would die as Romans. They would make the enemy pay a price he wouldn't soon forget.

"For Rome!" Maximus cried, his voice rough and hoarse.

"For the Second Augusta!" Brutus roared back, blood trickling from the corner of his mouth.

The remaining legionaries answered with a final, desperate battle cry, hurling themselves back into the slaughter.

Amidst this chaos, just as death seemed inevitable, something unexpected happened. A small group of legionaries, who had fallen slightly behind during the initial onslaught and now stood somewhat apart from the main fight, had been watching the scene. At their head stood Optio Decimus, his stocky body tense, his face an expression of determined fury.

Decimus had seen Flaccus's betrayal with his own eyes. He had seen the main body of the cohort abandon the vanguard. His heart filled with a mixture of burning rage and deep despair. He saw his Centurion, Brutus, whom he revered like an older brother, fighting wounded and surrounded. He saw the young Tribune, who had proven himself a worthy leader despite everything, facing certain death. He saw the handful of brave men fighting like lions, but doomed.

He could have retreated. Flaccus had signaled the withdrawal. He could have saved himself and his few men. No one would have blamed him. But Decimus was not a man to abandon his comrades. He was a soldier of the Second Legion, and his loyalty did not lay with a treacherous Tribune or a distant Emperor, but with the men at his side and the Eagle they had all served.

He made a decision, one that defied every order, all military logic, but came from the depths of his heart.

"Men!" he called to the roughly fifteen legionaries gathered around him. His voice was firm, clear, without a hint of doubt, ringing with the authority of an experienced Optio. "Do you see our brothers there? Do you see the Centurion? The Tribune? They will die if we do nothing! Flaccus betrayed us, left them to die!"

The men looked at him, their faces a mixture of shock, anger, and disbelief.

"We are legionaries of the Second!" Decimus continued, his voice rising, becoming passionate. "We do not abandon our comrades! Never! We don't fight for Flaccus; we don't fight for politicians in Rome! We fight for the men beside us! For the honor of the Legion!"

He drew his *gladius*. His father's wooden amulet, a simple good-luck charm, dangled on his chest. "Who is with me? Who fights with me to save our brothers, or die honorably at their side?"

For a moment, there was silence, only the distant echo of the battle audible. Then an older legionary, his face scarred, stepped forward. "I am with you, Optio."

"Me too!"

"And I!"

One by one, the men stepped forward, their resolve ignited by Decimus's words. They were not many, just a handful

XI. BLOOD IN THE FERN

against overwhelming numbers. But they were Romans.

"Good!" Decimus said, his heart swelling with pride. "Wedge formation! Aim for the flank of the bastards pressing the Centurion! We strike fast, break their lines, and pull back with our brothers as quickly as we can! No mercy! For Brutus! For Maximus! For the Second Augusta!"

With a thunderous war cry, the small group charged, Decimus at the point. They ran through the ferns, shields raised, swords ready. They were an unexpected arrow, shot into the enemy's flank.

The Celts, focused on annihilating the surrounded Roman circle, noticed the new threat too late. Decimus and his men crashed into their unprotected side with full force. The element of surprise was perfect. *Gladii* met exposed backs; shields slammed warriors to the ground. The Celtic line wavered; chaos erupted in their ranks.

"Decimus! By the gods!" Brutus cried in disbelief, seeing the unexpected reinforcement. Hope, which he had already abandoned, flickered within him.

"Retreat! Men, to me!" Maximus shouted instantly, recognizing the unique opportunity. "Decimus is creating a gap! Move!"

The surrounded legionaries, spurred by the sudden turn of events, gathered their last strength. They pushed against the weakened Celtic line, surged forward, while Decimus and his men attacked from the side, carving a bloody path.

For a brief, chaotic moment, they succeeded. The Celtic ring broke. The two Roman groups merged, forming a new, larger, though still desperate, formation.

"Fall back! Slowly! To the edge of the woods!" Maximus commanded, trying to bring order to the chaos.

But the Celts recovered quickly from the shock. Furious at the unexpected disruption, they reformed and pressed the Romans again, determined not to let their prey escape. The battle reignited, fiercer than before.

Decimus fought like a lion to cover the retreat. He stood between his rescued comrades and the charging Celtic mass, his sword a red whirlwind. He saw Maximus supporting the badly wounded Brutus, pulling him slowly backward. He saw the faces of his men, exhausted, bleeding, but resolute. He knew they wouldn't all make it.

A large warrior wielding a huge axe broke through the Roman line, charging directly at Maximus and the wounded Brutus. Decimus didn't hesitate for a second. With a loud cry, he threw himself into the attacker's path. He parried the first axe blow with his shield, which shattered under the impact. He thrust with his *gladius*, hitting the Celt in the chest, but the giant fought on. The axe fell again. Decimus dodged, but not fast enough. The blade struck him deep in the side. Searing pain shot through him, but he stayed on his feet, blocking the warrior's path. He saw two legionaries stab the Celt from behind, then his legs gave way.

He sank to his knees, the sword slipping from his grasp. He felt the life ebbing from him, vaguely saw the faces of his comrades slowly retreating. He saw Maximus turn one last time, his eyes filled with pain and gratitude. He saw Brutus trying to struggle upright. A final image flashed before his mind's eye: the small vineyard in Gaul, bathed in sunlight, his wife laughing, his daughter running towards him... *It was worth it,* he thought.

Decimus smiled faintly. He had done his duty. He had not abandoned his brothers. His wooden amulet pressed cold

XI. BLOOD IN THE FERN

against his chest. He closed his eyes, hearing the distant echo of battle, the rustle of rain in the ferns, then… silence.

XII. Flight Through the Woods

Decimus's cry, a mixture of pain and final defiance, still hung in the damp air. Then the full force of reality hit Maximus: they were alone, betrayed, and surrounded. Decimus's sacrifice had bought them a tiny, precious chance, a bloody gap in the Celtic encirclement, but it would close quickly. There was no time for grief, no time for anger, only the animal instinct for survival.

"Brutus!" Maximus yelled, his voice hoarse from battle and strain. He gripped the wounded Centurion tighter as Brutus struggled to stay on his feet. "We have to get out of here! Now!"

Brutus nodded, gritting his teeth against the pain radiating from his shattered shoulder. He leaned heavily on Maximus, his breath coming in short, ragged gasps. "Where... in Hades... are we supposed to flee?"

"Into the woods!" Maximus ordered the few remaining men of his and Brutus's centuries—perhaps twenty, if he was lucky, battered, bleeding, but still living legionaries. "Follow me! Stay together!"

He pushed Brutus forward, away from the center of the slaughter, towards the dense, dark edge of the forest that now represented their only hope. The legionaries followed

XII. FLIGHT THROUGH THE WOODS

instinctively, forming a loose but determined wedge around their two leaders, stumbling over the bodies of friend and foe, their shields offering a last, desperate protection against the spears and stones hurled by the pursuing Celts.

Plunging into the woods was like entering another world. The chaos of the battlefield fell away, replaced by the twilight beneath the dense canopy and the eerie silence of the undergrowth. But the silence was deceptive. Behind them, they heard the furious shouts of the Celts, the cracking of branches, the sound of men forcing their way through the thicket. The pursuit had begun.

"Faster!" Maximus gasped, dragging the staggering Brutus along. "We can't stop!"

The forest floor was a treacherous maze of roots, rocks, and deep, wet leaves that made every step a potential fall. Thorny vines tore at their clothes and skin. Low-hanging branches slapped their faces. The fine rain, barely felt here beneath the leafy roof, had turned the ground into slick mud. Men slipped, fell, scrambled back up, helping each other. Their heavy armor, normally their protection, now became a leaden burden, dragging them down, consuming their already dwindling strength.

Brutus groaned with every step, his face ashen, sweat and blood mingling on his forehead. The makeshift bandage someone had applied during the fight was long soaked through. His left shoulder was a red, painful mess. He leaned heavily on Maximus and a young legionary named Titus, who supported him on the other side.

"Leave me, Maximus," Brutus forced out, his voice barely a whisper. "I'm only slowing you down. Save yourselves... save the men."

"Never!" Maximus retorted with a vehemence that surprised even himself, gripping Brutus's arm tighter. "No one gets left behind! Decimus's sacrifice wasn't worth that! We get out of here together, or not at all!" An uncontrollable rage surged within him—rage at Flaccus, rage at the Celts, rage at this cursed land, but above all, rage at the hopelessness of their situation. He had to stay strong, for Brutus, for the men. He was the Tribune. The responsibility rested on his shoulders.

He tried to maintain a course, navigating by the sun—rarely glimpsed as a pale disk through the leaves—by the direction of the wind, and by instinct. He didn't know exactly where he was leading them, only away from the pursuers, away from the trap, deeper into the supposed safety of the woods. But were the woods truly safe, or just another kind of trap, a green labyrinth with no exit?

Behind them, the sounds of pursuit grew louder. Celtic war horns blared through the trees, their calls seeming to come from all sides, driving the Romans before them like hunted animals. They heard the snap of twigs, the shouts of men in their strange, guttural language. They were close, too close.

"They're gaining!" gasped Titus, the young legionary supporting Brutus, fear stark in his eyes.

"Then we must be faster!" Maximus replied. "Come on, men! Move! Think of Rome! Think of your families!" He tried to spur them on, but his own legs felt like lead. Exhaustion was a physical pain, a constant throbbing in his temples, a burning in his lungs.

They reached a small stream, its water flowing sluggishly and muddy between moss-covered stones. Not a major obstacle, but another hurdle in their condition. They had

XII. FLIGHT THROUGH THE WOODS

to descend into the streambed, wade through the cold water, climb the slippery bank on the other side.

"Careful!" Maximus called out. "Help each other!"

They made it across, but it cost precious time and energy. One legionary slipped on the bank, twisting his ankle. He gritted his teeth but couldn't put weight on it. Two comrades supported him, dragging him along, slowing the group again.

Maximus looked back. He counted eighteen men left, including himself and Brutus. They had been twenty when they entered the woods. Where were the other two? He hadn't seen them fall, hadn't heard them cry out. Had they gotten lost in the fog? Fallen behind, overwhelmed? Or taken silently from the rear? The thought sent ice through his veins.

"We need to rest, Sir," Brutus said, his voice little more than a croak. He leaned heavily against a tree trunk, his face ashen, sweat and blood mingling on his brow, his lips tinged blue. "Just… just a moment. I… I can't go on."

Maximus hesitated. Every halt increased the danger of discovery. But Brutus's condition was alarming. He wasn't just wounded; he was at the end of his strength. Pushing him further would be pointless, perhaps fatal. And the men needed it too. They were ghosts, barely able to stay on their feet.

"Alright," he said finally. "Ten minutes. No more. Take cover! Post guards! Quietly!" He helped ease Brutus carefully onto the damp, mossy ground, leaning him against the thick trunk of an old oak.

The men collapsed in exhaustion, panting, groaning, hiding behind trees, in the dense ferns. The sudden silence after the hectic flight was almost unbearable, broken only by the men's heavy breathing, the soft drip of rain from the leaves, and the eerie creak of branches in the wind. Maximus knelt beside Brutus, pulled out his nearly empty waterskin, and held it to the Centurion's lips. Brutus drank greedily, spilling half.

Maximus examined the wound on Brutus's shoulder. The arrow had penetrated the *lorica hamata*, the mail shirt Brutus favored, lodging deep in the muscle tissue. Brutus had broken the shaft, but the head was likely still embedded. The bleeding seemed to have lessened somewhat, but the wound gaped, surrounded by swollen, reddened flesh. It was a miracle Brutus could walk at all.

"We need a medicus," Maximus murmured, trying to clean the wound with a relatively clean scrap of cloth torn from his innermost tunic. It was a futile gesture, but he had to do something.

"We need... wine," Brutus rasped, attempting a smile that became only a painful grimace. "Good, strong Falernian... and a dry place to die."

"Nobody dies here, Brutus," Maximus said firmly, his voice rough with emotion. He leaned closer to his friend. "Do you hear me? Nobody! Not after what Decimus did." The Optio's name hung heavy between them.

Brutus closed his eyes, a single, pained sigh escaping his chest. "Decimus... Damned fool. Brave, damned fool." He opened his eyes again, looking directly at Maximus, an unaccustomed vulnerability in his gaze. "I'm sorry, Maximus."

"For what?" Maximus asked, surprised.

"For being so... cold. Since Rutupiae." Brutus breathed heavily. "I was angry, disappointed. I thought you... you were abandoning us, the men back at the outpost, because of an order from above, because of politics." He coughed, his face twisting in pain. "I should have trusted you, your judgment.

XII. FLIGHT THROUGH THE WOODS

You are the Tribune."

Maximus felt a lump in his throat. He placed a hand on Brutus's uninjured shoulder. "I understand your anger, Brutus. I doubted myself. It was an impossible decision." He sighed. "Maybe it was the wrong one. Maybe we should have faced the Celts. Maybe Decimus would still be alive." The guilt weighed heavily on him.

"No," Brutus said with surprising firmness. "No, Maximus. You obeyed the order. That is duty. Decimus… he did his duty too. He saved us. Bought us time." He swallowed. "He was a good Optio. The best I ever had. Always correct, always loyal. Even if sometimes…" A faint smile touched Brutus's lips. "Even if sometimes he got on your nerves with his damned old stories at the wrong time."

Maximus smiled too, despite the desperate situation, remembering Decimus—the solid, reliable Optio, always a step behind Brutus, ready to execute any command, but also possessing a dry humor and an unexpected penchant for telling anecdotes from his youth or previous campaigns at the most inopportune moments.

"He always tried to lift spirits," Maximus said softly, "even when everything was going to hell."

"Aye," Brutus agreed, his voice thick. "He was the heart of this century, more than I could ever be." He looked at Maximus, his eyes clear despite the pain. "We owe it to him to get out of here. We owe it to him to report to Vespasian what Flaccus did. That traitor must not go unpunished."

"He won't, Brutus," Maximus promised, his voice now filled with cold fury. "I swear it to you, by Jupiter and by Decimus's memory. Flaccus will pay."

A moment of deep connection passed between them,

stronger than rank, stronger than orders, forged in shared loss and shared danger. They were more than Tribune and Centurion. They were brothers-in-arms.

Maximus looked around, saw the exhausted but watchful faces of the remaining men. They had overheard the dialogue, felt the emotions. He had to lead them, give them hope.

"Listen up, men!" he said, his voice louder now, firmer. "We have suffered a heavy loss. Optio Decimus was a hero. His sacrifice gave us this chance. We will take it!" He rose painfully, pulling Brutus up with him, who leaned groaning against him. "We are still alive. We are soldiers of Rome! We will get out of here. We will reach Rutupiae. We will report what happened! Flaccus will pay for his betrayal! But to do that, we must keep fighting—for each other, for Decimus, for the honor of the Legion! Get up!"

Slowly, painfully, but with renewed determination in their eyes, the men rose. The words had worked. Shared anger at the traitor, the memory of their fallen comrade, the appeal to their honor—it had rekindled the fire. They were not broken yet. They were legionaries.

Just as they were about to move again, they heard it—the sound of war horns, closer this time, directly behind them. And then shouts, the noise of fighting.

"They've found us!" cried Titus, the young legionary supporting Brutus.

"Trap!" Brutus snarled. "They circled around while we sat here! Damned bastards!"

Maximus's heart sank. He had made a fatal mistake. The emotional pause, the moment of connection, had been too long. He should have listened to his instincts. "Formation!" he yelled. "Form circle! Defend yourselves!"

XII. FLIGHT THROUGH THE WOODS

But it was too late. Celts erupted from the thicket simultaneously from several sides. Not just Bryn's warriors, but also other, taller men with long swords—Durotriges. They outnumbered the Romans, were fresh, while the Romans were exhausted and wounded.

The fight was short, brutal, and one-sided. The Romans fought bravely, selling their lives as dearly as possible, but they stood no chance. Maximus saw Titus fall beside him, a spear piercing his chest. He saw another legionary overwhelmed by three Celts at once. He himself parried, stabbed, spun, but was pushed back, stumbling.

He felt a heavy blow to the back of his head. Stars exploded before his eyes. Then darkness.

When he regained consciousness, he was lying on the cold, wet forest floor, hands bound behind his back, a rough rope constricting his breathing. His head throbbed; blood seeped from a wound on the back of his skull. Around him lay the bodies of his men, still and lifeless in the bloody ferns. Only a few survived, bound like him. He saw Brutus, dazed but conscious, supported by two Celtic warriors. The arrow had been removed from his shoulder, replaced by a crude dressing of moss and leaves.

Celtic warriors stood around them, faces painted, eyes full of triumph and hatred, collecting the weapons and armor of the fallen Romans. Bryn, the gaunt leader of the marsh warriors, stepped before Maximus, regarding him with his cold, sharp eyes. He said something in Celtic, then spat in Maximus's face.

Maximus closed his eyes, a wave of despair washing over him, and lost consciousness again. They had fought, they had suffered, Decimus had died—and it had all been for nothing.

They were captives, deep in enemy territory, betrayed by their own people, at the mercy—or rather, lack thereof—of the barbarians. The flight through the trees was over. It hadn't led them to freedom, only deeper into the darkness.

XIII. In Chains

Darkness enveloped Maximus. Not the gentle blackness of sleep, but a brutal, painful nothingness. Slowly, he came to, his first conscious sensation a dull, pounding hammer in his skull, as if a smith were working an anvil directly on his helmet. He tried to move, but his limbs obeyed reluctantly. His hands were still painfully bound behind his back, the coarse ropes cutting deep into his wrists. A sticky feeling on the back of his head told him the wound from the blow was still bleeding.

He blinked, trying to make out his surroundings. He lay on cold, damp ground that smelled of earth, moss, and something more unpleasant—likely the blood and excretions of battle. It was dark around him, but not completely black. Pale moonlight occasionally filtered through the dense canopy, and the restless flicker of several campfires cast long, dancing shadows, making the scene even more surreal.

Maximus wasn't alone. Groans and stifled whimpers told him other Romans had survived the final confrontation, only to fall captive. With effort, ignoring the sharp pain, he turned his head. He saw the shapes of his men, huddled closely together, guarded by stocky Celtic warriors whose silhouettes loomed menacingly against the fires. The Celts spoke quietly in their guttural language, the silence occasionally broken by harsh laughter or a command. They seemed to be examining the weapons and armor of the fallen Romans, trading spoils.

Maximus's gaze searched for Brutus. He found him several paces away, leaning against the trunk of a large oak. The Centurion was conscious, his face a mask of pain and indomitable defiance. His injured shoulder was crudely bound with leaves and strips of animal hide. He sat upright, fixing the Celtic guards with undisguised contempt. In the dim light, their eyes met for a moment. Brutus gave the faintest nod. It was a silent message of acknowledgment, of endurance, but also of shared despair.

Maximus closed his eyes again, letting his head sink against the damp ground. Captured. Betrayed by Flaccus. Overwhelmed by the Celts. Deep in enemy territory, with no hope of rescue. This was the end. He thought of his men, of the dead now lying unburied in the woods. He thought of Decimus, whose sacrifice had been in vain. He thought of Vespasian, who had, however unknowingly, put him in this situation. A feeling of bitter hopelessness washed over him.

How had it come to this? He had obeyed orders, tried to do the right thing, fought, bled—and for what? To end up here in the mud, bound, humiliated, delivered to an uncertain fate at the hands of his enemies? Was this the glory of Rome? Was this the honor his grandfather had always spoken of? It felt only hollow and meaningless now.

He felt someone roughly tug at his bonds. He was hauled to his feet, the pain in his head exploding. Two burly Celts grabbed him by the arms and dragged him towards the group of other prisoners. He counted them fleetingly. Perhaps fifteen men, including himself and Brutus. The rest of the

XIII. IN CHAINS

small troop Decimus had rescued had fallen in the final fight. Fifteen Romans, surrounded by hundreds of Celts.

They were roughly shoved into the center of a makeshift camp the Celts had set up in a small clearing. The fires now burned higher, illuminating the scene. Maximus saw the faces of his men—young, old, veterans, recruits. Their eyes reflected fear, exhaustion, but also a spark of Roman defiance. They were beaten, but not broken. Not yet, anyway.

Celtic warriors surrounded them, prodding them with spear shafts, mocking them in their foreign tongue. Some already wore pieces of Roman armor—a helmet, a greave, a decorated belt. It was a bitter humiliation.

Then Bryn stepped forward, the gaunt leader of the marsh warriors. He now wore Maximus's Tribune's sword at his belt, a sight that filled Maximus with rage. Bryn regarded the captured Romans with his cold, sharp eyes, then said something to his men. Two warriors stepped forward, grabbed a young legionary from the group, and dragged him before Bryn. The boy didn't resist, his face pale, but he looked Bryn steadily in the eye.

Bryn spoke again, this time it sounded like a question. The young legionary didn't answer, just stared at him. Bryn chuckled softly, then slowly drew a long, thin knife from his belt. He traced the tip across the legionary's cheek, drawing a line of blood. The boy flinched but didn't cry out.

"Leave him alone, you filthy barbarian bastard!" Brutus suddenly shouted, his voice rough but strong. He tried to stand, but was immediately forced back down by his guards.

Bryn turned slowly towards Brutus, a cruel smile on his lips. He said something in Celtic that sounded like a question.

"He asks who you are to dare give him orders, Roman," an

unexpected voice translated.

Maximus looked up. Standing beside Bryn now was Adminius. The Celtic prince was unharmed, his clothes clean, his smile as charming and false as ever. So he hadn't fled or been killed. He was here, with the enemy. Brutus had been right.

"Adminius! You bastard!" Brutus snarled, spitting towards him on the ground. "You betrayed us!"

Adminius laughed softly. "Betrayed, Centurion? I merely weighed my options. Rome or Britannia? Flaccus or Maximus? I chose the side that offered me more." He stepped closer to Brutus. "And you, old dog, always had nothing but contempt for me. You'll regret that now."

"What do you want, Adminius?" Maximus asked, his voice surprisingly calm. He needed to buy time, understand what was happening.

Adminius turned to him, his gaze a mixture of curiosity and amusement. "Ah, Tribune Maximus. The mysterious riser, Vespasian's favorite. I want to know who you really are. Bryn here is only interested in revenge. He wants to have you all killed, slowly and painfully." He gestured towards the young legionary, whose throat Bryn now held the knife to. "But I... I have other plans. I believe you could still be useful to me."

"Useful? For what?" Maximus asked.

"To overthrow my foolish brother Caratacus, of course," Adminius said lightly. "And to take my rightful place as king—as king by Rome's grace, naturally, and Flaccus will help me in return for my assistance." He smiled. "You see, Tribune, I am a pragmatist, just like our friend Cogidubnus. We know which way the wind blows."

"You're a vulture," Brutus spat.

XIII. IN CHAINS

Adminius ignored him, focusing on Maximus. "Bryn will play his games. He needs his revenge. But he won't kill all of you, not immediately. He'll wait until Caratacus learns of our success here. Then he'll present you to him—or what's left of you." He leaned closer to Maximus. "But I could ensure you survive, Tribune, if you tell me what I want to know. Who are you really? Why does Vespasian protect you? What is your secret?"

Maximus remained silent. His mind raced. Adminius knew or suspected something. But how, and from where? And if he was in league with Flaccus, what did Flaccus know?

"I am Gaius Julius Maximus, Tribune of the Second Legion Augusta," he said firmly. "A soldier of Rome."

Adminius laughed again. "A nice story, but I don't believe it. You'll tell me what I want to hear eventually, reveal the secret of why Flaccus wants you dead." He turned to Bryn and spoke rapidly in Celtic. Bryn nodded grimly, then shoved the young legionary back towards the other prisoners. He gave orders to his men.

The Romans were hauled to their feet and led deeper into the woods, towards an area where several crude wooden cages stood beneath the trees, obviously intended for captured animals—or humans. They were shoved inside, the doors secured with heavy bolts. The stench of old excrement was overwhelming.

"Welcome to your new home, Romans," Adminius said mockingly through the bars, before turning away to follow Bryn, who had already returned to one of the larger fires where a victory feast was apparently being prepared.

Maximus sank to the damp floor inside the cage. Around him crowded the other surviving legionaries, their faces barely visible in the darkness, but he could feel their fear, their despair. Brutus leaned against the bars beside him, his breathing shallow.

"We should have listened to you, Brutus," Maximus said quietly, the bitterness in his voice unmistakable. "We should never have trusted Adminius."

"Too late for regrets now, Sir," Brutus replied wearily. "Now we have to survive." He looked through the bars at the celebrating Celts by the fire. "And figure out how to get out of here."

Maximus followed his gaze. The odds were poor, almost hopeless. But Brutus was right. They were Romans. Giving up was not an option. They were captives, but the fight wasn't over yet. He would find a way—for Brutus, for his men, for Decimus's sacrifice, and for himself.

XIV. The Blood Priest

The night in the marsh warriors' camp was a descent into the darkest abysses of human cruelty and despair. The surviving Romans' hope dwindled with each agonizing hour, locked in narrow, stinking wooden cages, exposed to the cold, the rain, and the mocking laughter of their Celtic guards. The din of the Celts' victory feast assaulted their ears incessantly—a cacophonous mixture of wild singing, the throb of drums, the shrill notes of bone flutes, and the occasional bloodcurdling howl of a warrior, a cruel torture for their frayed nerves. The Romans watched as the Celts drank, danced, boasted with looted Roman weapons, and recounted their heroic deeds in battle to one another.

Maximus huddled on the damp floor of his cage, beside him the feverish Brutus and three other legionaries, barely responsive. Maximus fought against nausea, the pounding pain in his head, and leaden fatigue, forcing himself to stay awake, listening into the darkness, searching for any sign, any weakness, any unlikely chance of escape. But there was none. They were surrounded, guarded, deep in enemy territory. Their only hope lay in a quick death, a release from this hell.

Brutus groaned softly in his troubled sleep, his hand groping for his aching shoulder. Maximus leaned towards him, whispering soothing words he didn't believe himself. The bond with his friend and mentor anchored him in this darkness. He thought of Decimus, of his sacrifice. Had it been worth it? For this?

As the night reached its nadir and the Celts' celebrations subsided into drunken roaring, the eerie chanting began. It came from the depths of the forest, deep, rhythmic, carried on an ominous melody that seemed to tell of old gods, of blood, and of sacrifice. The Celtic guards around the cages froze, their faces, moments before showing raw triumph, now displaying a mixture of superstitious awe and deep-seated fear. They turned their gazes towards the edge of the woods, waiting.

In the pale moonlight, falling like spectral fingers through the wet leaves, a figure emerged from the darkness of the trees. It was tall, gaunt, and shrouded in a long, dark robe that seemed to shimmer with complex patterns in the faint light. A deep cowl hid the face, revealing only a hint of pale skin and two glittering eyes that shone like a predator's in the night. The figure carried a long, gnarled staff of dark oak, which struck the damp ground softly with each slow, dignified step. The chanting followed it like an invisible choir, though the figure itself seemed silent.

A Druid! Maximus felt the hairs on his neck prickle. This was not human authority like a king's or chieftain's, but something different, older, connected to the dark powers of this land.

Bryn, the leader of the marsh warriors, approached the Druid reverently, bowed his head low, and murmured words of greeting in Celtic. The Druid did not reply immediately. Its cowled face turned slowly towards the cages, its gaze seeming to pierce the bars, weighing, measuring, assessing each Roman individually. Maximus felt naked, exposed under that cold, appraising stare.

After a long, unbearable silence, the Druid raised its staff and spoke. Its voice was surprisingly strong, deep, and resonant, echoing across the now-silent campsite, seeming to make the very air tremble. It spoke Celtic, but the tone of command was unmistakable. It demanded something.

Bryn nodded subserviently, without hesitation, and barked orders to his warriors.

Several Celts, their faces now serious, almost fanatical, approached the cages with torches and coarse ropes. The Romans' fate was sealed.

"No... by all the gods..." whimpered one of the young legionaries in the next cage.

"Quiet!" hissed an older veteran. "Die like a Roman!"

The Celts opened the first cage and dragged out three trembling legionaries. They were hauled to the center of the clearing, where the Druid waited beside a crudely hewn, bloodstained altar stone. The drums started again, a slow, dull rhythm mimicking the heartbeat of death.

The Druid resumed its chant, louder now, more insistent, a hypnotic singsong that numbed the senses. Bryn stepped beside it, drawing a long, bronze knife adorned with ritual markings.

The three legionaries were forced onto the altar. Their screams rent the night as Bryn raised the knife and slit their throats. Blood spurted, steaming in the cold night air, pooling in the depressions of the altar stone. The bodies twitched briefly, then were carelessly tossed aside by the warriors.

Maximus shut his eyes, clenching his teeth to keep from

crying out. The metallic stench of blood filled the air, mingling with the smoke and decay. Nausea rose in his throat.

But it wasn't over. The Druid pointed to the next cage. Again, three men were dragged out, and the brutal ritual repeated. Screams. Blood. Silence.

Maximus forced himself to watch. He had to bear witness. He had to remember. He had to absorb this horror, transform it into rage, into the absolute will to survive and take revenge.

Cage by cage was opened. The sacrifices continued relentlessly, accompanied by the Druid's monotonous chant and the dull thudding of the drums. The number of surviving Romans dwindled.

Finally, the Celts came to the cage where Maximus and Brutus huddled. The door was torn open. Two burly warriors grabbed the last remaining legionary with them and dragged him out. The man didn't scream; he just looked at Maximus with empty, resigned eyes before being hauled to the altar.

Now only the two of them were left. The warriors came for Brutus.

"No! Leave him! He's wounded! Take me!" Maximus yelled, throwing himself against the bars with his remaining strength.

The Celts just laughed, seizing the weakened Brutus. He cursed, kicked, tried to resist, but pain and exhaustion had overwhelmed him. They dragged him from the cage, hauled him towards the altar.

Helpless in his cage, Maximus watched as his friend, mentor, and brother-in-arms was forced onto the bloody stone. Brutus lifted his head and looked at Maximus. Despite the pain and imminent agony, there was no fear in his eyes, only deep, unshakable defiance and a silent message of farewell.

The Druid stepped beside the altar, its chant reaching an

XIV. THE BLOOD PRIEST

ecstatic peak. Bryn raised the ritual knife again. This time, however, he aimed not for the throat but placed the tip on Brutus's chest, directly over the heart, preparing to cut out the Roman centurion's heart—the ultimate sacrifice for his dark gods.

At that moment, as time seemed to stand still, another sound cut through the night—louder than the drums, shriller than the Druid's chant. It was the wild, piercing blare of several Celtic war horns, the *Carnyx*, followed by the thundering hoofbeats of dozens, perhaps hundreds, of horses.

Every head snapped around. From the darkness of the forest, from the direction they themselves had come, a phalanx of riders burst forth, torches casting restless light on their fierce faces and gleaming weapons. At their head rode an imposing figure in magnificent, but distinctly Celtic, armor, long hair streaming in the wind, his face bearing the unmistakable stamp of royal authority and burning anger—Caratacus.

He and his riders didn't hesitate. They galloped straight into the camp, their horses shying at the fires and bodies, but Caratacus drove them relentlessly forward, straight towards the group around the sacrificial altar. Surprised, the marsh warriors fell back uncertainly, almost fearfully. Bryn lowered the knife, his face mirroring disbelief and rage. Even the Druid interrupted its chant, taking a step back, its cowl slipping slightly to reveal an ascetic face marked by fanaticism.

Caratacus reined in his horse directly before Bryn, his gaze icy. A heated exchange in Celtic immediately erupted between the two leaders, Caratacus's voice thundering with fury and disgust across the clearing as he gestured angrily at the sacrificed legionaries, at Brutus still lying on the altar, and at Maximus in the cage. Bryn answered defiantly, defending himself, pointing towards the Druid. Caratacus turned to the Druid, his words now cutting, almost disrespectful of the spiritual authority. The Druid didn't reply but visibly withdrew, its dark power seeming to fade before the temporal might of the warrior king.

During this tense confrontation, with all eyes fixed on the leaders, Maximus noticed a fleeting movement at the edge of the firelight, near the sacrificial altar. A figure detached itself from the shadows and vanished silently into the forest thicket—Adminius. He was using the chaos to slip away before Caratacus could notice him and potentially execute him for his treachery. Maximus understood: the prince played his own game, always seeking his own advantage, loyal only to himself.

Finally, Caratacus seemed to have prevailed. His anger was still visible, but controlled. He gave his riders a curt command. Several dismounted, roughly shoving Bryn and his remaining warriors aside. They opened Maximus's cage and pulled him out. Others helped the dazed Brutus from the altar, supporting him.

"You are my prisoners now, Romans," Caratacus said, turning directly to Maximus, his Latin rough but understandable. He surveyed Maximus from head to toe, his eyes lingering briefly on his stature, his defiant gaze, the marks of battle. "Bryn and his priest may find satisfaction in senseless bloodshed. I do not." His gaze sharpened. "I prefer information, and perhaps a useful pawn in the game against Rome."

He gave his men another signal. The Romans were bound again, more securely this time, but without the marsh warriors' needless brutality. They were lifted onto some of the captured Roman horses. Brutus was carefully placed on a horse, supported by one of Caratacus's riders.

Caratacus cast a final, contemptuous glance at Bryn and the Druid, then gave the signal to depart. The riders left the marsh warriors' camp as swiftly and unexpectedly as they had arrived, leaving Bryn's humiliated and bewildered Celts behind in the bloody silence, taking their Roman prisoners with them—saved from the jaws of death, but now in the hands of Rome's most feared enemy in Britannia.

XV. In the King's Presence

The ride under Caratacus's command differed from the agonizing flight before. Though still prisoners, hands bound behind their backs, their treatment was markedly less brutal than under Bryn and his marsh warriors.

Caratacus's cavalrymen were disciplined, speaking barely a word. They were an elite force, recognizable by their superior armor, decorated helmets, and powerful horses. They moved swiftly and purposefully through the forest, following paths Maximus hadn't even glimpsed before, skillfully bypassing swamps and dense thickets. Night slowly yielded to another gray, rainy morning, but the riders seemed unaffected by the weather or terrain.

Maximus rode beside Brutus, who was supported on his horse by one of Caratacus's warriors. The Centurion was pale and weak but conscious. The bleeding from his shoulder seemed to have stopped, but he had lost a lot of blood and was clearly in severe pain. Maximus's own head injury throbbed dully, but shock and adrenaline had given way to a gnawing worry: What would Caratacus do with them? Why had he saved them only to take them captive himself?

The ride was surprisingly short. After only a few hours, perhaps three or four, they reached a large, hidden encampment nestled in a wide hollow, surrounded by dense woods and protected by natural rock formations. Thousands of Celtic warriors swarmed here, their campfires rising like countless smoke signals into the damp sky. It was a picture of impressive, if chaotic, military strength—far removed from Bryn's small band of marsh warriors. This was the heart of Caratacus's army.

But something wasn't right. Maximus, whose strategic eye immediately assessed the camp's size and layout, frowned. The camp was huge, yes, but it seemed… not fully occupied. He estimated the number of warriors at perhaps three, maybe four thousand men. Impressive, but nowhere near the entire force Plautius was supposedly hunting in the north. Where was the rest of Caratacus's army?

They were led to the center of the camp, towards a large tent significantly more elaborate than the warriors' simple shelters. Large fires burned before it, and guards with decorated shields and spears stood rigidly. They were lifted from the horses and shoved into the tent.

The interior was surprisingly spacious, laid out with animal hides and coarse rugs. In the middle stood a massive wooden table covered with maps similar to Roman ones but marked with Celtic symbols and runes. At this table sat Caratacus, engrossed in studying a map. He looked up as they entered, his face serious, his eyes piercing. Beside him stood several other Britons who looked like chieftains and warriors.

"Seat them," Caratacus ordered curtly in Celtic. His guards pushed Maximus and Brutus onto low stools. Their bonds were not loosened.

Caratacus studied the two Romans for a long time in silence, his gaze lingering on Brutus's wounded shoulder, then on

Maximus's blood-caked hair and the swelling on the back of his head. Finally, he turned to Maximus and spoke in surprisingly good, though rough, Latin.

"State your name and rank."

Maximus answered for both. "Tribune Maximus and Centurion Brutus."

"You are the Tribune and he the Centurion?" A hint of disbelief and grudging respect tinged his voice. He shook his head. "Your Roman hierarchies never cease to amaze me. You could be his son." He pointed a finger at Brutus.

Maximus seethed inwardly at the slight but didn't let it show, quickly changing the subject. "We were betrayed, Caratacus," Maximus retorted, his voice steady despite his situation. "By one of yours, and one of mine."

Caratacus nodded slowly. "Adminius. Yes, I know of his betrayal of you. Bryn told me. He serves Rome now, or rather, he serves himself under Rome's cloak." He paused. "And who was the Roman?"

Maximus hesitated. Should he betray Flaccus? What good would it do? "A Tribune named Flaccus," he finally said.

Caratacus didn't seem to recognize the name or attach any importance to it. He leaned back. "Betrayal is a dirty business, Tribune. On both sides." His gaze sharpened again. "But that is not important now. What is important is that you are here, my prisoners, and you will be useful to me."

"We are soldiers of Rome," Brutus said, his voice weak but firm. "We betray nothing."

Caratacus smiled thinly. "I don't expect you to, Centurion." He studied Brutus more closely, tilting his head. "Your face... seems familiar. Have we met before?"

Brutus stared back without answering. *He doesn't remember,*

XV. IN THE KING'S PRESENCE

Maximus thought. *He only saw Brutus from a distance when Togodumnus fell.*

Caratacus turned back to Maximus. "You must have wondered, Tribune, why my army is not in the north, where your General Plautius hunts it so eagerly."

Maximus's heart began to beat faster. This was the question that had been bothering him. "Indeed."

Caratacus smiled triumphantly. "Plautius hunts ghosts, shadows. Only about a third of my forces, perhaps five thousand men, lead him on a wild chase through the northern hills. Enough to keep him busy, tire him out, distract him from what truly matters."

"And where... where is the rest of your army?" Maximus asked, though he already suspected, and feared, the answer.

"Here, Tribune," Caratacus said, spreading his arms to encompass the bustling camp outside. "And on their way here. About fifteen thousand of my best warriors." He leaned over the map. "We returned in small groups, none larger than five hundred men, bypassing the Roman outposts widely, moving through forests and along forgotten paths. Your scouts didn't notice us. The Durotriges have joined the resistance. Even the dim-witted marsh warriors."

Maximus froze. Fifteen thousand men gathered here in the south, and no one had noticed.

Now it all made terrifying sense. The Celts with the carts they had pursued from Outpost Secundus weren't a raiding party; they had been one of Caratacus's units heading here. Vespasian's order of recalling Maximus to Rutupiae had prevented him from discovering their true strength and intent. The plundered village they found en route to the Atrebates, the scattered burned farmsteads—they were Caratacus's work

113

too. He should have recognized the signs earlier.

"If I had ordered the ambush back then," he thought bitterly, *"we might have stopped some of them, raised the alarm!"* The circle had closed, and he looked like a fool.

"You deceived us skillfully," Maximus said with difficulty, trying to suppress his shock and anger.

"War is deception, Tribune," Caratacus replied calmly. "Rome often forgets that, drunk on its own power."

"But why?" Maximus asked. "Why assemble this force here in the south? What is your objective?"

Caratacus regarded him for a long moment, his eyes probing. Then he smiled his thin, dangerous smile again. "You are a clever man, Tribune. You already know the answer." He tapped a point on the map with his finger, a place Maximus knew all too well. *"Rutupiae."*

The confirmation hit Maximus like a physical blow. Rutupiae. The port. The supply line. The lifeline of the Roman army in Britannia.

"You intend to take the port," he whispered, almost disbelievingly.

"Not just take it, Tribune. Destroy it," Caratacus corrected him gently. "We will burn the storehouses, sink the ships, render the docks useless. We will cut Rome's throat, here in the south, before winter even arrives."

Maximus thought of the garrison in Rutupiae. Vespasian was there, yes, but with how many men? Maximus had left half a legion behind, perhaps 2500 men, plus the harbor guards, some auxiliary units. Maybe 3000, 4000 fighting men at most. Against fifteen thousand determined Celts? Rutupiae was a fortress, yes, but not impregnable, especially not against such overwhelming numbers.

XV. IN THE KING'S PRESENCE

"You have no siege engines," Brutus interjected weakly.

Caratacus laughed. "We don't need them, Centurion. We have the numbers, we have the fury of our people, and we have surprise on our side. Your Legate Vespasian does not expect us. He believes we are in the north, fleeing from Plautius."

"When... when do you plan to attack?" Maximus asked, his voice barely a breath.

"Patience, Tribune," Caratacus said. "My warriors are still gathering. They come from all directions. In five days, we will be at full strength. Then," his gaze turned icy, "then we march on Rutupiae. And then Rome will learn what it means to challenge Britannia."

Five days. Maximus calculated frantically. Plus roughly six days' march to Rutupiae. There was no way to warn Vespasian in time. Even if they could escape, which was impossible, they would never make it. Rutupiae was doomed. And with Rutupiae, the entire Roman campaign in Britannia. Plautius would be cut off, without supplies, trapped in the hostile north. It would be a catastrophe, worse even than Varus's defeat in Germania.

Caratacus seemed to read Maximus's thoughts. "You see the truth now, Tribune. Rome is not invincible. You are far from home, in a land that hates you. Your strength is your discipline, your organization. But that is also your weakness. Destroy the organization, cut the lines, and you are lost."

He stood up and stepped closer to Maximus. "You and I, Tribune, we are enemies. But I will not have you tortured or sacrificed."

"What... what do you intend to do with us then?" Maximus asked, his voice barely a whisper, still trying to grasp the magnitude of the revelation.

Caratacus studied him for a moment, a hint of calculation in his eyes. "Bryn would have sacrificed you. A senseless waste. You are Roman officers, possessing knowledge of Vespasian, of Roman warfare, your value as hostages... all that is more useful to me than your blood on an altar. Dead, you can report nothing back to Rome." He smiled thinly again. "And alive, you will witness my greatest triumph."

"Caratacus," Maximus said, his voice as reasonable and calm as possible, "is this truly the only way? War, destruction, death? Rome is mighty, yes, but it also offers peace, trade, prosperity. Cogidubnus recognized that. Isn't an alliance, an honorable peace, better than this endless struggle that only brings suffering to both our peoples?"

Caratacus laughed, but this time it sounded harsh, devoid of humor. "Peace? With Rome? Tribune, you are either a fool or you take me for one. What peace does Rome offer? The peace of the slave under the master's whip? The peace of the farmer whose land is stolen and whose gods are defiled? The peace of my brother Togodumnus, who fell because he dared to defend our land?" His voice rose, filled with bitter anger. "Rome only takes; it gives nothing. It subjugates; it destroys. You speak of trade, but you mean exploitation. You speak of order, but you mean oppression. There can be no peace between the wolf and the lamb, Tribune. Not while the wolf is hungry, and Rome is always hungry." He leaned forward, his gaze burning into Maximus's eyes. "I will fight until the last Roman is driven from this island, or until I myself fall. There is no other way."

"You will be witnesses," Caratacus continued, his voice louder again, "witnesses to the fall of Rutupiae, witnesses to the beginning of the end of Roman rule in Britannia. And

XV. IN THE KING'S PRESENCE

then… then I will decide whether you return to Rome as messengers to report your defeat, or whether your bones rot here in Britannic soil."

He turned away. "Take them to the cages. Give them water and some food. Treat them… appropriately. They are officers, even if they are Romans."

The guards seized Maximus and Brutus and led them from the tent, back to the stinking cages that were now their world. Maximus's head spun. The truth was more staggering than anything he could have imagined. Rutupiae was the target. Flaccus and Adminius's betrayal had just been a sideshow, part of a much larger, bolder plan. Caratacus had outsmarted them all.

He looked at Brutus, sitting beside him on the cage's filthy floor, eyes closed, face contorted in pain. What could they do? They were trapped, powerless. Their only hope was a miracle, or a mistake by their enemy. Maximus clung to that tiny spark of hope as darkness and despair threatened to engulf him once more.

XVI. An Old Debt

The days following the conversation with Caratacus stretched into a leaden eternity. Confined in the narrow, stinking wooden cage, guarded by indifferent Celtic warriors, Maximus and Brutus were close to despair. The truth about Caratacus's audacious plan—an imminent attack on Rutupiae with an overwhelming force while Plautius chased ghosts in the north—weighed on them like a millstone. Rutupiae was the Roman army's lifeline. If the port fell, the entire campaign in Britannia was lost, Plautius's army doomed. They were the only Romans aware of the impending catastrophe, trapped here, powerless, delivered to an uncertain fate at the hands of their enemy.

Maximus tried to marshal his thoughts, searching for any weakness, any possibility of escape or warning, but his head ached, and hopelessness paralyzed him. He looked at Brutus. The Centurion leaned against the bars, eyes closed, his breathing shallower. The wound in his shoulder, despite the crude treatment by Caratacus's men, seemed to have become inflamed again; he was slightly feverish. A wave of fear for his friend washed over Maximus. Brutus was tough, a rock, but even the strongest rock could break under enough pressure. His initial anger and defiance had given way to

XVI. AN OLD DEBT

apathy.

The camp continued to bustle with activity, different from the disciplined efficiency of a Roman camp. It was the chaotic, loud swarm of a Celtic war host gathering. New groups of warriors constantly arrived, greeted with shouts and drumbeats. They came from various tribes, identifiable by their different tattoos, shield patterns, and hairstyles. The Durotriges were numerous, as were warriors of the Dobunni and several smaller tribes from the west and south. Their attire was less wild, their shields larger and often adorned with complex patterns, their horses looked better groomed. It was an impressive, yet frightening, spectacle of unity against the common enemy, Rome, orchestrated by Caratacus.

Four agonizing days had passed since their capture. Four days in the filth and stench of the cramped cage, under the incessant drizzle or the oppressive humidity when the sun briefly broke through. Time blurred into a gray monotony of waiting, pain, and growing hopelessness. Hunger and thirst became constant companions, barely alleviated by meager rations of dry bread and brackish water carelessly shoved towards them by the guards. Maximus felt his own strength waning but worried more about Brutus. The Centurion's fever had worsened; he often drifted in and out of consciousness, muttering names Maximus didn't recognize in his delirium. His initial fury had subsided into dull apathy, hope nearly extinguished. Just as Maximus believed only death or the cruel whim of Bryn and his Druid would release them from this misery, he noticed the new group approaching the center of the camp.

A middle-aged man led them. He was broad-shouldered, with short brown hair and a weather-beaten but honest face.

He wore a bearskin over his shoulders and surveyed the camp with a critical, almost disapproving gaze.

Maximus's heart leaped. He knew this man. He had met him and his warriors during the first year of the campaign, after the battle where they had defeated the Trinovantes under Vortigern. It was Bran, chieftain of the Iceni, the proud tribe from the east known for its fertile fields and relative independence. Brutus, under Vespasian's orders, had made contact with the Iceni back then.

It had been a delicate mission. The Iceni were suspicious, but they also hated the Trinovantes, their traditional rivals. Brutus, with his direct, unvarnished manner, had managed to win Bran's respect. Moreover, when a Trinovantian raiding party attacked Bran's village while Brutus was there, the Centurion hadn't hesitated. His men had repelled the attack, saving Bran's life and his village. From that act, an unexpected bond had formed, a pact of mutual respect, even though no formal alliance was struck. Bran had promised Brutus then that he would never forget that deed.

And now Bran was here, in Caratacus's camp. What did it mean? Had the Iceni finally joined the resistance? The Iceni were a powerful tribe; their participation would significantly strengthen Caratacus's army.

Bran seemed to be seeking Caratacus, disappearing with his closest advisors into the main tent. Maximus and Brutus waited, holding their breath. What would happen? Would Bran recognize them? And if so, what would he do?

After what felt like an eternity, perhaps half an hour, Bran emerged from Caratacus's tent, his expression serious, almost grim. He spoke briefly with his men, then his gaze swept over the camp—and stopped at the cages holding the Roman

XVI. AN OLD DEBT

prisoners. He seemed to hesitate, then slowly approached, followed by two of his warriors.

Bran stood before the cage holding Maximus and Brutus, briefly surveying Maximus before his eyes fell on Brutus, who had laboriously sat up, watching the Iceni chieftain with a mixture of pain and rekindled hope.

Bran's eyes widened in disbelief. He stepped closer to the bars, leaning forward. "By the ancestors... Centurion Brutus? Is that truly you?" His voice was an incredulous whisper.

"Bran," Brutus croaked, a faint smile touching his lips. "I didn't expect to see you here."

"What... what happened?" Bran asked, his gaze shifting over Brutus's wound, the bonds, the wretched surroundings, shock, and horror reflected in his face. "Why are you here? In Caratacus's camp? As a prisoner?"

"A long story, Chieftain," Maximus said before Brutus could answer, needing to control the conversation. "We were betrayed, led into an ambush."

Bran turned to him, his look suspicious. "And you are?"

"Tribune Gaius Julius Maximus. I command these men and also took part in the attack against the Trinovantes," Maximus replied, slightly offended that the chieftain apparently didn't remember him.

"The Tribune Caratacus spoke of," Bran murmured thoughtfully. He studied Maximus again, then looked back at Brutus, clearly concerned about his condition. "You are gravely wounded, Centurion."

"Just a flesh wound," Brutus lied through gritted teeth. "Nothing a Roman soldier can't handle."

Bran shook his head. "You saved my village, Centurion, my family, my life. I gave you my promise. I am in your debt." He glanced around nervously, lowering his voice. "This is a dangerous place for you. Bryn is a cruel man, and his Druid... he thirsts for Roman blood. Caratacus saved you for now, but he won't keep you alive forever. He needs you as pawns, but when you're no longer useful to him..." He left the sentence unfinished.

"Can you help us, Bran?" Maximus asked directly, feeling a first, fragile spark of hope.

Bran hesitated, visibly conflicted. He looked at his two warriors, waiting silently and loyally. He looked back at Brutus, whose eyes pleaded with him. "I... I am not here to support Caratacus," he finally said quietly. "I am only here to trade, to gather information. My tribe, the Iceni, we stay out of this war. We have made peace with Rome—with you, Centurion." He took a deep breath. "Helping you here is dangerous, very dangerous. If Caratacus or Bryn find out..."

"We do not ask you to endanger your people, Chieftain," Maximus said quickly. "But if you could just help us escape from here, show us the way back towards our lines..."

"It's more than just the way," Bran interrupted. "Caratacus's army is gathering. Thousands of warriors are heading for Rutupiae. They will attack the port in five days."

Maximus and Brutus nodded; Caratacus had already told them this.

"You must warn your people," Maximus urged. "If Rutupiae falls, Britannia is lost to Rome."

"We do not interfere," Bran said seriously. "We take no sides!" Bran looked around again, checking the guards lounging boredly by the other cages. He stepped even closer to the bars. "I cannot simply free you. That would be suicide. But... perhaps there is a way." He thought hard. "Tonight,

XVI. AN OLD DEBT

during the feasting. The guards will be careless, drunk on mead. My men and I must leave before dawn anyway." He looked them over critically. "Are you strong enough to ride, Centurion?"

Brutus nodded with effort. "If I must."

"Good." Bran made a decision. "I will get you weapons and ensure the guards at this cage are distracted. Shortly after midnight. You must be ready. You will have only a brief moment to escape. I cannot accompany you; that would be too conspicuous. But one of my men will guide you part of the way, to a hidden path that leads quickly out of this valley."

Hope, strong and unexpected, flooded Maximus. It was a daring plan, fraught with risk, but it was a chance. Their only chance. "We will be ready, Bran," he said, his voice firm with determination. "We thank you. Rome will not forget your help."

Bran shook his head. "I do not do this for Rome, Tribune. I do it for him." He gestured towards Brutus. "I repay an old debt." He looked Brutus deeply in the eyes one last time. "May your gods be with you, Centurion." Then he turned abruptly and walked away with his warriors, without looking back, returning to his place in the camp, the mask of the neutral chieftain firmly back in place.

Maximus and Brutus watched him go until his figure disappeared into the camp's bustle. A storm of emotions raged within them. Hope, sudden and unexpected like a sunbeam after a storm, fought against deep-seated fear and the bitter experience of betrayal. Could Bran be trusted? Was his offer genuine, or just another, subtler trap?

"What do you think, Brutus?" Maximus finally whispered, his voice barely more than a rough croak. He had to lean close to the Centurion to make himself heard over the cage's foul stench. "Do you believe him? Will he come back? Will he help us?"

Brutus was still staring in the direction Bran had disappeared. A strange expression was on his face, a mixture of exhaustion, pain, and something else, something Maximus interpreted as deep emotion. Slowly, Brutus turned his head and looked at Maximus. A faint, ironic smile twitched at his lips, despite the pain the movement caused him.

"Come back? Help us?" Brutus chuckled softly, a hoarse, rasping sound. "Of course. There's no doubt about it."

Maximus looked at him, surprised. This sudden confidence starkly contrasted with Brutus's usual suspicion, especially towards Celts. "Why such certainty, my friend?"

Brutus grinned wider, though it clearly cost him effort. "Simple, Maximus. Back when I saved his village from the Trinovantes, we sealed the peace." He paused briefly, grimacing. "With spit."

Maximus stared at him, then burst out laughing, the first time in days, perhaps weeks. He vaguely remembered the story Brutus had once told him by a campfire—about the strange Iceni ritual where agreements weren't sealed with blood or on wax tablets, but by a hearty handshake after both parties had spat into their palms. Brutus had recounted it then with feigned disgust but underlying respect.

"You mean... you actually...?" Maximus asked, still laughing and simultaneously appalled.

"Indeed," Brutus confirmed with mock seriousness. "I spat in my hand, he spat in his, and then we shook. A bond for life, Iceni style." He grimaced. "Scrubbed my hands for days afterward. But," his gaze turned serious again, "Bran is a

XVI. AN OLD DEBT

man of honor, in his own Celtic way. He swore an oath, acknowledged a debt. And he will repay it. I'd wager my life on it." He paused briefly. "Which, essentially, I am doing right now."

The laughter died on Maximus's lips. Brutus was right. Their lives now depended on the honor of a Celtic chieftain and a promise sealed with spit. It was absurd, unreal, but it was their only hope.

"Then let's hope the Iceni take oaths more seriously than some Romans take their orders," Maximus said quietly, a bitter undertone in his voice, thinking of Flaccus.

"They do, Sir," Brutus replied with surprising firmness. "They do." He closed his eyes again, leaning his head back against the cold bars. "Now we just have to survive until midnight."

Maximus nodded. The night would be long. But for the first time in days of captivity, he felt a tiny spark of genuine hope, nourished by the memory of a barbaric custom and the unexpected loyalty of a man who should have been their enemy. Bran had offered them a lifeline. Now it was up to them to cling to it and escape certain death. The night would be long.

XVII. Paths of the Night

The silence after Bran's departure was almost as oppressive as the earlier noise of the Celtic camp. Maximus and Brutus sat silently in the damp darkness of their cage, the Iceni chieftain's words echoing in their minds. A chance. A tiny, dangerous chance, forged from an old debt and a promise sealed with spit. Hope was a fragile seedling in an ocean of despair.

Maximus glanced at Brutus. The Centurion leaned against the bars with eyes closed, his breathing shallower but more regular than before. The brief, almost surreal conversation about Bran's spit-oath seemed to have offered him a moment of distraction, perhaps even a spark of dark humor. But now his face was again a mask of pain and deep exhaustion.

"Brutus?" Maximus whispered after a while. "Are you awake?"

The Centurion slowly opened his eyes. In the pale moonlight, they looked clouded, almost feverish. "Awake enough to know we're still sitting in this damned cage," he croaked.

"Not for much longer," Maximus said, trying to inject a confidence into his voice that he barely felt himself. "Bran will keep his word. I believe that."

Brutus was silent for a moment, his gaze shifting to Max-

XVII. PATHS OF THE NIGHT

imus. "We lost too many men, Maximus," he said quietly, his voice thick. "Too many good men. Decimus… he shouldn't have died."

"No," Maximus agreed, the guilt weighing heavily on him again. "He sacrificed himself. For us."

"Sacrifice," Brutus repeated bitterly. He closed his eyes again. "When I was lying on that… that damned altar, when that priest came with his knife…" His voice broke off, a shudder running through his body.

Maximus waited, sensing the darkness of memory enveloping his friend.

"I thought that was it," Brutus continued after a pause, his voice rough. "I thought of nothing. Just cold. And then… then I thought of her."

Maximus frowned. "Her?"

"Anwen," Brutus whispered, the name sounding strangely soft on his lips. "The healer. The one with the red hair and blue eyes who couldn't take her eyes off you in the field hospital." A faint, wistful smile appeared on his face. "Crazy, isn't it? Facing death, you don't think of battles or Rome… but of a woman you barely know."

Maximus was surprised. He knew Brutus hadn't forgotten Anwen after their encounter in Camulodunum, but the Centurion rarely spoke of personal feelings, especially ones like these. "She… she meant something to you?"

"Meant something?" Brutus snorted softly. "I don't know. She was… different. Strong. Stubborn. Stood up to me." He smiled again, a bit wider this time. "And she has eyes like the summer sky over Italy. I've missed her since we left Camulodunum. I should have sought her out. Just to… see if she was alright. But I was too proud. Too busy with the war."

His smile faded, replaced by deep regret. "Another mistake. Another missed chance. And now…" He left the sentence unfinished.

Maximus understood. At this moment of extreme danger, confronted with his own mortality, Brutus regretted not the lost battles or missed promotions, but the forsaken human connection, the unsaid word, the hand not taken. It was emotional honesty that deeply touched Maximus.

"You will see her again, Brutus," Maximus said with firm conviction. "We're getting out of here. I promise you. And then we ride to Camulodunum, and you will find her."

Brutus looked at him, a spark of hope dawning in his eyes, mixed with skepticism. "You're a hopeless optimist, Tribune."

"Someone has to be," Maximus retorted. "And now stop whining like some lovesick recruit. We need your strength, Centurion. Soon."

Brutus nodded slowly, seeming to regain some of his old composure. "You're right. Enough of that." He took a deep breath, despite the pain.

Time crept by, measured only by the slow crawl of the moon and the pounding of their own blood in their ears. The festivities in the Celtic camp continued to die down; most warriors retreated to their shelters or collapsed drunk by the fires. The guards became fewer, their steps heavier.

Maximus tried to estimate midnight by the moon's phases. His head still ached, but adrenaline and hope kept him alert. He looked at Brutus. The Centurion seemed to be dozing, but Maximus knew he was wide awake, every fiber of his body tense as a bowstring.

Then, finally, a sign: a soft scraping at the back of the cage, where the shadows were deepest. Maximus and Brutus exchanged a quick glance. One of Bran's men. He had come.

A stocky Iceni warrior, his clothing dark and inconspicuous, crouched in the shadows. He made a brief gesture, signaling them to be quiet. Using a simple but sturdy tool—a lever of hardened wood—he began working on the cage's crude wooden bolts from the outside. It was surprisingly quick and almost silent. The bolts gave way; the door swung open a crack.

The Iceni pushed a bundle through the opening. Maximus recognized *gladii* and daggers, wrapped in dark cloth to muffle any sound. He grabbed them, handing Brutus a sword. The familiar weight of the weapon in his hand gave him new strength, new resolve.

The Iceni pointed outside, then towards the guards at the front of the cage, who were currently turning towards a mead jug, laughing. He made a quick, slicing motion across his throat with his hand—an unmistakable message. Then he pointed to a dark gap between two huts behind the cage and vanished as silently as he had appeared.

Maximus and Brutus looked at each other. This was the moment. There was no turning back.

"Now," Maximus whispered. He helped Brutus painstakingly to his feet. The Centurion gritted his teeth, suppressing a groan. "Can you walk?"

"I have to," Brutus forced out.

Maximus carefully pushed the cage door further open. He peered out. The two guards still had their backs to them, engrossed in their conversation and their mead.

"Go," Maximus hissed. He slipped out of the cage, Brutus close behind him, limping but determined. They crouched low, moving silently as shadows. They reached the gap between the huts. Beyond lay a narrow, muddy path leading out of the camp, away from the fires, into the deeper darkness of the woods.

They didn't dare look back. They heard no shouts of alarm, no pursuit. Bran's diversion, whatever it was, seemed to have worked.

They followed the narrow path as it snaked through the undergrowth. It was pitch dark; only occasionally did a pale moonbeam break through the clouds, casting ghostly light on wet leaves and twisted roots. Maximus led the way, trying to feel the path, while supporting Brutus, who groaned softly with every step. The pain in his head wound was almost forgotten, replaced by a burning focus on escape.

After what felt like an eternity, perhaps twenty minutes of agonizing progress, they reached a small clearing. There, appearing as if from nowhere, waited the stocky Iceni warrior who had freed them. He held the reins of two horses—not magnificent Roman warhorses, but smaller, tough Britannic ponies that looked strong and sure-footed. Beside the horses lay a small bundle.

The Iceni pointed to the horses, then to the bundle. He spoke no Latin, but his gestures were clear. He gave them water from a leather flask, a piece of dried meat, and a simple map drawn on birchbark. He pointed to the map, then to a barely visible path leading further east, away from the camp, towards the territories they had crossed earlier. Then he pointed to himself and shook his head—he would not accompany them further. His task was done.

"Thank you," Maximus said sincerely, clapping the man on the shoulder. The Iceni merely gave a short nod, then vanished into the woods as silently as he had come.

XVII. PATHS OF THE NIGHT

Maximus helped the exhausted Brutus onto one of the ponies. The Centurion clenched his teeth as he swung himself into the simple saddle. Maximus secured the small bundle with supplies and the map and mounted the other pony.

"Ready?" he asked Brutus.

The Centurion nodded, his face a mask of pain and unwavering determination in the pale moonlight. "Lead us out of here, Maximus."

Maximus gathered the reins. He cast one last look back in the direction they had come, where somewhere in the darkness lay their enemies' camp. Then he turned east and urged his pony forward. They rode off, two lone riders on a narrow night path, uncertain freedom before them, but the horrors of captivity and the looming catastrophe of Rutupiae close behind. The escape had succeeded, but the journey back was still long and fraught with danger.

XVIII. Separate Ways

The flight was a race against time, a desperate ride through a hostile landscape under the cover of deceptive darkness. Maximus and Brutus pushed the tough ponies relentlessly, following the vague markings on the birchbark map Bran's warrior had given them. The path was narrow, often barely visible, winding through dense forests, crossing gurgling streams, and leading over windswept hilltops. Every shadow seemed to hold a threat; every sound made them flinch. They spoke little, their entire focus on the path ahead and listening for signs of pursuit.

Despite his aching shoulder, Brutus held his seat surprisingly well. The raw determination that had always characterized him seemed to grant him superhuman strength. Thoughts of Anwen, the memory of Decimus, anger at Flaccus, and the urgent need to warn Vespasian were a more potent elixir than any pain reliever from the Roman *medici*.

Maximus's head still throbbed, but the strategist's clear mind had taken over. He knew their escape was only the first step. The real challenge was delivering the message in time and averting the impending catastrophe. Caratacus had said five days. In five days, fifteen thousand Celts would march. That had been four days ago. They would likely need another

XVIII. SEPARATE WAYS

five or six days for the march to Rutupiae.

They rode through the entire night, allowing themselves and the animals only short, necessary rests. In the first light of dawn, as the eternal drizzle began again, they reached a fork in the path. The map showed one way leading southeast, back towards the coast and Rutupiae. The other turned north, towards the main road leading to Camulodunum, where Sabinus, Vespasian's brother, was stationed with the Fourteenth Legion.

Maximus reined in his pony; Brutus did the same. They looked at each other, the same realization in their eyes.

"We have to separate," Maximus said quietly but firmly. The decision had come to him during the last hours of the night.

Brutus nodded slowly, his expression serious. "I ride to Rutupiae. I warn Vespasian."

"And I ride to Camulodunum," Maximus continued. "I inform Sabinus. If Caratacus attacks the port, we'll need every available legion to repel him. Sabinus must march troops south immediately."

It was a risky plan. They would halve their already small number. Each would travel alone, through potentially hostile territory. But it was the only logical course. They had to alert both headquarters as quickly as possible.

"You're badly wounded, Brutus," Maximus said with concern. "Can you make the ride alone? It's still at least two, maybe three days' march to Rutupiae."

Brutus straightened in the saddle, his eyes flashing defiantly. "I am a Roman Centurion, Tribune. I reach my objective. Don't worry about me. Worry about yourself. The road north is longer, and who knows what scattered groups of Caratacus's men you might encounter."

"I'll be careful," Maximus assured him. "And fast."

They looked into each other's eyes once more. The coolness of the past days had vanished, replaced by the deep bond of men who had been through hell together. Now, they had to prevent another, greater nightmare.

"Take care, Maximus," Brutus said gruffly, extending his uninjured arm.

Maximus grasped it firmly. "You too, my friend. May the gods be with you."

"And with you." Brutus hesitated a moment, then said, "If… if you see Anwen… tell her…" He broke off, shaking his head. "No. Tell her nothing. I'll tell her myself when I get back."

Maximus nodded. "You will."

With a final, firm handshake, they parted. Brutus turned his pony southeast, Maximus north. Maximus cast one last look back, watching Brutus's lone figure disappear into the fog. A sense of loss and worry tightened his throat, but he shook it off. There was no time for sentiment. He had to ride.

His ride north became a merciless test of endurance and willpower. The pony was tough, but Maximus pushed it to the limits of its capability. He rode day and night, taking only brief pauses to water the animal and choke down a few bites of dried meat himself. The rain was his constant companion, the mud his greatest enemy. He avoided the main roads, following smaller paths instead, navigating by the stars when the clouds allowed, and by his military instinct.

He knew he could be watched. He constantly scanned for tracks, for signs of presence. Once, he heard the distant blare of Celtic war horns; another time, he thought he briefly saw a group of riders crosses his path in the twilight woods, but he wasn't sure. He forced down the fear, focusing only on the

XVIII. SEPARATE WAYS

goal: Camulodunum. Sabinus. The warning.

After a day and a half of continuous riding, he reached a small Roman outpost, little more than a fortified timber fort manned by a handful of auxiliary soldiers. He was exhausted, his pony likewise. The Decurio on duty recognized the Tribune instantly and reacted with professional haste. Maximus received water, some warm porridge, and most importantly, a fresh horse, a strong animal from the legion's stock. He briefly explained the urgency of his mission to the Decurio, warned him of possible Celtic troop movements, and ordered maximum vigilance. Then he swung onto the fresh horse and rode on, allowing himself no rest.

The second leg of the journey was faster; the terrain gradually flattened, the forests thinned. He was now entering territory more firmly under Roman control. He encountered scattered patrols, passed larger farmsteads where life seemed to be proceeding normally.

On the evening of the second day since parting from Brutus, he finally reached the familiar outlines of Camulodunum. The former Catuvellaunian capital, now a major Roman base, lay before him, its newly erected but still incomplete walls silhouetted against the evening sky. Smoke rose from chimneys; the muted sounds of a busy town reached his ears.

Exhausted but relieved, Maximus rode through the main gate, guarded by vigilant legionaries of the Fourteenth Legion. He gave his name and rank and demanded to be taken immediately to Legate Sabinus. The guards, impressed by the urgency and the state of the high-ranking officer, obeyed without question.

He was led through the bustling but orderly streets of the Roman quarter to the *praetorium*, a solid stone building that had once been part of the Celtic royal palace. Titus Flavius Sabinus, Vespasian's older brother, was known as a capable but also stern and somewhat arrogant commander. Maximus prayed Sabinus would believe his warning.

He was ushered into a large room where Sabinus stood bent over maps, surrounded by his staff officers. Sabinus looked up as Maximus entered, his eyebrows rising slightly at the sight of him.

"Tribune Maximus? What brings you here? I thought you were with my brother in Rutupiae? By Jupiter, don't tell me you've had another dream?" Sabinus's voice was cool, formal. The rivalry between the brothers was well-known, though overlaid with familial loyalty.

"Legate Sabinus," Maximus said, trying to hide his exhaustion and shame at his filthy appearance, forcing authority into his voice. "I come directly from the south. I bring urgent, alarming news. Caratacus… he has deceived us. His main army is not in the north. It is gathering here in the south. His target is Rutupiae."

An icy silence fell in the room. The officers stared at Maximus in disbelief. Sabinus's expression became unreadable. "Those are serious claims, Tribune. On what basis?"

Maximus reported briefly, concisely, militarily: his capture, the huge camp he had seen, Caratacus's own words, the planned attack in—now only—three days. He mentioned the betrayal by Flaccus and Adminius only peripherally, focusing on the immediate military threat.

When he finished, silence reigned again. Sabinus paced slowly back and forth, stroking his chin, his gaze turned inward, weighing the information. Finally, he stopped before Maximus.

XVIII. SEPARATE WAYS

"Fifteen thousand men? Against Rutupiae? In three days?" His voice was low but intense. "If this is true, Tribune, then not only Rutupiae but the entire Roman campaign is at stake." He looked Maximus firmly in the eye. "Can you vouch for this information? With your life?"

"With my life, Legate," Maximus replied without hesitation.

Sabinus nodded slowly. He seemed to have made a decision. "Very well, Tribune. I believe you." He turned to his officers. "The Fourteenth Legion moves out immediately! South! Utmost haste! Send riders ahead, secure the bridges over the smaller rivers! Notify all outposts! We must reach Rutupiae before Caratacus strikes!"

A whirlwind of activity erupted in the *praetorium*. Orders were shouted, messengers dispatched, officers hurried away.

Sabinus turned back to Maximus. "You have done your duty, Tribune. More than your duty. Go, rest. You've earned it."

"No, Legate," Maximus replied, though his knees trembled with exhaustion. "My place is with my men and with your legion. I ride with you."

Sabinus studied him again, this time with a hint of respect in his eyes. "As you wish, Tribune. As you wish."

Maximus saluted and left the *praetorium*. Outside, the blare of *tubae* and *cornua* filled the air, the signal for immediate assembly. Legionaries streamed from the barracks, forming up in the streets. News of the imminent danger and the marching orders spread like wildfire. The earlier orderly bustle had given way to feverish urgency. Maximus leaned against a cool stone wall for a moment, closing his eyes. He had made it. He had reached Sabinus, convinced him. The Fourteenth Legion was on its way. But would it be enough?

Would they arrive in time? And what about Brutus? Had he reached Rutupiae? Was he still alive? The uncertainty was almost unbearable. He pushed himself off the wall. There was no time for doubt. He had to keep going. The race against time had just begun.

* * *

Brutus didn't look back. His focus was on the path ahead, not the pain radiating from his shoulder, only the burning urgency of his mission. Vespasian had to be warned. Rutupiae must not fall. He gritted his teeth, ignoring the throbbing in his wound, the nausea from exhaustion and blood loss. He was a Roman Centurion. Pain was an old acquaintance; weakness a luxury he couldn't afford.

He urged his pony on, as fast as the treacherous terrain allowed. The path was narrow, often waterlogged, visibility severely limited by the fog and incessant rain. He relied on the animal's instinct and his own decades of experience surviving in hostile territory. He knew the Celts were likely following him, even if he couldn't see them. They were like shadows in the swamp, silent and deadly.

The pain in his shoulder worsened. The makeshift bandage of moss and leather strips was long soaked through; the wound throbbed with his heartbeat. He felt fever rising, a cold sweat breaking out on his forehead despite the damp chill in the air. He clenched his teeth harder. He couldn't give in. Not now.

He thought of Maximus. The young Tribune who had developed so quickly into a capable commander. The man who, despite his background and rank, was willing to fight

XVIII. SEPARATE WAYS

in the mud and risk his life for his men. The man who had become his friend. Had it been right to let him ride north alone? The way was longer, more dangerous. Brutus felt a pang of concern, which he immediately suppressed. Maximus was strong, clever; he would make it. He had to.

He thought of Decimus, the loyal Optio who had sacrificed himself to allow their escape. His face appeared clearly in Brutus's mind's eye—the honest smile, the determined gaze, the final, desperate battle cry. Anger and grief boiled up inside Brutus. Decimus's death must not be in vain. Flaccus had to pay. But first, Rutupiae had to be saved.

He thought of Anwen. Her image appeared unexpectedly clear—the red hair like a flame in the fog, the clear blue eyes that had met his so directly, so fearlessly. Her smile, her courage, the unexpected tenderness of her touch. He had missed her, more than he cared to admit. The thought of perhaps never seeing her again constricted his throat. He shook his head, trying to banish the sentimentality. He was a soldier, not a poet. But the thought of her gave him new strength, a reason to keep riding, keep fighting, survive.

After hours that felt like days, he finally reached a small, fortified watchtower at a crossroads, manned by a handful of tired auxiliary soldiers. He was utterly spent; the pony beneath him trembled with exhaustion.

The guard commander, a bearded German, recognized the Centurion and his plight immediately. "Centurion Brutus! By Wotan, you look terrible!"

"Water… and a fresh horse," Brutus gasped. "Now! I must get to Rutupiae. Urgent message for the Legate!"

The Germans reacted quickly. They helped him off the pony, gave him water, redressed his wound crudely. They brought him their best horse, a strong animal that looked rested.

"Have you seen any enemies?" Brutus asked, swinging himself painfully into the saddle.

The German shook his head. "Quiet here, Centurion. Too quiet."

"Stay alert," Brutus warned. "Large groups of Celts are on the move. Report anything unusual immediately to Rutupiae and fall back if things get serious." He nodded gratefully to the German, then spurred the new horse on, galloping away, back into the rain and fog.

The rest of the ride was a blurred nightmare of pain, exhaustion, and iron will. Brutus lost track of time, focusing only on staying in the saddle, pushing the horse onward, bringing the goal mile by mile closer. He changed horses once more at a larger supply post, giving the surprised officers curt orders for heightened vigilance.

Finally, after nearly two days of continuous riding since parting from Maximus, he reached the outskirts of Rutupiae. The massive earth ramparts of the coastal fortress emerged from the haze like a promise of safety. He urged his horse through the main gate, ignoring the startled shouts of the guards, and galloped directly to the *praetorium*.

He leaped from the horse, staggered for a moment, but found his balance. He shoved aside the guards at the *praetorium* entrance and stormed inside, his face a mask of dirt, blood, and deadly determination.

Vespasian stood bent over a map, talking with Centurion Longinus and several other officers. He looked up in surprise as Brutus burst in.

"Brutus! By all the gods, what happened? Where is

XVIII. SEPARATE WAYS

Maximus?" Vespasian's voice was sharp with concern.

"Betrayed, Legate!" Brutus gasped, leaning heavily on a table. "Flaccus... Adminius... a trap!" He took a deep breath, struggling for words. "Caratacus... his army... it's not in the north! It's here! Fifteen thousand men! They march on Rutupiae! Attack... in three days!"

An icy silence descended upon the *praetorium*. The officers stared at Brutus in disbelief. Vespasian's face became an impenetrable mask, but his eyes betrayed the shock. He slowly approached Brutus.

"Are you certain, Centurion? Fifteen thousand men, here?"

"I heard Caratacus himself, Legate," Brutus said with his last strength. "Maximus... Maximus rode to Camulodunum to warn Sabinus. I came here." His legs gave way. He sank to his knees before Longinus could catch him.

"*Medicus!* Quickly!" Vespasian called. He knelt beside Brutus, placing a hand on his uninjured shoulder. "Keep talking, Centurion. Tell me everything."

While the hurried *medicus* tended to Brutus's wound, the Centurion recounted, in a weak but clear voice, the ambush, the betrayal, the captivity, the sacrifice, Caratacus's arrival, Bran's help, the escape, and the terrible truth about the impending attack.

When he had finished, silence reigned again. Vespasian slowly stood up, his face now hard as stone. He looked at the map of Britannia, then at the faces of his officers. "Highest alert," he said finally, his voice calm but filled with deadly determination. "Immediate mobilization of all available troops! Reinforce the ramparts! Prepare the defenses! Send the fastest ships to Gaul with calls for aid! Caratacus is coming. And we will be ready!"

A whirlwind of activity erupted in the *praetorium*. Vespasian turned once more to Brutus, who was being attended to. "You have done greatly, Centurion. You warned us. You may have saved Rutupiae." He hesitated. "Rest now."

"I only did my duty, Legate," Brutus whispered.

Vespasian nodded slowly, looking towards the door, out into the bustling camp where the horns were already blowing the assembly call.

XIX. Before the Storm

A sharp smell of herbs, linen, and the sickly sweet stench of gangrene dragged Brutus from a deep, feverish sleep. He blinked, trying to focus on the blurred shapes around him. He was no longer on the cold floor of the *praetorium*, but on a narrow, yet relatively comfortable, caught in a large tent. Through the open tent flaps came the muffled sounds of a busy camp and the pale light of another rainy day in Britannia. He recognized the field hospital.

His head throbbed. His shoulder ached infernally, a dull, incessant pounding that stole his breath. But he was alive. He was in Rutupiae. He had made it.

A *medicus* leaned over him, an older Greek with tired eyes and skillful hands. "Ah, Centurion, awake at last. You've slept nearly a full day. The fever has dropped, a good sign." The *medicus* began changing the dressing on Brutus's shoulder, his touch practiced and surprisingly gentle.

"A day?" Brutus croaked, his throat dry. "How long until the attack?"

The *medicus* shrugged, applying ointment to the cleaned wound. "Who knows, Centurion? The camp is like a stirred-up anthill. Orders flying back and forth. The men reinforce the ramparts day and night. The Legate seems to believe you." He applied a fresh bandage. "But you should rest. The wound is deep, but clean. With luck, it won't become further inflamed. But you lost a lot of blood. Stay down."

"Stay down?" Brutus grumbled, trying to sit up, a pained groan escaping him. "By Mars' bloody spear, the enemy is at the gates, and I'm supposed to lie here like a sick woman?"

"The Legate expressly ordered rest, Centurion," the *medicus* said sternly, gently pushing Brutus back onto the cot. "You're more useless than a one-legged gladiator right now if you try to play the hero. Rest, gather your strength. You'll need it later."

Brutus ground his teeth, but he knew the Greek was right. He was weak, too weak to do much at the moment. He closed his eyes, trying to ignore the pain, but his mind raced. *Five days*, Caratacus had said. Likely another five or six days' March until they arrive. Four days in captivity, three fleeing. Another day had passed while he slept. That left two or three days. Two days to defend a fortress against an army fifteen thousand strong. Two days until Sabinus and the Fourteenth Legion arrived—if Maximus had made it in time, if Sabinus had believed him, if they were fast enough. Too many ifs.

He dozed fitfully, images of the forest battle, Decimus's death, Adminius's betrayal, and Caratacus's triumphant face mingling with fever dreams. The next time he opened his eyes, Vespasian stood beside his cot. The Legate had shed his parade armor, wearing simple leather instead. His face was marked by fatigue and worry, but his eyes were alert and clear.

"Brutus," Vespasian said quietly. "Good to see you awake. How do you feel?"

XIX. BEFORE THE STORM

"Ready for duty, Legate," Brutus answered immediately, trying again to sit up, but Vespasian restrained him with a gesture.

"Stay down, old friend. You've done enough. The *medicus* says you need rest." Vespasian pulled over a stool and sat. "But I need your mind. Tell me again what you heard in Caratacus's camp. Every detail."

Brutus gathered his thoughts. Calmer now, and in more detail, he recounted the conversations with Caratacus—the number of warriors, the planned attack on Rutupiae in likely just two more days, the goal of cutting supply lines and isolating Plautius in the north.

Vespasian listened intently, nodding occasionally, asking precise questions. "Fifteen thousand… That's more than our scouts previously estimated. Caratacus has concentrated his forces skillfully." He thoughtfully stroked his clean-shaven chin. "He targets Rutupiae. A bold, but logical, strike."

"Can we hold the fortress, Legate?" Brutus asked directly. "Two days? Against such overwhelming numbers?"

Vespasian sighed. "It will be… difficult, Brutus. Very difficult. We have perhaps four thousand fighting men here, counting ship crews and auxiliaries, against fifteen thousand. The odds are poor." He paused. "I have sent messengers to all remaining outposts ordering immediate withdrawal here. Messengers to Plautius in the north as well, though I doubt he can arrive in time. His army is too far, the route too long and dangerous. It would take weeks."

"And Sabinus?" Brutus asked hopefully. "Maximus…"

"I have also sent an express courier to Camulodunum," Vespasian confirmed. "As a precaution, in case Maximus didn't make it or Sabinus hesitates." He shook his head. "But even if Sabinus marches immediately, the Fourteenth Legion needs at least three, more likely four, days to get here. If Caratacus attacks in two days as reported, they will be too late to repel the first wave."

Brutus felt hope dwindle again. "What about Gaul? Can we expect reinforcements from there?"

"Unlikely," Vespasian said grimly. "The sea is rough this time of year. The crossing is dangerous, especially for troop transports. And even if they set sail, it takes days for them to arrive. No, Brutus." He looked the Centurion firmly in the eye. "We are on our own. Everything depends on whether we can hold these walls until Sabinus arrives."

"But the Celts have no siege engines," Brutus interjected, clinging to that straw. "They can't breach the walls easily."

"That is our only advantage," Vespasian agreed. "They will try to overrun us with sheer numbers, scale the palisades, smash the gates. They will suffer heavy losses, but they have enough men to absorb those losses. We do not." His gaze hardened. "We must make every man, every arrow, every stone count. We must organize the defense perfectly. Everyone must know what to do."

"I want to help, Legate," Brutus said emphatically, trying again to sit up. "I can't lie here while my men fight! Give me a section of the wall! Anything!"

Vespasian gently pushed him back. "Your time will come, Brutus, but only when you're back on your feet. Right now, I need you alive and clear-headed. You've borne the brunt of the fighting these past weeks. Grant yourself this brief rest. The men will need you later, when the real storm breaks." He stood. "I have temporarily given Centurion Longinus command of your century. He is a good man."

XIX. BEFORE THE STORM

Brutus nodded reluctantly. He knew Longinus, respected him, but it was *his* century. His place was with his men.

"One more question, Legate," Brutus said as Vespasian turned to leave. "What... what about Flaccus and Adminius?"

Vespasian froze for a moment, his back to Brutus. Then he slowly turned, his expression unreadable. "They are here. In Rutupiae."

Brutus felt a chill. "Here? How...?"

"They arrived last evening, shortly after you collapsed," Vespasian explained calmly. "The cohort was... decimated. They reported a heavy ambush shortly after being separated from you."

"An ambush?" Brutus asked incredulously. "We were the ones in the trap!"

"That is their report," Vespasian continued, his gaze meeting Brutus's unflinchingly. "Tribune Flaccus and Centurion Longinus report consistently: they were unexpectedly attacked by a large group of Celts while following the supposed Druid path. They were cut off from your vanguard. Flaccus claims he saw your position overrun. He invokes Tribune Maximus's last order—retreat upon heavy enemy contact—to justify his own withdrawal."

Brutus was speechless with rage. Flaccus's audacity was breathtaking. He had betrayed them and now lied to save his own skin. And Longinus? Had Flaccus threatened him? Bribed him? Or had Longinus been part of the plan from the start?

"And Adminius?" Brutus forced out.

"Vanished," Vespasian said curtly. "Supposedly lost in the chaos of the ambush. Flaccus deeply regrets his loss." A hint of sarcasm touched Vespasian's voice.

"That's a lie, Legate!" Brutus choked out. "Flaccus betrayed us! He led us into that trap deliberately! Adminius was his accomplice! I saw Adminius flee when Caratacus arrived!"

"I know what you saw, Brutus," Vespasian said quietly. "And I know what Flaccus reported. For now, it is his word against yours. Flaccus is a Tribune from an influential family. You are a Centurion." The unspoken reality of Roman hierarchy hung heavy in the air.

"What… what will you do?" Brutus asked, his voice barely a whisper.

"For the moment… nothing," Vespasian replied. "We face a siege. I need every capable officer, including Flaccus. His time will come, Brutus. But only after this battle is won. Only when Maximus returns and can give his testimony." He leaned forward. "Until then: not a word of this to anyone. Concentrate on recovering. That is an order."

Brutus closed his eyes, swallowing his rage and helplessness. He understood. Politics. Intrigue. Even here, at the edge of the world, facing annihilation, the dirty games of Rome continued. He nodded silently.

"Good." Vespasian straightened. "Rest, Centurion. The storm breaks soon." With those words, he left the hospital tent. Brutus remained alone with his pain, his anger, and the agonizing uncertainty about the future. Two days. Only two days left.

* * *

A dull throbbing in his skull and the familiar, unpleasant scent of herbal salves pulled Maximus from deep unconsciousness. He blinked, the bright light hurting his eyes. It streamed through a tent opening. Slowly, his senses returned, and with them, memory: the grueling ride, the arrival in Camulodunum, the tense report to Legate Sabinus, the swelling activity in the camp as the Fourteenth Legion prepared for a hasty departure. Then: blankness. He must have collapsed, overwhelmed by the exhaustion of the past days and the nerve-wracking ordeal.

He tried to sit up, but a gentle pressure on his shoulder held him back. "Easy, Tribune. You overexerted yourself. You need another moment."

The voice was soft, melodious, but with a familiar, slightly rough undertone. Slowly, he turned his head, blinking again until his vision cleared. Then he saw her: Anwen. The Celtic healer with the flame-red hair, clear blue eyes, and small, upturned nose stood beside his makeshift cot in the crowded hospital tent of Camulodunum. She wore her simple, practical clothes, sleeves rolled up, her hands preparing a fresh bandage for a groaning legionary beside him.

"Anwen?" Maximus whispered disbelievingly. "What are you doing here?"

Anwen looked up, a warm smile lighting her face as she addressed him. "Maximus! By the ancestors, you're awake! I was worried." She set aside her work and stepped closer to his cot. "I am here because Legate Sabinus summoned all available healers and *medici* for the march south. The news you brought changed everything here."

"The news…" Maximus repeated, memory returning with full force. "Caratacus. Rutupiae. How much time do we have left?"

"Not much," Anwen said seriously, her smile vanishing. "Legate Sabinus ordered immediate departure. The Fourteenth Legion marches in less than two hours, right after breakfast." She glanced briefly towards the tent opening, where the sounds of the assembling army could be heard. "It will surely be a forced march."

Two hours. Maximus felt a fresh surge of adrenaline. He had to get to Sabinus, discuss final details, ensure everything was ready. He tried again to sit up.

"Slowly, Maximus," Anwen said, placing a cool hand on his forehead. "You completely exhausted yourself. You must conserve your strength."

"No time for that," Maximus replied, gently pushing her hand away and managing to sit up. His head throbbed, but his mind was clear. "I must get to the Legate." He swung his legs over the side of the cot. "How… how is Brutus? Have you heard anything?" The concern for his friend was evident in his voice.

Maximus's expression softened, a hint of worry entering his eyes. "I don't know for sure, Anwen. We separated after escaping captivity. He went to Rutupiae, I came here." He didn't mention Brutus was wounded.

"He is a strong man," Anwen said quietly, her cheeks flushing slightly. "Stubborn as an old boar, but strong."

Maximus smiled faintly. "That he is." He looked at Anwen, noticing the fatigue in her eyes, but also the determination. "And you? Are you coming with us? On this forced march?"

"Of course," she answered, as if it were obvious. "Where there are wounded, healers are needed, whether Roman or Celt." Her blue eyes flashed briefly. "Even if your Roman *medici* still scoff at my methods."

"They are fools if they do," Maximus said seriously. "You saved my life." He now stood, swaying slightly but finding his

XIX. BEFORE THE STORM

balance. "I... I must thank you, Anwen. For everything."

"Save your thanks, Tribune," she said with a slight smile. "Just ensure you and your Centurion survive this war. I'd rather not see either of you on a cot like this again." Her tone was light, but the concern in her eyes was real.

"I will do my best," Maximus promised. He felt an unexpected warmth, a connection to this Celtic healer who possessed more courage and decency than some Roman Tribunes. "I must go now, to Legate Sabinus, for the final briefing before departure."

"Take care, Maximus," Anwen said softly.

"You too, Anwen." He hesitated a moment, then turned and left the hospital tent, his steps still somewhat unsteady, but his will firm.

Outside, the camp was a picture of organized chaos. Centurions bellowed orders, legionaries formed dense ranks, pack animals were loaded, the air filled with the clang of weapons and the blare of horns sounding the assembly. Maximus took a deep breath of the cool morning air, pushing aside exhaustion and personal worries. He was the Tribune again. He had a duty to perform.

He made his way through the throng to the *praetorium*. He stopped first at a rain barrel to wash his face and, as best he could, his body. Arriving at the *praetorium*, Sabinus was already standing outside, surrounded by his key officers, giving final instructions. He nodded to Maximus as he approached.

"Tribune Maximus, are you ready to depart?"

"Yes, Legate," Maximus replied. "I am ready."

"Good." Sabinus looked out at the forming legion, his face a mask of hard determination. "It will be a forced march.

We must reach Rutupiae before Caratacus can deploy his full strength. Every man must give his utmost. No negligence, no delay." He turned back to Maximus. "You know the situation in the south better than anyone here. You ride beside me. Your counsel will be valuable."

"I am at your disposal, Legate," Maximus said.

"But report to my slave at the first halt. He will give you fresh clothes; you look dreadful," Sabinus said, wrinkling his nose, then called to his officers: "Move the Fourteenth Legion out! For Rome! For our brothers in Rutupiae!"

A thunderous cry echoed through the city: "For Rome!" The standards rose. The long column of the Fourteenth Legion Gemina began to move, a steel serpent winding its way south, into the rain, into uncertain battle, into the storm threatening to break over Britannia.

Maximus rode beside Sabinus, his body aching, but his gaze fixed forward, his heart full of worry, yet filled with a cold, hard determination. The race had begun.

XX. The King's Wrath

The first rays of sunlight struggled through the dense fog that still lay like a shroud over the hidden valley where Caratacus's main army was gathering. The pale light revealed a camp pulsing with life and restless energy, a vast, sprawling city of hide tents and lean-tos. The air was thick with the tang of wood smoke from countless campfires, the smell of damp wool and unwashed bodies, the scent of horses, and the low murmur of thousands of voices speaking in the varied dialects of Britannia. Thousands of warriors from diverse Britannic tribes had assembled here, a daunting, if chaotic, picture of Celtic military power. Men honed the edges of swords and axes, checked spear points, mended crude shields, or boasted of past glories, their breath misting in the cool air. Smoke mingled with the mist, creating a gray-brown pall that hung heavy with anticipation. They were preparing, body and spirit, for the impending strike against the Roman eagle.

Caratacus stood alone on a small rise at the edge of the camp, a solitary figure gazing eastwards. There lay Rutupiae, the hated Roman foothold, the strategic heart of their supply in Britannia. His face, usually marked by a noble, almost philosophical calm, was today a mask of tense anticipation and iron will. The lines around his eyes and mouth were deeper than usual, etched by sleepless nights and the immense burden of responsibility that weighed upon him like his mail shirt. He was the commander-in-chief, the King of the Catuvellauni, the chosen leader of the resistance, the man who had dared to defy mighty Rome, leading his people in this desperate fight for freedom.

The recent victory over the cut-off Roman cohort, the capture of the young Tribune Maximus and his experienced Centurion Brutus, had been a welcome, if minor, triumph. It had undeniably boosted his men's morale and provided valuable prisoners—potential pawns in the game against Rome, or perhaps even sources of vital information about Vespasian's defenses, troop strength, and spirit. He planned to interrogate them more thoroughly today, perhaps separately. Surely, he thought with grim satisfaction, their arrogant Roman demeanor must have softened somewhat after days penned like beasts in the cage. Hunger, fear, and the recent horrors they'd witnessed would make them more talkative, more pliable.

His greatest satisfaction, however, came from the confirmation that his bold, overarching strategy was working flawlessly. Plautius, the Roman governor, was still chasing the shadow of his army far to the north, lured away by a third of Caratacus's forces, bogged down in the rugged hills, far from the true center of action. Meanwhile, Caratacus gathered his true fighting strength here in the south, unnoticed, ready to strike Rome at its most vulnerable point. Small, disciplined groups of warriors, led south along winding, forgotten paths, continued to arrive day after day, swelling his host. The trap for Rutupiae was almost set. Tomorrow, they would begin the

XX. THE KING'S WRATH

final march; in six days, they would fall upon the port, conquer it, burn the storehouses, sink the ships, thereby strangling Roman supply and isolating Plautius in the north. It was a daring plan, a high-stakes gamble conceived in the desperate days after the Medway, but it was his only real chance to turn the tide of the war and free Britannia from the eagle's shadow.

A muffled sound behind him—a footstep on the damp earth—tore him from his thoughts. He turned. Branwen, the cool, strategically minded warrior woman who had become one of his most trusted and indispensable advisors, approached with swift, purposeful steps, her expression serious, almost alarmed. Her usual calm composure seemed strained.

"Caratacus," she said without preamble, her voice low but urgent, cutting through the morning air. "There is... a problem."

Caratacus faced her fully, a shiver tracing a path down his spine at her tone. He had learned to trust Branwen's instincts implicitly. "What has happened?"

"The Roman prisoners..." Branwen met his gaze directly, her eyes troubled. "The Tribune and the Centurion... they are gone."

The words struck Caratacus like an unexpected physical blow. He felt the air leave his lungs. "Gone?" he repeated, the word catching in his throat. "What do you mean, *gone?*"

"Escaped," Branwen explained curtly, her voice clipped. "Sometime during the night. The guards before their cages were... overpowered. Silently. No one heard a thing, noticed nothing until the changing of the guard at dawn. Their tracks, what little we could find in the mud and mist, lead east."

An icy rage, cold and sharp as the winter wind, surged

within Caratacus, instantly banishing the morning chill. A visceral heat climbed his neck. He clenched his fists, his knuckles turning white beneath the tanned skin. "Escaped?" His voice was dangerously quiet now, laced with suppressed fury. "By all the gods, Branwen, how could two wounded Romans, one gravely so, escape from a guarded cage in the heart of my army? Who was responsible for the watch?"

"Bryn's men," Branwen confirmed, her lips thinning in distaste. "They were… negligent. Drunk from the victory feast, most likely. Arrogant fools." She paused, hesitating for a fraction of a second. "But… there is more. The tracks suggest they had help. From inside."

Caratacus froze, the implication hitting him with the force of a second blow. "Help? From *whom*?"

"We don't know for certain," Branwen admitted, "but the timing is… suspicious. Bran of the Iceni and his men left the camp early this morning, well before sunrise. They claimed they had to return urgently to attend to trade matters back in their own lands."

Bran. The Iceni chieftain. The trader. The man who walked a careful line between tribes, who profited from Roman trade routes even while lamenting Roman presence. Caratacus thought bitterly of the man's feigned neutrality, his careful courtesies, his refusal to fully commit to the cause. Bran, who always acted in a friendly way towards Rome, fulfilled his treaty obligations, but never truly took sides. Whose sudden departure under the thin pretext of "trade matters" now reeked of deceit. Caratacus cursed inwardly, a black tide of fury rising. He had always distrusted Bran, viewing him as a cautious opportunist, a man ruled by gold rather than honor, but he hadn't suspected him capable of such active treachery—freeing Roman officers, potentially jeopardizing the entire campaign. He had been wrong. Terribly wrong.

The contained rage in Caratacus finally exploded. With a roar, he slammed his fist against the trunk of a nearby ancient oak, the impact sending splinters of bark flying and pain shooting up his arm, though he barely registered it. "Traitor!" he bellowed, startling nearby warriors. "That Iceni fox! That dung-eating merchant! By the gods, I will hunt him down! I will burn his fields and put his head on a spike! He has betrayed us all! Betrayed Britannia!"

"Calm yourself, Caratacus," Branwen said, her voice calm but firm, placing a soothing hand on his trembling arm. The physical contact helped ground him slightly. "Anger is a poor counselor now. We cannot catch Bran at the moment; he is long gone, swallowed by the mists. What matters more, much more, is this: the Romans have escaped. The Tribune and the Centurion. They know our plan. They know our strength. They ride for Rutupiae even now, to warn the legion."

The full, disastrous implication of the situation hit Caratacus with brutal force, chilling his rage. His meticulously crafted plan, his carefully constructed deception, his one chance to deal Rome a decisive blow—all of it was now in jeopardy. If the legion was warned, if Vespasian knew what was coming, he would reinforce Rutupiae's defenses, call for aid, perhaps even summon Sabinus and the Fourteenth Legion from Camulodunum. The vital element of surprise, the cornerstone of his strategy, was lost.

"How much of a head start do they have?" he asked, his voice hoarse, fury yielding to cold, gnawing fear.

"Hard to say," Branwen replied, her brow furrowed in thought. "Given when the escape was likely discovered…

perhaps six, seven hours. But there are only two of them, one badly wounded. We have fast riders, men who know these paths."

"Send them out!" Caratacus ordered immediately, his voice sharp with urgency. "The best riders we have! Cadeyrn! Send Cadeyrn! Have them pick up the trail! They must not reach Rutupiae! Bring me their heads!"

Several of his advisors, alerted by his earlier outburst, had approached, including Cadan, the old, cautious tribal elder. "Caratacus," Cadan said, his voice slow and deliberate as always, "even if your riders catch them, what then? A chase deep into Roman territory? That is risky. And what of our main plan? Should we advance the attack on Rutupiae now, immediately, before the Romans are fully warned and can prepare?"

Caratacus hesitated, the tactical dilemma warring with his lingering fury. His first impulse was to strike now, immediately, use the remaining sliver of time before the Romans could fully react. But his army wasn't completely assembled. Many warriors were still arriving, weary from long marches. A hasty, potentially disorganized attack on a fortified position like Rutupiae, even if the defenders were not fully prepared, would be an enormous risk, potentially trading one disaster for another.

"We cannot wait!" shouted Cadeyrn, the young cavalry leader, striding forward, his face flushed not just with anger but with impatience and a burning desire to prove himself in battle. "We must attack now! With the strength, we have! We've seen them bleed already before our walls! If we hesitate, we give them time to recover, time to reinforce! Momentum is on our side; we must use it! Do we cower here while they laugh at our caution? Let's overrun the Romans before they know what hit them! Revenge for Togodumnus! Revenge for our fallen brothers! Let us show that Britannic courage is stronger than Roman walls!" His passion was infectious; several younger chieftains nodded in vigorous agreement, murmuring their assent.

"Silence, Cadeyrn!" Caratacus snapped, though he understood the young man's fire, an impatience shared by many of his warriors eager for glory or vengeance. "This is no time for blind rage or impetuous courage alone. We must act wisely." He turned back to Cadan and Branwen, his expression seeking their counsel. "What do you think? Advance now, or wait as planned?"

"Wait," Cadan said decisively, his gaze steady. "Our strength lies in overwhelming numbers and the shock of the attack's timing, even if they might now be warned. Give the arriving men one more day to assemble fully, to rest properly. A rested warrior fights better than ten exhausted ones, and Rutupiae isn't going anywhere. Even warned, the Romans cannot make the fortress impregnable overnight. We still hold the advantage of numbers, and we can still choose the exact moment of attack, perhaps striking where they least expect it."

"Cadan is right," Branwen agreed, her analytical mind assessing the situation. "A hasty attack now would be a mistake; it would only increase our losses unnecessarily. We stick to our plan. We attack in two days, at full strength. By then," she added, a thoughtful look in her eyes, "your riders may have caught the Tribune and the Centurion. And if not," she shrugged slightly, "then the legion will indeed be warned, but they will also know the true might marching against them. Perhaps fear will make them withdraw behind their walls entirely, or perhaps the other Roman legion from Camulodunum will march straight into our arms, allowing us to destroy them both."

Caratacus wrestled with himself. The anger at Bran's betrayal still burned; the fear of the Fourteenth Legion's intervention gnawed at him. Cadeyrn's passionate appeal resonated with his own warrior heart, the desire to strike swiftly, decisively. But he also knew Cadan and Branwen were wise counselors, their cool judgment a necessary counterpoint to the heat of battle lust. A rash, ill-prepared attack was not his way. He was a strategist, a king, not merely a hotheaded chieftain. The burden of command settled heavily upon him; the fate of thousands rested on his decision. He could not afford weakness or error.

"Very well," he said finally, his voice calmer again, though filled with an iron resolve that silenced all further debate. "We wait one more day. Let the arriving men rest fully, sharpen their weapons, prepare their spirits. Send scouts ahead to closely observe Rutupiae, report any Roman movement, any sign of reinforcements arriving by sea or land." He looked directly at Cadeyrn, whose face darkened momentarily with disappointment. "Your riders will hunt the two fugitives. Ride like the wind itself is chasing you, Cadeyrn, but be careful and clever, not just fast! No rest for you or your mounts until they are found! I want them alive, if possible; their information could still be valuable. But dead is also acceptable." His voice hardened. "The main thing is, they do not reach Vespasian."

Cadeyrn nodded grimly, the anticipation of the hunt mixing with his frustration at the delay. "Consider it done, Caratacus." He turned sharply and hurried off to gather his best men and horses.

Caratacus watched him go, then turned his gaze east again towards the unseen Roman fortress. The sun climbed higher, burning through the fog like a baleful eye, revealing the vastness of his assembled host but doing little to warm the chill in his heart. Bran's betrayal had struck him personally; the Romans' escape had jeopardized his grand design. But he was not beaten. He was Caratacus, leader of the Britannic resistance. He would adapt. He would fight. He would prevail. The burning rage yielded to an icy, focused determination. Rutupiae would fall. Rome would bleed. And he would be the one holding the knife. The storm he intended to unleash was merely delayed, not stopped.

XXI. Walls and Memories

A gray dawn broke over Rutupiae, no different from the day before. Yet today, a new tension hung in the air. The rain had eased, but the sky remained overcast. The wind from the sea carried the salty tang of the incoming tide and the ominous foreboding of impending battle to the farthest corners of the vast Roman camp, which now felt like a besieged fortress.

In the crowded hospital tent, Brutus opened his eyes to the smell of herbs and human suffering. The feverish haze of the past days had lifted somewhat. The pain in his shoulder had become a dull but bearable throbbing. He had slept for almost a full day, his body using the forced rest to heal. His mind, however, was restless. Worry about Maximus, anger at Flaccus, and the pressing awareness of time running out consumed him. Caratacus and his fifteen thousand warriors were out there, somewhere in the fog. They were coming.

He sat up with effort, ignoring the protest from his injured shoulder and the warning glance from the Greek *medicus*, who was applying a bandage to another legionary. "Enough lying around," Brutus muttered. "A Centurion belongs on the wall, not on a cot."

"Centurion, you should rest!" the *medicus* called out, but

XXI. WALLS AND MEMORIES

Brutus was already tuning him out. He pulled on his tunic and laboriously buckled his *balteus* with one hand, his *gladius* hanging at his side. He felt weak, his legs unsteady, but his will was stronger. Brutus left the hospital tent, blinking in the gray morning light, and took a deep breath of the cool, salty air.

He walked through the busy streets of Rutupiae. The town, or rather the fortified port complex, was an impressive example of Roman engineering and military organization, even if hastily constructed. Massive earth ramparts, partially reinforced with stone and surrounded by deep ditches, formed the outer defensive ring. Behind them rose strong timber palisades with walkways and regularly spaced watchtowers. Inside crowded tents, barracks, storehouses, workshops, and the central *praetorium*. Everything bustled with activity, yet remained orderly. Legionaries hauled building materials, reinforced the ramparts, dug more ditches. Engineers worked on the gates, strengthening hinges and bolts. Archers and slingers took positions on the towers. The air filled with the noise of labor—hammering, sawing, shouted commands, the groaning of carts.

Brutus felt a mixture of pride and deep concern—pride in the unwavering discipline and work ethic of his comrades, who didn't falter even facing overwhelming odds, but also concern whether these walls, these men, would be strong enough. He knew the Celts, knew their fierce determination. Fifteen thousand of them... that was a tidal wave threatening to break even the strongest Roman dams.

His path led him to the northern gatehouse, the most massive part of the fortifications, guarding the main landward approach. He knew this would likely be a primary point of attack. As he neared, he saw a group of officers standing on the rampart walkway, surveying the forward defenses. Among them, he recognized the stocky figure of Legate Vespasian.

Brutus climbed the wooden ramp to the walkway. The guards saluted curtly, letting him pass. Vespasian turned as he heard him approach, a flicker of surprise but also approval in his eyes.

"Brutus? Back on your feet already? I thought the *medicus* ordered bed rest."

"A scratch, Legate," Brutus downplayed it. "I wanted to inspect the defenses. See where I can help."

Vespasian nodded slowly, his gaze sweeping over the men working feverishly below. "Good to have you here. Your eye for weaknesses is valuable." He gestured towards the ditch before them. "We are deepening the ditches, setting up additional *cippi* (sharpened stakes) and *lilia* (concealed pit traps). But against sheer numbers…" He left the sentence unfinished.

"The walls are strong, Legate," Brutus said. "The palisades are solid oak, the ramparts wide enough for two ranks of defenders." He knew the standard construction of Roman field camps; Rutupiae was more than that, a permanent fortress, but it had never been designed for a siege of this magnitude. It spanned roughly 800 by 600 paces, a considerable area requiring many men to defend.

"Strong enough against men, yes," Vespasian replied thoughtfully, "but what about ladders? Rams they might improvise? They have no heavy siege engines, that's our luck, but they are resourceful and desperate."

Brutus thought, looking out at the wide, clear strip of land

XXI. WALLS AND MEMORIES

before the ditch, deliberately cleared to deny attackers cover. "We need something to break their charge before they even reach the ditches. Something to disrupt their formations, sow chaos." His gaze sharpened. "Caltrops!"

Vespasian raised an eyebrow. "*Tribuli*? Yes, a good idea. Small, four-pronged iron spikes. No matter how they land, one point always faces up. Devastating against charging infantry and cavalry."

"Exactly, Legate," Brutus said eagerly. "We need to have as many made as possible. Thousands! We scatter them in a dense field before the main points of attack, especially before the gates and weaker sections of the palisade. If the Celts attack at dawn, perhaps in the fog, they'll run into them before they see them. It will break their initial charge, inflict heavy casualties, and buy us precious time."

Vespasian nodded approvingly. "An excellent idea, Brutus. Pragmatic, effective. Roman." He smiled thinly. "We must order the forges to begin production. Currently, they are fully occupied repairing weapons, making arrowheads and bolts."

"I will see to it, Legate," Brutus said firmly. "I can't do much heavy lifting right now anyway." He gestured to his bandaged shoulder. "But I can give orders and push the smiths. There are three forges in the camp, aren't there? I'll visit them personally."

"Good," Vespasian said. "Do that. Every caltrop counts." He turned back to the wall, his gaze shifting to the warships in the harbor. "I must speak with the *nauarchi*. I want their ballistae up here on the walls. They can provide additional firepower, especially against massed formations." He sighed. "They won't be thrilled about removing their precious machines from the ships, but they have no choice."

The two men stood silently side-by-side for a moment, each with his own plans and worries, but both determined to hold Rutupiae.

"May the gods help us, Brutus," Vespasian said quietly, so no other legionaries could hear.

Brutus replied, "The gods help those who help themselves, Legate." He added, "We will fight." Then he gave a curt salute and headed back into the camp, towards the forges.

He walked through the busy streets, observing the feverish preparations. Legionaries hauled heavy stones for the walls, others practiced formation drills in small groups, still others meticulously cleaned their equipment. The air vibrated with tension, but also with focused calm. It was the quiet before the storm, the calm of men who knew their fate and prepared to meet it. Brutus felt pride in these men, in their resilience and discipline. They were the best Rome had to offer.

He reached the first of the three forges, an open workshop near the western wall. The rhythmic hammering of metal filled the air. Sparks flew from anvils, and the smell of hot iron and coal fires was almost overpowering. Several half-naked, sweat-drenched men worked glowing metal—likely local recruits or slaves under the supervision of a Roman master smith.

Brutus approached. The master smith was a stocky man with a soot-blackened face and powerful arms. He glanced up briefly, wiped sweat from his brow, and returned to his work, shaping the blade of a *gladius*, apparently a custom order for an officer.

"Smith!" Brutus called over the noise.

The master looked up again, this time with a hint of annoyance at the interruption. "What is it, Centurion? I have work to do! Weapons for the defense!"

"I have new orders for you," Brutus said firmly. "Effective immediately, cease work on all other orders. Your sole task is to forge caltrops. As many as possible, as quickly as possible."

The smith lowered his hammer, staring at Brutus incredulously. "Caltrops? *Tribuli*? Are you mad, Centurion? It's simple work, yes, but time-consuming! And we need swords, spearheads, arrowheads! The men need weapons, not... little iron stars!"

"You have your orders, smith," Brutus replied icily. "Legate Vespasian himself authorized them. Every caltrop you forge can stop a Celt before he reaches the wall. That saves lives. More lives than another sword in the hand of a man who might fall tomorrow. Now, get to work!"

The smith hesitated, his expression a mixture of disbelief and defiance. He was a civilian under military authority, but also a master of his craft, clearly proud of his work. "But... Centurion Clodius's order..."

"Centurion Clodius can wait!" Brutus cut him off. "The defense of Rutupiae cannot! If you refuse, I'll have you put in chains and your assistants will take over!"

The smith swallowed. He saw the unyielding expression in Brutus's eyes, felt the authority radiating from the Centurion. He was a stocky man, but he limped slightly as he stepped back, an old affliction that had likely rendered him unfit for regular military service.

Brutus noticed the limp. His gaze softened fractionally. "Where did you get the injury, smith?"

The man seemed surprised by the sudden question, the change in tone. He looked down at his left leg. "Old wound, Centurion. From the war. Long time ago."

"Which war? Which legion did you serve?" Brutus pressed, a sudden curiosity stirring within him.

The smith hesitated, then answered with a hint of old pride in his voice, "I was a Centurion in the Fourteenth Gemina, under Legate Sabinus, in the cohort of *Primus Pilus* Sextus Pompeius Magnus."

Brutus froze. *Magnus.* His old mentor, the man who had shaped him, taught him everything he knew about the craft of war. The man who had perished in the flames of Camulodunum. "You... you served under Magnus?"

The smith nodded, a shadow crossing his face. "Aye. A great man. A hard man, but just. His death was a heavy blow to the Fourteenth." He looked Brutus over more closely. "How do you know him, Centurion?"

"He was my first Centurion, my trainer," Brutus said quietly, the memories returning with unexpected force. "In the Second Augusta. A long, long time ago. He was my mentor."

The smith's eyes widened. "You... You are Brutus? The Brutus Magnus always spoke of?"

Now Brutus was surprised. "He spoke of me?"

The smith nodded eagerly, the earlier hostility vanished. "Aye, often! Always said you were the stubbornest mule and the toughest nut he ever had under his command!" He chuckled softly. "But he was proud of you, Centurion. Very proud. Said you'd make a great commander one day."

Brutus felt an unexpected warmth in his chest, a mixture of grief and pride. Magnus had believed in him. He swallowed the lump in his throat. "He was a good man. And a stubborn bastard himself."

"The best," the smith agreed. His gaze fell on the unfinished sword blade, then back to Brutus. His posture changed.

XXI. WALLS AND MEMORIES

"Caltrops, you say, Centurion?"

Brutus nodded. "As many as possible."

"Consider it done," the smith said firmly. He called his assistants together, explained the new task. Then he turned back to Brutus. "One more thing, Centurion. If you really want these things to be effective… forge barbs on them. Small, backward-facing points. Once they dig into flesh or boot leather, they don't come out easily. Slows the enemy down even more."

Brutus looked at the smith, giving an appreciative nod. "A good idea, smith. Very good. See that it's done."

"Count on it, Centurion. For Magnus."

The two men looked at each other for a moment, an unexpected connection forged between them by the shared memory of a fallen comrade.

"Thank you," Brutus said. "I'll let you get to work."

He left the noisy forge, the rhythmic hammering following him for a few steps before fading into the general din of the camp. Brutus headed towards the next forge, located closer to the harbor area. His path now took him through parts of Rutupiae that were less military in character, where soldiers' barracks mingled with the makeshift shelters of merchants, craftsmen, sailors, prostitutes, and a growing number of civilian refugees who had streamed in from the surrounding countryside in the deceptive hope of Roman protection.

The atmosphere here differed from the purely military section of the camp. The tense discipline of the legionaries gave way to a louder, more chaotic nervousness. People crowded the narrow, muddy lanes, their faces marked by fear and uncertainty. Merchants desperately tried to sell their remaining goods at inflated prices. Craftsmen offered their services, often for little more than a meager meal. Everywhere, Brutus saw signs of panic: families carried their few belongings on carts or backs, children cried, women stared blankly into space.

The situation was particularly bad down at the harbor, in the area designated for civilian ships. A noisy, desperate crowd had gathered there, pressing against the quays where a few private merchant vessels lay anchored, their captains hesitant to set sail. Shouts and angry cries filled the air as people tried to force their way onto the ships, offering the sailors their last money, jewelry, anything they owned, for passage to Gaul, away from the impending siege, away from the feared Celtic vengeance.

Brutus saw how the ship captains, mostly hardened Gallic traders, shamelessly exploited the situation, demanding exorbitant sums for a place onboard, playing the desperate against each other, laughing at their pleas. Scuffles broke out as men fought for space. Guards from the harbor command struggled to maintain a minimum of order, pushing back the throng with their spear shafts. It was an ugly picture of human greed and desperation in the face of danger.

Some wealthier merchant families had apparently managed to secure passage and were now being brought aboard under the protection of private mercenaries, while the poorer refugees remained behind, filled with rage and envy. Disgust rose in Brutus. This aspect of war—the civilian panic, the profiteering of individuals—was as repugnant to him as the betrayal of a Flaccus or the senseless brutality of a Celtic raid. He was a soldier. His world was orders, discipline, combat. He couldn't, and wouldn't, deal with this civilian chaos. Yet, he felt a pang of pity for the common people caught innocently between the fronts. Brutus shook his head, turned away, and continued towards the second forge.

XXII. Moves in the Shadows

The departure of the Fourteenth Legion Gemina from Camulodunum occurred with the impressive efficiency characteristic of a well-oiled Roman war machine. Beneath the surface of discipline, however, lay a feverish urgency. The news of Caratacus's massive army in the south and his planned attack on Rutupiae had spread through the ranks like shockwaves. Every legionary, from the common *miles* to the experienced Centurion, knew what was at stake. Rutupiae was more than just a port; it was the umbilical cord connecting them to Rome, their only guarantee of supplies and reinforcements in this hostile land. Failure would not only doom their comrades of the Second Augusta but likely seal the fate of the entire Britannic campaign.

Maximus rode beside Legate Titus Flavius Sabinus at the head of the long marching column. The thunder of thousands of hobnailed boots on the worn path, the rhythmic clank of armor and weapons, and the snorting of horses and mules from the baggage train created a familiar yet tense soundscape. The sky was still gray, but the rain had stopped for now, making the march on the muddy ground slightly easier.

Maximus felt exhaustion deep in his bones. The hard ride from Bryn's camp to Camulodunum had taken its toll. His

XXII. MOVES IN THE SHADOWS

head still ached slightly, and his muscles were stiff. But the urgency of the situation and the knowledge of the looming danger to Brutus, Vespasian, and the men in Rutupiae drove him on, leaving no room for weakness. He observed the deploying legion around him, trying to gauge its strength.

After a period of silence, Maximus began, "Legate Sabinus, the legion doesn't appear to be marching at full strength. Are units missing?" His voice was rough but respectful. He had a good eye for numbers and formations, and the column seemed thinner than expected for a full legion of over five thousand men, even accounting for previous losses.

Sabinus, who had been staring straight ahead with a grim expression, briefly turned his head. His face was angular, features sharp like his brother Vespasian's, but lacking the warmth Vespasian sometimes showed. Sabinus seemed harder, more uncompromising. "Your eye is sharp, Tribune," he said coolly. "You are correct. I had to leave a garrison behind in Camulodunum."

"A garrison, Legate?" Maximus asked, surprised. "Given the threat in the south?"

Sabinus explained patiently, yet with a hint of condescension, "The city was only recently conquered, Tribune." It sounded as if he were explaining basics to an inexperienced recruit. "The populace is subdued but not loyal; discontent simmers beneath the surface. An uprising would be a disaster, especially now, with Caratacus operating in the south." Sabinus paused. "I had to leave a full cohort in the city to maintain order and crush any spark of resistance. Additionally, I deployed another cohort among the smaller outposts along the route north. We cannot leave Plautius completely unprotected, in case Caratacus only sent part of his army south and threatens Plautius's supply lines with the rest."

Maximus nodded slowly. The decision was militarily sound but significantly weakened their own force. "So how many men are marching to Rutupiae, Legate?"

"About four and a half thousand legionaries," Sabinus replied, "plus some auxiliary units, mainly cavalry for reconnaissance. Just under five thousand men in total."

Five thousand against fifteen thousand. The odds were still poor, but better than those facing the garrison in Rutupiae alone. Time was critical.

Maximus urged, "Legate, we must be faster. The men can endure a forced march. If we march day and night, with minimal breaks, we might reach Rutupiae on the third day, not the fourth. That single day could make the difference."

Sabinus shook his head decisively. "No, Tribune. Out of the question."

"But Legate…"

"No buts, Maximus!" Sabinus interrupted sharply, his tone brooking no argument. "I understand your concern for your comrades, for my brother. But what use are five thousand men so exhausted they can barely lift their swords when we reach Rutupiae? They would be easy prey for Caratacus's rested warriors." He reined his horse slightly to look directly at Maximus. "A forced march would break our fighting strength before the real battle even begins. We would lose more men to exhaustion and stragglers left behind than we could save by the time gained."

"But what if Rutupiae falls before we arrive?" Maximus countered, his voice full of worry. "If Caratacus destroys the port? Then all is lost! Our arrival will be meaningless! We'd

XXII. MOVES IN THE SHADOWS

be cut off, just like Plautius!"

"I am aware of the risk, Tribune," Sabinus replied, his voice calmer now but still firm. "I know my brother. Vespasian is a tough, experienced commander. He has the Second Legion Augusta, one of Rome's finest units, at his side." A rare hint of acknowledgment touched his voice as he mentioned the legion's name. "They will hold Rutupiae. They must hold it, at least for one, perhaps two days. They know we are coming. That hope will give them strength."

He looked asses singly at Maximus. "The crucial question is not whether we reach Rutupiae, but in what condition. I will not decimate this legion with a pointless forced march. We march fast, but orderly. We build a fortified marching camp every evening. We conserve our strength for the decisive battle. Vespasian must withstand the initial assault. That is what I am counting on."

Maximus fell silent, torn internally. Sabinus's logic was militarily sound; the arguments against a forced march were valid. But his heart cried out for haste, for immediate action. Images of Brutus, wounded and feverish, of the few remaining men of their cohort, stood clearly before him. Would they hold out?

Sabinus seemed to guess his thoughts. "There is another consideration, Tribune," he said after a while, his tone becoming thoughtful, almost suspicious. "Are you absolutely certain about what you heard and saw in Caratacus's camp?"

Maximus looked at him, surprised. "Legate? I reported what Caratacus himself said! Fifteen thousand men, attack on Rutupiae in… now only two days!"

"Yes, you did," Sabinus nodded slowly. "But think, Tribune. Caratacus is cunning. He successfully deceived Plautius.

Could it not be that he deceived you, either? That your capture, your 'coincidental' rescue by this Iceni chieftain, your escape—that it was all part of a larger plan?"

Maximus froze. The thought hadn't occurred to him, too focused had he been on the immediate threat and the escape. But now that Sabinus voiced it...

"What do you mean, Legate?" he asked, a new, cold fear creeping into him.

"Just think!" Sabinus continued, ticking off points on his fingers. "You and your Centurion are lured into an ambush—by betrayal, you say. Most of your men die, but you two, the highest-ranking officers, survive and are captured. Coincidence? Then you are taken to Caratacus, who—what a surprise!—reveals his entire plan of attack on Rutupiae to you. A plan that would hit Rome hard. And then, coincidentally, an old acquaintance of your Centurion appears, a Celtic chieftain who helps you escape out of pure gratitude? A Roman Tribune and Centurion? From the middle of the enemy's main camp?" Sabinus shook his head. "Forgive me, Maximus, but that doesn't just sound improbable; it sounds like a poorly staged farce."

Maximus felt the ground shift beneath him. Sabinus's words struck a nerve, awakening doubts he had suppressed. Bran's appearance... was it really just an old debt? Or had Caratacus sent him? Had Caratacus *wanted* them to escape? Wanted them to carry this information to Rutupiae and Camulodunum? But why?

"Why? Why would he do that?" Maximus stammered.

Sabinus replied intently, "To lure us exactly where he wants us! Perhaps Rutupiae isn't his real target at all. Perhaps it's a feint. Perhaps he wants us to divide our forces: I rush south

XXII. MOVES IN THE SHADOWS

with the Fourteenth Legion, while he, with his main force…" Sabinus glanced north, the direction they had come from. "…attacks Camulodunum, which is now weakly defended. Or," his gaze darkened further, "he lies in wait for us right here, on this road. Perhaps he intends to annihilate the Fourteenth Legion in an ambush, far from any support."

A strong internal conflict erupted within Maximus. Sabinus's theory sounded plausible, terrifyingly plausible. The ease of their escape, Bran's sudden appearance, Caratacus's unusual openness—did it all fit together too well? Had he been deceived? Blinded by concern for Brutus and Rutupiae, had he fallen for a false warning, potentially triggering an even greater catastrophe? The responsibility weighed unbearably upon him. His head began to throb again.

He looked at Sabinus, whose eyes studied him intently. "Legate… if you believe that… why did you set out? Why are we marching south?"

Sabinus sighed deeply. "Because I don't know for sure, Tribune. That is the damned truth of war—you never know for sure." He looked south again. "I believe you. I believe Caratacus does indeed plan to attack Rutupiae. It is a logical, strategically valuable target. It fits his boldness. Your warning feels genuine." He paused. "But I cannot rule out the possibility of a ruse. Caratacus is intelligent enough for it. Therefore," he looked directly at Maximus again, "we march south to aid my brother. But we do it cautiously. We conserve our strength. We build a fortified marching camp every evening. We constantly send out scouts, not just ahead, but also to the flanks and rear. We are prepared for anything—for a siege in Rutupiae, and for an ambush on the way there."

Maximus listened, and slowly his inner turmoil gave way to

a growing admiration for the elder Legate's strategic foresight and cool rationality. Sabinus was not driven by panic, neither by Maximus's warning nor his own doubts. He weighed the risks, made a sound, albeit difficult, decision, and took precautions for all eventualities. He conserved his men not out of weakness, but out of strategic necessity.

"I... I understand, Legate," Maximus finally said, and for the first time, felt genuine respect for Vespasian's older brother. "Your approach is... wise."

Sabinus merely gave a curt nod, a gesture conveying both acknowledgment and a warning for caution. "Wisdom comes with age, Tribune. And with scars." He turned his gaze forward again. "You still have much to learn. But you learn quickly. That is good." He added casually, gaze still fixed on the path, "And your grandfather? Vespasian once mentioned knowing him. A certain Prosonius, if I recall correctly. Also a simple man?"

Maximus's heart skipped a beat. *Prosonius.* His grandfather's cover name. Sabinus knew. Or he was testing him, laying bait. A wave of cold sweat ran down his back despite the cool air. He felt Sabinus's probing, though indirect, gaze. What did Sabinus really know? Had Vespasian revealed more than he should have? Or was it just the usual game of the powerful in Rome, rumors, half-truths seeping all the way to Britannia? Flaccus? They all seemed to be pulling strings whose ends he couldn't see. He was a piece in their game, his life, his origins a weapon or a danger. He couldn't show weakness, couldn't confirm suspicion.

"I barely knew my grandfather, Legate," Maximus lied, forcing his voice to remain steady though his insides churned. "He died when I was very young." Maximus hated the lie,

XXII. MOVES IN THE SHADOWS

forced by fear. Hated the feeling of constantly having to be on guard, even with men like Sabinus, whom he was beginning to respect.

"A pity," Sabinus said tonelessly. "The wisdom of the elders is priceless, they say." He fell silent again, leaving Maximus alone with his racing thoughts.

They rode on in silence, but the atmosphere between them had changed. Maximus still felt the weight of responsibility, but felt less alone. He was part of a larger machine, led by experienced men who pursued their course despite all uncertainties and dangers. Maximus had to learn to trust orders, even when his instincts disagreed. He had to learn to see the bigger picture. And he had to learn to live with the doubts—and with the constant, hidden danger of his own existence. The march south was not just a race against time, but also a lesson in humility, leadership, and the perilous game of power.

XXIII. The Price of Haste

The forests swept past as a blurred green and brown veil under a merciless gray sky. Caratacus relentlessly pushed his large, dark warhorse, knees pressed tight against the animal's flanks, gaze fixed eastward towards Rutupiae—the hated symbol of Roman power and the strategic heart of their presence in Britannia. Behind him thundered the hooves of his personal cavalry guard, followed by the first waves of his vast army: an endless stream of warriors on foot and horseback, snaking resolutely through the landscape.

They had been marching for two days since leaving the hidden assembly camp, two days of continuous forced march that exacted a heavy toll. Caratacus felt the exhaustion in his own limbs, a dull ache in his back, a leaden heaviness in his arms. He had barely slept since the news of the two Roman officers' escape struck him like lightning. Anger at Bran still burned hot within him, but it was overlaid by a cold, pressing fear: the fear that his bold, carefully planned strike against Rutupiae might now fail because the Romans were warned.

He knew every hour counted. The Tribune and the Centurion were dangerous men. They knew his plan, his strength, his objective. They would do anything to reach their fortress

XXIII. THE PRICE OF HASTE

and sound the alarm. Cadeyrn's riders were surely hot on their trail, but the Romans had a head start, and the terrain favored fugitives. Caratacus could only hope his riders were faster, that they could intercept the escapees before they reached Rutupiae or, worse, Camulodunum.

"Maintain the pace! No rest!" he shouted to his men, his voice rising above the panting of warriors and the tramp of thousands of feet. "Rutupiae is near! Victory is near!"

He saw the tired faces of his warriors, mud clinging to their legs and hides, exertion etched into their features. They were brave, loyal, ready to follow him to the death, but they were also only human. Two days of forced march through difficult terrain, in damp, rainy weather, had left their mark. Many limped, leaning on their spears, their breathing ragged. Even the horses of his cavalry guard snorted heavily, flanks flecked with foam.

At midday on the second day, they crossed a wider ford through a sluggish, muddy river. Cadan, the old, farsighted advisor, rode beside him, his face calm as ever, but his eyes showing deep concern.

"Caratacus," he said quietly, his voice barely audible over the splashing water, "the men are exhausted. They need a break, a proper rest. Otherwise, many will collapse on the way before we even reach Rutupiae."

"We cannot stop, Cadan!" Caratacus retorted sharply, his gaze fixed forward. "Every hour we lose gives the Romans another hour to prepare. We must exploit the element of surprise as much as possible!"

"What element of surprise?" asked Branwen, riding on Caratacus's other side, her voice cool and pragmatic as always. "The Tribune and the Centurion have escaped. Vespasian has long been warned. He will be reinforcing the walls, gathering his men. The surprise is lost, Caratacus."

"Not entirely!" Caratacus insisted. "Vespasian may be warned, but he doesn't know exactly when we are coming. He doesn't know how we will attack. And he cannot triple his garrison overnight. We still have the advantage of numbers. But that advantage melts away with every passing hour! If the legion from Camulodunum arrives…"

"Precisely why we need our men at full strength," Cadan interjected. "What good is superior numbers if half our warriors can barely lift a spear from exhaustion? Assaulting a Roman fortress is no stroll, especially without siege engines. We need rested, battle-ready men."

"Give them an hour's rest, Caratacus," Branwen urged. "Just one hour, enough to draw water, eat some dried meat, tend to their feet. It will do more good than an hour gained marching with exhausted men."

Caratacus hesitated. He saw his advisors' faces, saw the truth in their words. He looked back at the endless column of his army, saw the tired but determined men. They would follow him whatever he commanded, he knew that. But at what cost? He was their leader, their hope. He couldn't sacrifice them needlessly.

"Alright," he finally said reluctantly. "One hour's rest after we cross the river, but not a minute longer! Then we march on until nightfall."

A murmur of relief went through the officers nearby who had overheard the conversation. Cadan and Branwen nodded in agreement.

After the army reached the far bank, they settled down to rest on a wide meadow. Sentries were posted, and the first

XXIII. THE PRICE OF HASTE

small fires kindled. Suddenly, a small troop of riders galloped into the camp at full tilt, their horses utterly spent, close to collapse. It was Cadeyrn and the men he had sent in pursuit of Maximus and Brutus.

Caratacus's heart tightened. He immediately rode towards them, followed by his advisors. Cadeyrn's face was dark, his breath coming in ragged gasps.

"Report, Cadeyrn!" Caratacus commanded. "Did you catch them?"

Cadeyrn swung himself from his horse; the animal swayed and nearly fell. "No, Caratacus," he said bitterly. "They escaped us. We tracked them day and night. They rode like the wind, changed horses at their outposts." He spat on the ground. "The Centurion reached Rutupiae last evening. The Tribune... he rode north, towards Camulodunum."

Caratacus felt the blood freeze in his veins. *Camulodunum.* The Fourteenth Legion. If the Tribune reached the Legate and convinced him...

"When did he reach Camulodunum?" he asked sharply.

"We don't know for sure," Cadeyrn replied. "We lost his trail shortly before the town, but he had almost a day's lead on the Centurion. He must have arrived there this morning."

"Cursed!" Caratacus yelled, slamming his fist into his palm again. "So the Fourteenth Legion knows too! They will march!"

"They already are, Caratacus," said another of Cadeyrn's riders, a scout who had been observing the area around Camulodunum. "We saw the signals, the dust clouds. The Fourteenth Legion broke camp this morning. They march south."

An icy silence fell over the group. The situation had changed dramatically. It was no longer just an attack on a surprised garrison; it was a race. A race against Sabinus and the Fourteenth Legion.

"How long will it take them to reach Rutupiae?" Caratacus asked Branwen, valuing her knowledge of Roman marching speeds.

Branwen calculated quickly. "From Camulodunum to Rutupiae, on the main roads, a disciplined legion on a forced march... three, maybe four days, if they hurry."

"Four days," Caratacus repeated. "We need another day to reach Rutupiae if we keep marching now. That gives us... two days' head start at most." His gaze hardened, resolute. "Two days to take Rutupiae before Sabinus arrives."

"That's impossible!" Cadan cried out, appalled. "Storm a Roman fortress in two days? With exhausted men? Without siege equipment? That's suicide!"

"It's our only chance!" Caratacus retorted, his voice cutting. "If Sabinus reaches Rutupiae before we take it, we are trapped. The two legions together... they would crush us!" He looked around, his eyes burning with intensity. "We no longer have a choice. The time for caution is over. The time for deception is over. Now, only speed and brute force matter!"

He turned to his chieftains. "The rest is over! Immediate departure! We march day and night! No more breaks! Any man who falls behind is left to the wolves!" He saw the shock and protest in their faces but gave them no time to object.

"We reach Rutupiae tomorrow evening!" he shouted, his voice echoing across the camp. "And at dawn the day after, we attack! With all our might! We throw everything we have against those walls! We will overrun them before the Fourteenth Legion is even in sight!"

XXIII. THE PRICE OF HASTE

He drew his own sword, holding it high, the blade flashing dully in the gray light. "For Togodumnus! For Britannia! For freedom! We will conquer, or we will die! But we will fight!"

A wild roar of assent rose from thousands of throats, carried on a mixture of fear, anger, and the infectious determination of their leader. Fatigue seemed forgotten for a moment. The army surged into motion again, faster this time, more driven, a desperate yet resolute onslaught against time and the might of Rome.

Caratacus rode at the head, his heart pounding, his mind working feverishly. The plan was risky, almost insane. But it was the only way. He had underestimated the Romans, allowed his prisoners to escape. Now he had to pay the price—with the haste that pushed him and his men to the brink of collapse. But the thought of Rutupiae, of the chance to deal Rome a devastating blow, drove him onward. He would succeed. He had to succeed.

XXIV. Waiting and Longing

Gray dawn broke over Rutupiae, no different from the day before, yet today a new tension charged the air. The rain had eased, but the sky remained overcast, and the wind from the sea carried the salty tang of the incoming tide and the ominous foreboding of battle into the farthest corners of the vast Roman camp, which now felt truly like a besieged fortress.

In the crowded hospital tent, Brutus opened his eyes to the smell of herbs and human suffering. The feverish haze of the past few days had somewhat lifted; the pain in his shoulder had subsided to a dull but bearable throbbing. He had slept nearly a full day, his body using the forced rest to heal, but his mind was restless. Worry for Maximus, anger at Flaccus, and the pressing awareness of time running out consumed him. Caratacus and his fifteen thousand warriors were out there, somewhere in the fog. They were coming.

He sat up with effort, ignoring the protest from his injured shoulder and the warning glance from the Greek *medicus*, who was applying a bandage to another legionary. "Enough lying around," Brutus muttered. "A Centurion belongs on the wall, not on a cot."

"Centurion, you should conserve your strength!" the

medicus called, but Brutus wasn't listening. He pulled on his tunic and, with difficulty, fastened his *balteus* with one hand, his *gladius* hanging at his side. He felt weak, his legs unsteady, but his will was stronger. Brutus left the hospital tent, blinking in the gray morning light, and took a deep breath of the cool, salty air.

He walked through the busy streets of Rutupiae. The town, or rather the fortified port complex, was an impressive example of Roman engineering and military organization, albeit hastily erected. Massive earth ramparts, partly reinforced with stone and surrounded by deep ditches, formed the outer defensive ring. Behind them rose sturdy timber palisades with walkways and regularly spaced watchtowers. Inside crowded tents, barracks, storehouses, workshops, and the central *praetorium*. Everything bustled with activity, yet remained orderly. Legionaries hauled building materials, reinforced the ramparts, dug more ditches. Engineers worked on the gates, strengthening hinges and bolts. Archers and slingers took positions on the towers. The air filled with the noise of labor—hammering, sawing, shouted commands, the groaning of carts.

Brutus felt a mixture of pride and deep concern: pride in the unwavering discipline and work ethic of his comrades, who didn't falter even facing overwhelming odds, but also concern whether these walls, these men, would be strong enough. He knew the Celts, knew their fierce determination. Fifteen thousand of them... it was a tidal wave threatening to break even the strongest Roman dams.

His path led him to the northern gatehouse, the most massive part of the fortifications, guarding the main landward approach. He knew this would likely be a primary point of attack. As he neared, he saw a group of officers standing on the walkway, looking out over the forward defenses. Among them, he recognized the stocky figure of Legate Vespasian.

Brutus climbed the wooden ramp to the walkway. The guards saluted curtly, letting him pass. Vespasian turned as he heard him approach, a flicker of surprise but also approval in his eyes.

"Brutus? Back on your feet already? I thought the *medicus* ordered bed rest."

"A scratch, Legate," Brutus downplayed it. "I wanted to inspect the defenses. See where I can help."

Vespasian nodded slowly, his gaze sweeping over the men working feverishly below. "Good to have you here. Your eye for weaknesses is valuable." He gestured towards the ditch before them. "We are deepening the ditches, setting up additional *cippi* and *lilia*. But against sheer numbers…" He left the sentence unfinished.

"The walls are strong, Legate," Brutus said. "The palisades are solid oak, the ramparts wide enough for two ranks of defenders." He knew the standard construction of Roman field camps; Rutupiae was more than that, a permanent fortress, but it had never been designed for a siege of this magnitude. It spanned roughly 800 by 600 paces, a considerable area requiring many men to defend.

"Strong enough against men, yes," Vespasian replied thoughtfully, "but what about ladders? Rams they might improvise? They have no heavy siege engines, that's our luck, but they are resourceful and desperate."

Brutus thought, looking out at the wide, clear strip of land before the ditch, deliberately cleared to deny attackers cover. "We need something to break their charge before they even reach the ditches. Something to disrupt their formations, sow chaos." His gaze sharpened. "Caltrops!"

Vespasian raised an eyebrow. "*Tribuli*? Yes, a good idea. Small, four-pronged iron spikes. No matter how they land, one point always faces up. Devastating against charging infantry and cavalry."

"Exactly, Legate," Brutus said eagerly. "We need to have as many made as possible. Thousands! We scatter them in a dense field before the most vulnerable sections of the wall. You just need to throw them; they always land with one spike up. Hide them under a thin layer of mud and leaves for surprise—a nasty shock for the charging Celts, especially before the gates and weaker parts of the palisade. If the Celts attack at dawn, perhaps in the fog, they'll run into them before they see them. It will break their initial charge, inflict heavy casualties, and buy us precious time."

Vespasian nodded approvingly. "An excellent idea, Brutus. Pragmatic, effective. Roman." He smiled thinly. "We must order the forges to begin production. Currently, they are fully occupied repairing weapons, making arrowheads and bolts."

"I will see to it, Legate," Brutus said firmly. "I can't do much heavy lifting right now anyway." He gestured to his bandaged shoulder. "But I can give orders and push the smiths. There are three forges in the camp, aren't there? I'll visit them personally."

"Good," Vespasian said. "Do that. Every caltrop counts." He turned back to the wall, his gaze shifting to the warships in the harbor. "I must speak with the *nauarchi*. I want their ballistae up here on the walls. They can provide additional firepower, especially against massed formations." He sighed. "They won't be thrilled about removing their precious machines from the ships, but they have no choice."

The two men stood silently side-by-side for a moment, each with his own plans and worries, but both determined to hold Rutupiae.

"May the gods help us, Brutus," Vespasian said quietly, so no other legionaries could hear.

Brutus replied, "The gods help those who help themselves, Legate." He added, "We will fight." Then he gave a curt salute and headed back into the camp, towards the forges.

He walked through the busy streets, observing the feverish preparations. Legionaries hauled heavy stones for the walls, others practiced formation drills in small groups, still others meticulously cleaned their equipment. The air vibrated with tension, but also with focused calm. It was the quiet before the storm, the calm of men who knew their fate and prepared to meet it. Brutus felt pride in these men, in their resilience and discipline. They were the best Rome had to offer.

He reached the first of the three forges, an open workshop near the western wall. The rhythmic hammering of metal filled the air. Sparks flew from anvils, and the smell of hot iron and coal fires was almost overpowering. Several half-naked, sweat-drenched men worked glowing metal—likely local recruits or slaves under the supervision of a Roman master smith.

Brutus approached. The master smith was a stocky man with a soot-blackened face and powerful arms. He glanced up briefly, wiped sweat from his brow, and returned to his work, shaping the blade of a *gladius*, apparently a custom order for an officer.

"Smith!" Brutus called over the noise.

The master looked up again, this time with a hint of

XXIV. WAITING AND LONGING

annoyance at the interruption. "What is it, Centurion? I have work to do! Weapons for the defense!"

"I have new orders for you," Brutus said firmly. "Effective immediately, cease work on all other orders. Your sole task is to forge caltrops. As many as possible, as quickly as possible."

The smith lowered his hammer, staring at Brutus incredulously. "Caltrops? *Tribuli*? Are you mad, Centurion? It's simple work, yes, but time-consuming! And we need swords, spearheads, arrowheads! The men need weapons, not... little iron stars!"

"You have your orders, smith," Brutus replied icily. "Legate Vespasian himself authorized them. Every caltrop you forge can stop a Celt before he reaches the wall. That saves lives. More lives than another sword in the hand of a man who might fall tomorrow. Now, get to work!"

The smith hesitated, his expression a mixture of disbelief and defiance. He was a civilian under military authority, but also a master of his craft, clearly proud of his work. "But... Centurion Clodius's order..."

"Centurion Clodius can wait!" Brutus cut him off. "The defense of Rutupiae cannot! If you refuse, I'll have you put in chains and your assistants will take over!"

The smith swallowed. He saw the unyielding expression in Brutus's eyes, felt the authority radiating from the Centurion. He was a stocky man, but he limped slightly as he stepped back, an old affliction that had likely rendered him unfit for regular military service.

Brutus noticed the limp. His gaze softened fractionally. "Where did you get the injury, smith?"

The man seemed surprised by the sudden question, the change in tone. He looked down at his left leg. "Old wound,

Centurion. From the war. Long time ago."

"Which war? Which legion did you serve?" Brutus pressed, a sudden curiosity stirring within him.

The smith hesitated, then answered with a hint of old pride in his voice, "I was a Centurion in the Fourteenth Gemina, under Legate Sabinus, in the cohort of *Primus Pilus* Sextus Pompeius Magnus."

Brutus froze. *Magnus.* His old mentor, the man who had shaped him, taught him everything he knew about the craft of war. The man who had perished in the flames of Camulodunum. "You... you served under Magnus?"

The smith nodded, a shadow crossing his face. "Aye. A great man. A hard man, but just. His death was a heavy blow to the Fourteenth." He looked Brutus over more closely. "How do you know him, Centurion?"

"He was my first Centurion, my trainer," Brutus said quietly, the memories returning with unexpected force. "In the Second Augusta. A long, long time ago. He was my mentor."

The smith's eyes widened. "You... You are Brutus? The Brutus Magnus always spoke of?"

Now Brutus was surprised. "He spoke of me?"

The smith nodded eagerly, the earlier hostility vanished. "Aye, often! Always said you were the stubbornest mule and the toughest nut he ever had under his command!" He chuckled softly. "But he was proud of you, Centurion. Very proud. Said you'd make a great commander one day."

Brutus felt an unexpected warmth in his chest, a mixture of grief and pride. Magnus had believed in him. He swallowed the lump in his throat. "He was a good man. And a stubborn bastard himself."

"The best," the smith agreed. His gaze fell on the unfinished sword blade, then back to Brutus. His posture changed. "Caltrops, you say, Centurion?"

Brutus nodded. "As many as possible."

"Consider it done," the smith said firmly. He called his assistants together, explained the new task. Then he turned back to Brutus. "One more thing, Centurion. If you really want these things to be effective… forge barbs on them. Small, backward-facing points. Once they dig into flesh or boot leather, they don't come out easily. Slows the enemy down even more."

Brutus looked at the smith, giving an appreciative nod. "A good idea, smith. Very good. See that it's done."

"Count on it, Centurion. For Magnus."

The two men looked at each other for a moment, an unexpected connection forged between them by the shared memory of a fallen comrade.

"Thank you," Brutus said. "I'll let you get to work."

He left the noisy forge, the rhythmic hammering following him for a few steps before fading into the general din of the camp. Brutus headed towards the next forge, located closer to the harbor area. His path now took him through parts of Rutupiae that were less military in character, where soldiers' barracks mingled with the makeshift shelters of merchants, craftsmen, sailors, prostitutes, and a growing number of civilian refugees who had streamed in from the surrounding countryside in the deceptive hope of Roman protection.

The atmosphere here differed from the purely military section of the camp. The tense discipline of the legionaries gave way to a louder, more chaotic nervousness. People crowded the narrow, muddy lanes, their faces marked by fear and uncertainty. Merchants desperately tried to sell their remaining goods at inflated prices. Craftsmen offered their services, often for little more than a meager meal. Everywhere, Brutus saw signs of panic: families carried their few belongings on carts or backs, children cried, women stared blankly into space.

The situation was particularly bad down at the harbor, in the area designated for civilian ships. A noisy, desperate crowd had gathered there, pressing against the quays where a few private merchant vessels lay anchored, their captains hesitant to set sail. Shouts and angry cries filled the air as people tried to force their way onto the ships, offering the sailors their last money, jewelry, anything they owned, for passage to Gaul, away from the impending siege, away from the feared Celtic vengeance.

Brutus saw how the ship captains, mostly hardened Gallic traders, shamelessly exploited the situation, demanding exorbitant sums for a place onboard, playing the desperate against each other, laughing at their pleas. Scuffles broke out as men fought for space. Guards from the harbor command struggled to maintain a minimum of order, pushing back the throng with their spear shafts. It was an ugly picture of human greed and despair in the face of danger.

Some wealthier merchant families had apparently managed to secure passage and were now being brought aboard under the protection of private mercenaries, while the poorer refugees remained behind, filled with rage and envy. Disgust rose in Brutus. This aspect of war—the panic of the civilians, the profiteering of individuals—was as repugnant to him as the betrayal of a Flaccus or the senseless brutality of a Celtic raid. He was a soldier. His world was orders, discipline, the fight. He couldn't, and wouldn't, deal with this chaos of civilian society. Yet, he felt a pang of pity for the common people caught innocently between the fronts. Brutus shook his head, turned away, and continued towards the second forge.

Later that evening, as the last light faded, Brutus stood again on the northern rampart, watching the horizon. The fog had lifted slightly, revealing the darkening landscape. Vespasian joined him.

"Any sign yet, Centurion?"

"No, Legate. Quiet. Too quiet."

"They will come with the dawn," Vespasian stated, more a fact than a question. "Caratacus favors attacking in the morning mist."

"We will be ready," Brutus said, his hand resting instinctively on the hilt of his *gladius*.

Vespasian nodded slowly. "One more piece of news. A fast galley arrived from Gaul just before dusk."

Brutus looked at him sharply. "Reinforcements?"

Vespasian shook his head. "No. A dispatch. From Rome." His expression became guarded. "From Narcissus."

"Narcissus?" Brutus frowned. Claudius's powerful freedman. What business did he have here?

"He sends… inquiries," Vespasian said carefully. "About Tribune Maximus. Asking for reports on his conduct, his background. Unusual interest."

A cold premonition touched Brutus. Narcissus, Flaccus's mysterious orders, the interest in Maximus… It felt connected, dangerous. "Why would Narcissus care about a junior Tribune?"

"That," Vespasian said, his eyes meeting Brutus's in the dim light, "is a question I have been asking myself, Centurion. A question I intend to answer. But first," he gestured towards the dark land beyond the walls, "we have a battle to win."

The horns blew the signal for the night watch change. Torches flared along the ramparts. The final night of waiting had begun. Tomorrow, the storm would break.

XXV. Shadows of Doubt

The third day of the march south began, scarcely different from the previous two. Relentless, cold rain fell from a leaden sky, turning the worn paths and open fields into deep, tenacious mire that clung to the hobnailed soles of boots, making every step an exertion. Like a steel serpent, the long column of the Fourteenth Legion Gemina wound through the bleak Britannic landscape—nearly five thousand men, a picture of indomitable Roman discipline amidst a hostile world.

Maximus rode silently beside Legate Titus Flavius Sabinus. The exhaustion of the past days sat deep in his bones, but it wasn't the physical strain that tormented him most. It was the uncertainty, the gnawing worry that crept like a cold poison through his veins. They were still a full day's march from Rutupiae. Tomorrow evening, they would reach the fortress—if everything went according to plan. But what would they find there?

The report from the mounted scouts, which Sabinus had received the previous day, had been both disturbing and a faint comfort. The scouts had sighted Caratacus's huge army before Rutupiae the day before yesterday. They had surrounded the camp but had not yet launched a major assault. Minor skirmishes, volleys of arrows, attempts to test the palisades—but the feared onslaught had not occurred. Vespasian and the Second Legion were holding out. For now.

But the report was from yesterday, the sighting from the day before that. What had happened in the last twenty-four hours? Had Caratacus waited to gather his full strength? Or had the attack already begun? Was Brutus still alive? Was Vespasian still in control? The questions hammered in Maximus's head, synchronized with the throbbing of his old head injury, which always flared up under stress and fatigue.

He glanced at Sabinus, riding calmly and focused beside him, his angular face beneath the helmet a mask of professional composure. Maximus admired the elder Legate's stoic calm, his ability to keep a clear head even under immense pressure. At the same time, Sabinus's cautious, almost deliberate, approach drove him to despair. Every step seemed too slow, every pause too long. His instinct screamed to spur the horses, force the men into a grueling march to reach Rutupiae as quickly as possible.

"Legate," Maximus finally began, unable to suppress his worry any longer, "the report is over a day old. Caratacus could have attacked already. Every moment counts. Can we not increase the pace after all? The men… they could manage it."

Sabinus slowly turned his head towards him, his gaze probing but not unfriendly. "I understand your concern, Tribune. You worry about your friend, the Centurion, and for my brother." He paused, his gaze sweeping over the seemingly endless column of his legionaries struggling through the mud. "But look at the men. They are already near their limit. This march is taking its toll. If we force them into a grueling march now, we might reach Rutupiae a few hours earlier, but with an army barely able to stand, let alone fight."

"But Legate, if we arrive too late…"

"Then we arrive too late," Sabinus interrupted calmly, but with unmistakable finality. "That is the risk of war, Maximus. We cannot control everything. We can only do what is within our power, and that is to bring this legion to Rutupiae as combat-ready as possible. A rushed march would be strategically unwise and militarily irresponsible."

He looked directly at Maximus. "Trust me, Tribune. I want to aid my brother just as much as you want to aid your friend. But I will not sacrifice thousands of men merely to gain a few hours that might ultimately make no difference." His words were harsh, but the logic was relentless.

Maximus fell silent, swallowing his frustration. Sabinus was right. Once again, he had to learn to subordinate his own impulses, his personal worries, to military necessity. It was a bitter lesson.

They rode on in silence for a while, only the monotonous sound of the march and the patter of rain audible. Then Sabinus said unexpectedly, "You did well to come to Camulodunum, Maximus. Your warning was crucial. Without it, we would have been unaware."

Maximus looked up. "I only did my duty, Legate."

"More than that," Sabinus countered. "You showed initiative, took a significant risk. Not every Tribune would have done that." He studied Maximus thoughtfully. "My brother seems to have a good eye for men."

A faint smile touched Maximus's lips. "Legate Vespasian taught me much."

"I am sure of it," Sabinus replied dryly.

The rest of the day passed in physical torment and inner conflict. Maximus battled mud, fatigue, growing doubts, and fears. Worry for Brutus and Rutupiae mingled with anxiety about his own future and the secret that perhaps was no longer a secret. What would happen when they reached Rutupiae? Would he be celebrated as a hero or eliminated as a threat?

In the evening, they made their marching camp, a temporary settlement of tents and earthworks, erected with the exhausted precision of men who knew their lives depended on it. After the meager meal in the *praetorium* tent with Sabinus and his staff officers—where conversation revolved coolly and professionally around the next day's arrival and possible scenarios—Maximus withdrew. He could find no rest.

Maximus walked through the camp, lying under the flickering firelight and the gray sky. The smell of wet wood, sweat, and latrines hung heavy in the air. He saw the faces of the men of the Fourteenth Legion, whom he barely knew, their fatigue and the underlying tension before the impending battle.

His steps led him involuntarily towards the rear of the camp, where the auxiliary units and civilian support staff were quartered, including healers and *medici* requisitioned by Sabinus. He knew Anwen must be here and hesitated. Should he seek her out? Was it fair to burden her with his worries? The throbbing pain in his head and the need for a familiar face, for a moment of human connection amidst this military machine, drove him onward.

He finally found her near a small tent serving as a makeshift infirmary for minor cases. She was applying a fresh herbal dressing to a legionary's chafed arm, her slender fingers moving deftly and surely, her expression focused. In the light of a single oil lamp, her red hair glowed like dark copper.

XXV. SHADOWS OF DOUBT

"Anwen?" Maximus said softly, not wanting to startle her.

She looked up, surprise then a flicker of concern crossing her face as she recognized him in the dim light. "Maximus? What is it? Are you injured?" She immediately stood, wiping her hands on her apron. The legionary raised his eyebrows slightly in annoyance but relaxed instantly upon recognizing the Tribune before them.

"No, no," he quickly reassured her. "Just… exhaustion and a headache." He rubbed his temples. "I thought… perhaps you had something for it? One of your Celtic miracle cures?" He attempted a smile, but it felt forced.

Anwen studied him searchingly, her clear blue eyes seeming to pierce his facade. "I have no miracle cures, Tribune, only herbs." She indicated a stool beside the tent. "Sit. I'll see what I can do."

Maximus sat gratefully. The legionary thanked them, exchanged a military salute with Maximus, and trudged off. Anwen disappeared briefly into the tent and returned with a small clay cup containing steaming, strong-smelling herbal tea. "Drink this. It's willow bark and valerian. It eases pain and calms the mind."

He took the cup, the warmth soothing his clammy fingers. The tea tasted bitter, but he drank it obediently. They sat in silence for a while, hearing only the patter of rain on the tent roof and the muffled sounds of the camp.

"You are worried about Brutus," Anwen finally said quietly. It wasn't a question.

Maximus nodded, staring into the cup. "He was wounded when we parted. He's on his way to Rutupiae to warn Vespasian. But the ride… it's long and dangerous."

"He is strong," Anwen said, her voice soft. "Stronger than

an ox."

Maximus looked at her. "You... you seem to have gotten to know him well in that short time."

A slight smile played around Anwen's lips. "I got to know his stubbornness." Her smile faded slightly. "He... he misses you, Maximus, though he would never say it. When you were unconscious back in the hospital... it hit him hard."

"We've been through a lot," Maximus murmured. "He's more than just my Centurion. He's my friend." He hesitated, then added, almost reluctantly, "I think... I think he misses you too, Anwen."

Anwen's cheeks flushed slightly, but she didn't look away. "I... I care for him too. Very much." She sighed softly. "But he is a Roman, a Centurion, and I am a Celt, a healer. Our worlds are too different." A trace of sadness was in her voice. "He hasn't contacted me since we parted in Camulodunum. Not a word. I was... disappointed." Her smile vanished, and lines of anger formed on her brow.

Maximus understood the unspoken hurt. He knew how proud and sometimes clumsy Brutus could be in such matters. "War leaves little room for... personal things, Anwen. Brutus carries a heavy burden. But," he searched for the right words, "I know your meeting meant a lot to him. He spoke of you when we were captives, just before..." He broke off, the memory of the sacrificial altar too painful.

Anwen gently placed a hand on his arm. "I understand, Maximus. War changes everything." She paused for a moment, then asked, "What will happen now? When we reach Rutupiae?"

Maximus looked up, his face serious again, the brief personal interlude over. "A hard fight awaits us. Caratacus has

XXV. SHADOWS OF DOUBT

assembled a huge army. We are greatly outnumbered." He looked her firmly in the eyes. "Anwen, listen to me: When we reach Rutupiae, stay away from the fighting. Find a safe place. If... if things look bad for us, if the legion falls... then flee. You are a Celt. You can blend in, find a way to survive. Promise me that!"

Anwen looked at him for a long moment, her blue eyes filled with a mixture of fear and determination. "I am a healer, Maximus. My place is with the wounded. I will not flee as long as there are men who need my help."

"But, Anwen..."

"No buts, Tribune," she interrupted him gently but firmly. "That is my duty, just as it is your duty to fight." She stood up. "The tea seems to be working. Your brow isn't so furrowed anymore." A faint smile returned to her face. "Rest some more. Tomorrow will be a long day."

She took the empty cup from him. "And Maximus," she added before disappearing back into the hospital tent, "I pray you both return, Brutus and you."

Maximus watched her go, a lump in his throat. Her strength, her compassion, her quiet determination were both shaming and inspiring. He slowly stood up. The headache had indeed eased; his mind felt clearer. He knew what he had to do. He had to reach Sabinus, ensure the legion was ready. He had to fight for Brutus, for Anwen, for the men who followed him, and he had to survive—not just for Rome, but also for the quiet hope of a future that might hold more than just war and loss.

With renewed determination, he made his way back to the *praetorium*, ready for the final briefing before the march south resumed the next morning.

XXVI. The Call of Ancestors

The sun sank low over Britannia, a blood-red orb fighting through ragged clouds, bathing the hills, forests, and the turbulent sea before Rutupiae in dramatic light. The last rays refracted off the wet palisades of the Roman fortress, making the watchtower tips gleam golden and casting long, ominous shadows across the land. It was the evening of the second day since Brutus's arrival, the eve of the expected storm.

Brutus stood on the wide walkway of the northern rampart, the section facing inland. The wind from the sea tugged at his cloak and whipped cold spray into his face, but he barely noticed. His gaze was fixed westward, where a spectacle unfolded on the plain before the fortress that made even a battle-hardened veteran like him shudder.

As far as the eye could see, the Celtic camp stretched out. Not an orderly Roman marching camp, but a vast, sprawling sea of tents, simple shelters made of branches and hides, countless campfires, and a seemingly endless mass of warriors. Hundreds of smoke columns rose towards the sky, mingling with the evening fog into a dense, gray-brown veil hanging over the land. Noise drifted from the camp: a deep, constant rumble of shouts, chants, the throb of drums, and

XXVI. THE CALL OF ANCESTORS

the occasional howl of war horns. It was like the breathing of a huge, awakening beast.

Brutus tried to estimate the enemy's numbers, but it was impossible. Caratacus had said fifteen thousand. It might be more or less, but it was too many. They seemed to be everywhere, their movements like an anthill, bustling but lacking the visible order of the legions. Brutus saw groups of warriors sharpening weapons, others leaping in ritual dances around fires, still others just standing, silently staring at the Roman walls, their fire-lit faces contorted into grim masks. He saw cavalry patrolling the camp's edge, their spears a prickly fence against the horizon.

"An impressive sight, isn't it, Centurion?"

Brutus turned. Legate Vespasian had quietly stepped beside him, his gaze also sweeping over the vast enemy camp. The Legate wore his full armor, helmet resting nearby on the parapet. His face was calm, but his eyes reflected the gravity of the situation.

"Impressive… and unsettling, Legate," Brutus replied gruffly. "I've rarely seen such a force gathered in one place, especially not barbarians."

"They are more than just barbarians, Brutus," Vespasian said thoughtfully. "They are a people fighting for their homeland, led by a man who knows how to unite them." He sighed softly. "Caratacus. We underestimated him. Plautius underestimated him."

"And now we stand here," Brutus continued, "a handful of men against a tidal wave." The old bitterness resurfaced. "If Sabinus and the Fourteenth don't arrive in time…"

"They will arrive," Vespasian said with a conviction Brutus couldn't entirely share. "Maximus reached Sabinus. Sabinus will march. But," he paused, his gaze meeting Brutus's, "we must buy them time. We must hold, tomorrow, the day after, as long as necessary."

"We will hold, Legate," Brutus said firmly, doubt again yielding to the soldier's iron resolve. "These walls are strong. The men are ready. We've laid caltrops; the ballistae are in position. They will pay a high price for every step they take on Roman ground."

"I know that, Brutus." Vespasian placed a hand on his uninjured shoulder, pausing for a moment, his gaze lingering on Brutus's scarred, weary face. The Centurion was a rock, loyal, unshakable in battle. But Vespasian also knew his direct, sometimes inconvenient manner, his deep bond with his men—and his growing friendship with Tribune Maximus. A friendship Vespasian observed with a mixture of goodwill and strategic calculation.

"Tell me, Brutus," Vespasian began casually, his tone barely changing, but his eyes now fixed the Centurion more intently. "Tribune Maximus… he is an unusual young man. Educated, strategically brilliant, but also… reserved. Has he ever mentioned anything to you about his family, about his origins before joining the legion?"

Brutus was visibly surprised by the sudden, personal question. He frowned, thinking briefly. "His family, Legate? No, not much." He hesitated. "He rarely speaks of his past, more about his time in the *ludus*, the training there. Why do you ask, Sir?" His gaze turned suspicious. He sensed this was no casual inquiry.

Vespasian smiled thinly, an inscrutable smile. "Just curiosity, old friend. One hears rumors in Rome. And Maximus… he has that certain something, an aura not solely derived from

XXVI. THE CALL OF ANCESTORS

training." *And a grandfather named Tiberius,* Vespasian thought, but didn't voice it. He watched Brutus's reaction closely. The Centurion seemed genuinely confused, unaware. Good. Maximus had apparently kept his secret, even from his closest confidant. That spoke to the young Tribune's discipline, but also made the situation more complex.

Vespasian believed Brutus, as the Centurion was a poor liar when it came to important matters. Consequently, he knew nothing of Maximus's imperial lineage. Vespasian had long pondered how to exploit this fact. A grandson of Tiberius, undiscovered and loyal, was a potentially powerful weapon in Rome's game of intrigue. If Claudius stumbled and the time was right, a candidate with imperial blood, backed by a loyal legion and an experienced legate, could make the difference. This, however, was a dangerous game, bordering on treason. If Narcissus or others at court got wind of it before Vespasian was ready to reveal his hand, it meant his own ruin, and Maximus's.

For now, he had to guard the secret, protect and promote Maximus, secure his loyalty. The young Tribune was valuable, not just as a capable officer, but as a potential key to power. Simultaneously, he represented a danger, an uncontrollable variable. Vespasian decided to let the matter rest for the time being; the impending battle for Rutupiae required his full concentration. Nevertheless, the thought remained in the back of his mind, a strategic option for the future.

"Forget my question, Brutus," he said finally, clapping the Centurion on the shoulder again. "Just an old man's thoughts. Let us focus on what matters." They stood silently for a moment, two experienced soldiers bound by countless battles and shared danger, both looking down at the sea of enemies as the sun sank into the sea, casting night's shadows over the land. The fires in the Celtic camp now seemed to burn brighter, their light reflecting ominously off the low-hanging clouds. The noise swelled again, becoming a thundering, rhythmic war chant sung by thousands of throats—a call to their gods and an oath to their ancestors.

"They call upon their ancestors," Vespasian said quietly, breaking the silence. "They prepare for battle."

"Let them," Brutus growled. "We have our own gods. And we have steel."

"And we have Rome," Vespasian added, his voice full of authority again. "Never forget that, Brutus. We fight not just for our lives. We fight for something greater." He straightened, putting on his helmet. "It is time. Assemble the Centurions and have the men stand to. I will speak to them."

Brutus nodded. He knew what came next: the pre-battle speech. It was a ritual as old as war itself. At this moment, a commander had to inspire his men, banish their fears, prepare them for the impending death. Brutus had heard many such speeches, good and bad. He wondered what Vespasian would say.

A short time later, the available cohorts of the Second Legion Augusta and the attached auxiliary units stood assembled on Rutupiae's central parade ground. There weren't many, perhaps three and a half thousand men. They stood disciplined, shoulder to shoulder, shields polished, spears and swords ready. Torches cast flickering light on their tense faces. An almost palpable silence filled the air, broken only by the howling wind and the distant, booming chant of the Celts.

Vespasian stepped before them, flanked by Brutus, Longinus, and the other Centurions and Tribunes not on duty at

XXVI. THE CALL OF ANCESTORS

the walls. He wore his full armor, his purple cloak whipping in the wind. Vespasian waited until absolute silence fell, then began to speak. His voice was calm at first, yet carried across the entire square, clear and unmistakable.

"Soldiers of Rome! Legionaries of the Second Augusta! Auxiliaries!" His gaze swept over the ranks, seeming to take in every single man. "You see the fires out there. You hear the chants of our enemies. They are numerous, yes. They are savage and determined to destroy us. They believe their hour has come. They believe Rome is weak, far away, unable to hold this island."

He paused, letting the words sink in. "They are wrong!" His voice grew louder, more powerful. "They see only our small number here in Rutupiae. But they do not see the power that stands behind us! They do not see the legions already marching to our aid! They do not see the invincible strength of the Roman Empire, which stretches across the entire known world!"

A murmur of agreement went through the ranks.

"They call us invaders," Vespasian continued, his voice now filled with passionate anger. "But who are they? Warring tribes fighting amongst themselves, living in darkness and superstition! We bring them order! We bring them law! We bring them the Pax Romana, the peace and prosperity only Rome can guarantee! But they reject our gifts! They cling to their barbaric customs, their bloody rituals!" He thought of the sacrificed men Brutus had described. "They slaughtered our comrades, not in honest combat, but like animals on a sacrificial altar!"

An angry growl rose from the soldiers.

"Tomorrow, they will attempt to storm these walls!" Vespasian cried. "They will come like a tidal wave, roaring, raging, full of hate! They will try to overwhelm us with their sheer numbers!" He raised his fist. "But they will fail!"

"YES!" some men roared back.

"They will fail because they will hit a wall! Not just a wall of wood and earth, but a wall of Roman steel, Roman discipline, Roman courage! They will hit *you*!" His finger pointed at the soldiers. "Every single one of you is worth ten of these barbarians! You are trained, you are equipped, you are experienced! But your greatest weapon is not your sword or your shield! Your greatest weapon is the man standing next to you! Your comrade! Your brother!"

He paced before the front rank, his gaze compelling. "Hold the line! Trust your Centurion! Trust the man beside you! Protect him, and he will protect you! Fight as one unit, and no power on earth can break you!"

"We fight not just for our lives!" his voice reached its full volume now, thundering across the square. "We fight for the honor of Rome! We fight for the Emperor! We fight for our families waiting for us back home! We fight for our fallen brothers, whose sacrifice must not be in vain! We fight for the future! For a future where the Roman eagle watches over this island too, bringing peace and order!"

He drew his *gladius*, the blade flashing in the torchlight. "Tomorrow, when the sun rises, we will show them what it means to trifle with Rome! We will hold! We will fight! We will conquer!" He thrust the sword into the air. "For Rome! For the Emperor! For the Second Augusta!"

A deafening roar erupted from thousands of throats: "FOR ROME! FOR THE EMPEROR! FOR THE AUGUSTA!" The cry echoed off the walls, rising to the dark sky, a wave of defi-

XXVI. THE CALL OF ANCESTORS

ance, determination, and unwavering courage, momentarily drowning out even the war chants of the Celts.

Vespasian slowly lowered his sword, an expression of grim satisfaction on his face. He looked into his men's eyes. He saw no hesitation there now, only the fire of battle, the iron will to conquer or die with honor. The commander had reached them, awakened the spirit of the legion.

Brutus stood beside him, heart pounding proudly in his chest, the hairs on his neck standing on end. It had been a good speech, a damned good speech. He felt the energy flowing through the men, the bond uniting them at that moment. They were ready. Whatever the morning brought, they would meet it as Romans. The call of their ancestors—their Roman ancestors—had been answered. The storm could come.

XXVII. The Assault

The night was an agony of waiting, time stretching endlessly, filled with the howl of the wind, the drumming of rain on tent roofs, and the ominous war chants of the Celts echoing like a promise of death across the plain. As the first pale hint of dawn lit the eastern sky, fear gave way to cold, steely resolve. The legionaries of the Second Augusta and their auxiliaries stood shoulder to shoulder on the ramparts of Rutupiae, their faces beneath wet helmets frozen into impassive masks. They were ready.

On the walkway of the north gate stood Brutus, his bandaged shoulder throbbing with his heartbeat. Ignoring the pain, he gazed out at the vast, surging sea of the Celtic army now forming up in the twilight. Torches danced among the ranks, casting restless light on thousands of determined, often wildly painted faces. The noise was deafening: commands in guttural tongues, the throb of countless drums, the shrill blast of *Carnyx* horns, and the deep, threatening chant swelling into a single, immense battle cry.

"They're coming," he muttered, his hand gripping the hilt of his *gladius*, so tightly his knuckles turned white. He felt the ground vibrate beneath his feet as the first wave of Celts surged forward.

XXVII. THE ASSAULT

It wasn't an orderly Roman assault, but a human tsunami. A roaring, raging mass of warriors wielding axes, spears, long swords, and simple clubs rolled towards the Roman fortress. They seemed to know no fear, only blind hatred and a savage determination to overcome the walls and slaughter the hated invaders. At their forefront ran the most fanatical warriors, some nearly naked despite the cold, their bodies painted with blue war-swirls and blood-red symbols.

"Hold fast!" Brutus bellowed to the men on his section of the wall. "Let them come closer! Archers, ready! Scorpions, take aim!"

The Roman defenders remained calm, a steel line on the walkway. They raised their large *scuta*, forming an impenetrable wall. Archers nocked arrows, their bowstrings taut. The crews of the *scorpiones*, the smaller, precise torsion engines, adjusted their machines, heavy bolts ready. On the towers, the larger *ballistae* groaned as crews cranked the massive throwing arms, loading arm-thick bolts into the firing troughs.

The first wave of Celts reached the open field before the walls, their roar swelling to a deafening crescendo. They charged blindly, driven by fury.

Then they ran into the caltrops.

The screams changed then. No longer war cries, but shrieks of pain and surprise. Men stumbled, fell, their feet and ankles pierced by the vicious, four-pronged iron stars forged day and night by the smiths. The recommended barbs did their cruel work, snagging in leather and flesh, making swift advance or retreat impossible. The front ranks of the charging Celts collapsed, dissolving into a chaotic tangle of falling, screaming men on the ground. Warriors behind tripped over their fallen comrades, tried to swerve, faltered. Thousands of small, inconspicuous iron spikes turned the first assault into a bloody shambles before it even reached the Roman ditches.

"Now!" Vespasian roared from one of the main towers, his voice clear and piercing. "Loose!"

A deafening inferno erupted. The *ballistae* on the towers thundered, launching their heavy, solid bolts into the densely packed Celtic ranks beyond the caltrop field. Bodies were pulverized, limbs torn off. The force of the impacts swept away entire groups of warriors. The *scorpiones* on the walkways fired their crossbow-like bolts with deadly precision, punching through shields and bodies. From the battlements, an incessant rain of arrows fell upon the confused and decimated attackers, Roman archers, protected behind the crenellations, loosing volley after volley, their arrows finding gaps in the Celtic defense with deadly accuracy.

The first Celtic wave was mown down, shredded, and repulsed before it posed any real threat to the walls, leaving hundreds dead and wounded in the muddy field before the Roman ditches—a gruesome testament to the efficiency of Roman defensive engineering and the lethal effect of Brutus's simple but ingenious idea.

A cheer went up from the Roman ramparts but was immediately suppressed by the Centurions. "Reload! Hold positions! The bastards are coming again!" Brutus yelled.

He was right. Caratacus was no fool. He had sacrificed the first wave to test the Roman defenses, to feel their firepower. Now the second wave formed, larger, more determined, and this time carrying protection.

Large, crudely built wooden shields were carried forward. Men held thick animal hides before them. Others carried

XXVII. THE ASSAULT

improvised battering rams—massive tree trunks borne by dozens of warriors. And among them, Brutus saw what he had feared most: scaling ladders. Long, hastily constructed wooden ladders, enough to attack dozens of points along the palisade simultaneously.

"They mean to storm the walls!" Longinus shouted, now commanding a section further east, his voice barely audible over the blare of horns. "Concentrate fire on the rams and ladder bearers!"

Again, the Roman bombardment began, more targeted this time. *Ballistae* tried to smash the rams before they reached the gates. *Scorpiones* and archers aimed for the men carrying the heavy ladders. From the walkways, defenders hurled stones, heavy amphorae filled with burning oil, even old millstones down onto the advancing Celts.

The second wave was more determined, better prepared. Under the cover of their improvised shields and a hail of their own spears and stones, they reached the ditches. They threw in branches, rubble, even the bodies of their fallen comrades to fill them and create crossings. The battering rams began to thud against the main gates with dull impacts. The first scaling ladders were leaned against the palisades.

Now the real fight for the walls begun. Wild determination drove the Celtic warriors up the ladders, axes and swords ready.

On the walkways, Romans shoved the Celts back with long poles, poured boiling water and pitch down, stabbed at the climbers with their *pila*. Ladders were pushed over, crashing down with their human cargo, men screaming as they fell into the ditches or onto the sharpened stakes below.

Again and again, some Celts managed to reach the walkway.

Brutal hand-to-hand combat immediately erupted on the narrow wooden planks. *Gladius* met long sword, *scutum* met Celtic shield. Better armored and more disciplined, the Romans fought with the efficiency of killing machines, forming small shield walls, thrusting coordinately, pushing the attackers back or throwing them over the parapet.

Brutus was in the thick of it. His shoulder ached, but he barely felt it. He roared commands, parried a blow, thrust, his *gladius* red with enemy blood. He saw his men fight, saw them fall, saw new men take their places. He saw the hate and desperation in the Celts' eyes, but also their indomitable courage. He killed to keep from being killed, a bloody dance on the narrow edge between life and death.

He saw the ram at the north gate splinter under concentrated *ballista* fire. A cheer from his men. But at the west gate, the other ram held, its dull blows thudding relentlessly; the heavy wooden gate began to groan, splinters flying.

"More men to the west gate!" he bellowed to an Optio. "Hold that gate at all costs!"

Hours passed in bloody chaos. The sun climbed higher, beating down on the combatants, its light mingling with the smoke from fires now breaking out inside the fortress, ignited by Celtic fire projectiles. The stench of blood, sweat, burnt flesh, and excrement became unbearable. The defenders were exhausted, arms aching from holding shields, throats raw from shouting, bodies covered in minor wounds. Yet they held.

Again and again, new waves of Celtic warriors crashed against the walls. Again and again, they were beaten back, both sides suffering horrendous losses. The field before the walls was now a carpet of dead and dying, Roman and Celt

XXVII. THE ASSAULT

thrown together in a grotesque tableau of destruction, the ditches in places filled with bodies.

Late in the afternoon, the Celtic onslaught seemed to lessen slightly. The attacks became less frequent, less coordinated. Caratacus's men were also exhausted; their losses had been enormous. Perhaps their morale was beginning to crack?

Brutus allowed himself a moment of hope. He looked out over the wall, saw the ebb and flow of battle, the relentless coming and going. Then he saw something that made his blood run cold: a new group of warriors forming up in the Celtic camp, different from the others. They were taller, wore better armor, carried long spears and heavy shields. At their head rode Caratacus himself, his boar-crested helmet gleaming in the late afternoon sun. It was his personal guard, his elite warriors, preparing for the final push.

"Legate!" Brutus yelled to a messenger. "Report to the Legate! Caratacus attacks personally! He gathers his elite at the west gate! We need reinforcements immediately!"

The messenger nodded and ran off. Brutus knew this was the decisive moment. If the west gate fell, all was lost. He drew his *gladius*, checked his helmet. He looked at the remaining men in his section, their faces exhausted, blood-smeared, but their eyes still burning with determination.

"Men of the Second Augusta!" he shouted, his voice hoarse but firm. "The enemy throws in his last reserve! Caratacus himself leads them! They mean to break the west gate! We cannot let that happen!" He raised his sword. "This is the moment we live for! Die for! Hold the line! Fight like Romans! Fight like the sons of Mars! For Rome! For the Emperor! For our fallen brothers!"

A final, desperate battle cry answered him. The men raised

their shields, closed ranks. They were ready for the last act of this bloody drama. Brutus looked west where Caratacus and his elite warriors now moved forward, a final, desperate assault on the walls of Rutupiae.

XXVIII. The Blood Price

The air over the battlefield before Rutupiae was a suffocating mix of smoke, dust, the metallic tang of blood, and the pervasive stench of burnt flesh and excrement. Setback slightly from the main fighting, Caratacus stood on a small rise, surrounded by his personal guard and closest advisors: Branwen, Cadan, and the cavalry leader Cadeyrn. His gaze was fixed on the Roman fortress, on the unyielding timber and earth walls from which death and destruction rained incessantly upon his men.

Hours of assault had passed since dawn. Hours of relentless charges against a wall of steel and discipline, hours of suffering, dying, and growing desperation. The initial optimism, the hope of overwhelming the Romans with sheer numbers and fierce determination, had long since given way to a bitter realization: Rome was an adversary unlike any Britannia had ever faced before.

The first assault had been a catastrophe. His bravest warriors, the men of the leading wave, had run into the treacherous Roman caltrops. A murderous hail of arrows, bolts, and heavy stones had mown them down before they even reached the ditches. Helplessly, Caratacus had watched hundreds of his men bleed out in the no-man's-land before the walls, their screams swallowed by the din of battle. It was a cruel price for a miscalculation: he had underestimated the effectiveness of Roman defenses and their cold, calculating brutality.

The second wave was better prepared, with improvised shields, battering rams, and scaling ladders, and managed to reach the walls. Fierce fighting erupted on the narrow walkways, man against man. Driven by hatred and the courage of desperation, his warriors fought like the lions of their ancestors, climbing over heaps of corpses, hurling themselves against the Roman shields, trying to tear open gaps and break through. Some briefly gained a foothold on the walkway, only to be immediately struck down by the short, lethal thrusts of Roman *gladii* or *pila*, or thrown from the battlements.

Caratacus watched the slaughter with a mixture of pride and growing horror: pride in the indomitable spirit of his people, refusing to bow to Roman might, but also horror at the horrendous losses. The meadow before the walls was stained red with the blood of his warriors. For every fallen Roman, ten Britons seemed to die. Roman discipline, superior armor, murderous efficiency in close combat—it was an uneven fight.

"We are losing too many men, Caratacus!" Cadan stepped beside him, his face a mask of worry. "This assault is futile. We shatter against their walls like waves on a cliff. We must break off the attack, regroup, find another tactic."

"Break off? Now?" cried Cadeyrn, the young cavalry leader, full of impatience and battle lust. "Never! We almost have them! Look, the west gate is faltering! One more push, and we're in! Send my riders! Let us break through!"

"Your riders are useless against fortified walls, Cadeyrn,"

XXVIII. THE BLOOD PRICE

Branwen retorted coolly, her eyes fixed unblinkingly on the battlefield. "Cadan is right. The losses are too high. We are bleeding out here before their gates. We must withdraw, lick our wounds, plan anew."

Caratacus remained silent, torn internally. His advisors were right; the losses were appalling. The plan to take Rutupiae by storm before the Fourteenth Legion arrived seemed to be failing. But retreat? That felt like defeat. He had promised his people victory, led them here vowing to drive Rome out. A retreat now would break their morale, perhaps shatter the fragile alliance of tribes.

And time was against him. The legion was marching. In two, maybe three days, it would be here. Then all chance would be lost. No, he couldn't fall back. He had to maintain pressure, force the Romans to expend their reserves, find a weak point, force a breakthrough.

"No," he said finally, his voice firm, though his heart was heavy. "We do not break off. Not now." He looked resolutely at his advisors. "We have suffered losses, yes. But so has Rome. Don't you see their ranks thinning? Don't you hear their defense weakening? They are tired, just like us. But we have the will of our people behind us! We have the gods on our side!" He pressed on, trying to project his own confidence onto the others. "Concentrate the attack on the west gate! Send fresh warriors! Break that gate down! Once we are inside, the town is ours!"

Cadan shook his head resignedly. Branwen watched him assessingly but said nothing. Cadeyrn, however, beamed. "Yes! I will gather my men!" He hurried off to organize fresh attacks.

Caratacus turned back to the battlefield, watching as new

waves of his warriors surged against the west gate and adjacent walls. He watched them fall, watched them die, but forced himself not to look away. Every death was a sacrifice for Britannia, a price for freedom. But how high could that price be? Doubt gnawed at him, a cold serpent in his heart.

The sun sank lower, bathing the bloody field in an eerie red light. The battle raged unabated. The west gate still held, though it groaned and trembled under the blows of the battering rams. The Roman defenders on the walls seemed inexhaustible, their arrows and bolts finding targets again and again.

Caratacus sensed his men's morale beginning to crumble. The attacks grew slower, less determined. More warriors hesitated, no longer throwing themselves into the fight with the same disregard for death. They saw the mountains of corpses before the walls, heard the screams of the wounded, felt the unyielding hardness of the Roman defense. Hope for a swift victory faded.

"They are wavering," Branwen observed soberly. "If we do not break through now, they will flee."

Caratacus knew she was right. The moment of decision had come. He could order the retreat now, gather his remaining forces, seek another path. Or he could put everything on one card, make one last, desperate attempt.

He made his choice. He turned to the commander of his personal guard, the *Teulu*, a troop of about five hundred of the best and most loyal warriors from his own tribe, the Catuvellauni—men who had grown up with him, trusted him blindly, were ready to die for him.

"Gather the men!" he commanded, his voice different now, no longer the strategic leader but the warrior throwing

XXVIII. THE BLOOD PRICE

himself into the fray. "We attack ourselves! We lead the final push! We break this damned gate or die trying!"

A surprised murmur went through his advisors, but no one dared object. The *Teulu* commander merely gave a grim nod and relayed the orders. The elite warriors formed up quickly, their faces a mixture of deadly determination and fanatical devotion to their king.

Caratacus drew his own sword, an ancient heirloom whose blade had tasted blood in many battles. He put on his helmet, the one crested with a boar's head that had brought him luck in countless fights. He swung himself onto his warhorse, which danced restlessly beneath him, as if sensing its rider's tension.

He looked one last time at the walls of Rutupiae, at the smoking ruins, at the unyielding Roman defenders. Then he looked at his men, his *Teulu*, ready to follow him. One last, deep breath. Then he let out a piercing war cry, a cry that echoed across the entire battlefield, making both friend and foe shudder.

"For Britannia! Follow me!"

With that cry, he spurred his horse forward, charging at the head of his bodyguard towards the groaning west gate of Rutupiae, into the heart of the storm, ready to risk everything for one last, desperate assault on the fortress.

XXIX. Blades in the Rain

The cry tore across the battlefield, different from the chaotic roar of the attacking masses before. It was a single, clear call, full of authority and fierce determination, seeming to cut through even the din of battle for a moment. Brutus, having just shoved back a Celt trying to climb over the parapet, instinctively looked up.

Through the smoke, dust, and incessant rain, he saw him: an imposing figure on horseback, taking the lead of a dense phalanx of elite warriors forming up before the groaning west gate. The rider wore magnificent, though foreign, armor, and his helmet bore the unmistakable silhouette of a charging boar. Even at this distance, through the chaos of battle, Brutus recognized him—Caratacus, King of the Catuvellauni, leader of the Britannic resistance, personally entering the fray.

An icy shiver ran down Brutus's spine, unrelated to the cold rain. This was the enemy's last, desperate gamble. Caratacus was putting everything on the line, throwing his personal guard, his best warriors, into the battle to force a breakthrough at the west gate. If they failed, the assault was likely over. But if they succeeded, if the gate fell and these elite warriors poured into the city, then Rutupiae was lost.

"By all the gods!" Brutus cursed. He saw the men around

XXIX. BLADES IN THE RAIN

him had also recognized Caratacus. A murmur of concern, almost fear, rippled through the ranks. The presence of the enemy king himself on the battlefield had an enormous psychological impact.

"Hold the line!" Brutus roared, trying to suppress the budding panic. "He's just a man! Flesh and blood, like us! Show him Roman steel!" But he knew words alone wouldn't suffice. Caratacus's attack had to be stopped, at all costs.

His gaze fell on the *scorpio* positioned on the tower beside the gate. The crew was currently reloading the torsion engine after a shot, their movements swift but practiced. An idea, risky but potentially decisive, formed in Brutus's mind.

"Optio! Take command here!" he yelled to his nearest subordinate, not waiting for a reply. He ran, ducking low across the walkway, dodging arrows and spears impacting the palisades, and scrambled up the ladder to the tower.

The *ballistarius*, the *scorpio*'s gunner, an experienced legionary named Balbinus, looked up in surprise as the Centurion suddenly appeared beside him. "Centurion?"

"Balbinus!" Brutus gasped, pointing over the parapet at the forming Celtic elite unit. "See that man there? The leader with the boar helmet? That's Caratacus!"

Balbinus squinted. "Yes, Centurion. I see him."

"I want you to take him out," Brutus commanded, his voice icy. "Forget the rams, forget the ladders. Aim the *scorpio* at him. One precise shot. If Caratacus falls, their morale breaks."

The gunner hesitated. "Centurion, that's a single, moving target at long range, the wind, the rain... the chances are slim." *Scorpiones* were accurate against larger targets or at short range, but hitting a single rider in this chaos...

"That's an order, Balbinus!" Brutus cut him off. "I take

responsibility. Aim carefully. Wait for the right moment. But shoot!"

Balbinus swallowed, then nodded resolutely. "Yes, Centurion." With the help of his crew, he began realigning the heavy engine, cranking the tensioning gears, adjusting the angle. It was precision work under extreme pressure.

Below, Caratacus had raised his sword. With another piercing cry, he gave the signal to charge. His bodyguard, the *Teulu*, surged forward, a wedge of determined warriors, straight for the west gate. They ran over the bodies of their fallen countrymen, ignoring the caltrops thinning their ranks, their sole objective the breakthrough.

"Now, Balbinus! Fire!" Brutus roared.

With a loud crack, the *scorpio*'s throwing arm snapped forward. The heavy, almost man-high bolt whirred through the rainy air, straight towards Caratacus.

For a heartbeat, Brutus held his breath. Would it hit?

The bolt struck with tremendous force—but not Caratacus. It hit the horse directly beside him, piercing the animal's neck, dropping it instantly. The rider, one of Caratacus's closest retainers, was buried beneath the falling horse. Caratacus himself was caught in the chaos, his own horse shying, rearing; he fought to stay in the saddle.

Missed. By a hair's breadth. A curse escaped Brutus's lips. "By Minerva's tits." A unique chance, wasted.

Caratacus regained control of his horse. His gaze snapped up to the tower, meeting Brutus's for a split second. Hate, cold and implacable, flared in the Celtic king's eyes. Then he turned back to the gate, driving his men forward with renewed fury.

The *Teulu*'s charge hit the west gate with the force of a

XXIX. BLADES IN THE RAIN

battering ram. They threw themselves against the groaning timber, hacked at the hinges with axes, tried to smash the heavy bolts. Simultaneously, new scaling ladders reached the walls on either side of the gate. Caratacus's elite warriors, taller, stronger, better equipped than the previous attackers, began to climb the palisades.

The fighting on the walkway reached a new, desperate intensity. The Romans now faced not just exhausted tribesmen, but the best of the best, men fighting for their king and honor to the last drop of blood. The noise was deafening, the slaughter gruesome. Men fell on both sides every second.

Brutus leaped back onto the walkway, throwing himself into the melee again. He fought like a man possessed, his injured shoulder a distant, dull ache. He had to hold the position. They had to hold. For Rome, for his comrades, for Maximus, for Decimus, for Anwen.

He saw Caratacus down by the gate, urging his men on, fighting with his own sword, a beacon of inspiration for his warriors. The man was a true king, Brutus had to admit reluctantly: brave, determined, charismatic. But he was the enemy.

"Target him!" Brutus yelled to some archers. "Shoot the man with the boar helmet!"

Arrows whizzed down towards Caratacus, but his bodyguard closed ranks around him, their shields forming a roof. The arrows glanced off harmlessly or stuck fast.

The pressure on the gate became unbearable. It groaned, splintered, the bolts buckled. It was about to give way. Soon the Celts would pour into the city.

"Hold the gate!" Brutus yelled desperately. "More men here!"

Legionaries rushed over, throwing themselves against the gate, trying to barricade it from the inside, while Celtic axes thundered from without.

At that moment, when all seemed lost, Brutus heard a new sound above the din of battle. Not heavy artillery this time, but the clatter of pottery and specific shouts from the towers and wall sections around the west gate. He looked up.

Then he saw it. At a signal from Vespasian, legionaries on the walkways began hoisting large, heavy clay pots over the parapet. Other men passed them up from below. With coordinated swings, they hurled the pots down, directly into the densely packed masses of Celtic elite warriors and the advancing reserves before the west gate. The pots shattered on shields, helmets, and the muddy ground, spilling their contents—a thick, dark, oily liquid.

Before the Celts, surprised by this unusual attack, could comprehend what was happening, another command echoed from the towers. "Archers! Fire arrows! Aim for the oil!"

Hissing, dozens of arrows, their tips dipped in pitch and ignited, flew down from the Roman walls. They struck the oily pools rapidly spreading among the warriors.

All hell broke loose.

A sea of flames exploded amidst the Celtic ranks. The oil ignited instantly, turning the area before the west gate into a blazing inferno. Men and horses, soaked in oil, went up in flames, screaming, running panic-stricken, their burning bodies setting others ablaze. The smell of burning flesh and hair filled the air, overpowering the stench of blood and sweat. The fire spread with terrifying speed through the oil-soaked mud, forming an impassable barrier of roaring agony.

Caratacus's elite warriors, moments from breaking through,

XXIX. BLADES IN THE RAIN

panicked. Their formation dissolved. Men tried to escape the fire, trampling their comrades. Caratacus himself was thrown back by the force of the explosion, the human panic, and the desperate flight of his men, his horse shying, nearly unseating him.

A tremendous cheer erupted from the Roman walls. The defenders stared in disbelief at the flaming inferno consuming their enemies. Vespasian's plan, his final tactical reserve—oil and fire arrows—had worked.

Caratacus, his face a mask of soot, rage, and incredulous horror, desperately tried to rally his fleeing men. But it was too late. Morale was broken. The attack had failed. He saw the mountains of dead his army had left before the walls of Rutupiae. He saw the unyielding Roman defense. He saw the flames devouring his last hope.

Slowly, reluctantly, he gave the signal to retreat. The Celtic war horns blew one last time, not for the attack, but for assembly, for withdrawal. The surviving Celts disengaged from the walls, pulled back, leaving their dead and wounded behind, vanishing again into the fog and smoke.

On the Roman walls, silence fell for a moment, then cheering broke out again, louder this time, full of relief. They had held. Against all odds, they had held.

Brutus leaned exhaustedly against the palisade, his *gladius* slipping from his hand. He looked down at the battlefield, at the gruesome evidence of the fight. The rain now fell harder again, washing the blood from the walls, slowly extinguishing the last flames. He had survived; his men had survived. Rutupiae had held. But the price had been high, and he knew, though this battle was won, the war in Britannia was far from over.

XXX. The Breaking Point

The darkness over Rutupiae was different from the night before. The thundering war chants of the Celts and the paralyzing fear of the unknown were gone, replaced by deep exhaustion and the macabre silence after the slaughter. The rain had stopped, but the wind from the sea howled around the watchtowers, carrying the acrid smell of smoke, burnt flesh, and death across the fortress.

Inside the *praetorium*, oil lamps burned brightly, casting restless shadows on the grim, soot-smeared faces of the officers. It served again as the command center. Legate Vespasian sat at the head of the wooden table, his stoic calm replaced by fatigue, though his eyes were vigilant. His key commanders had gathered around him: Brutus, his left arm splinted and resting in a sling; Centurion Longinus, his armor bearing the marks of hard fighting; the tribunes of the auxiliary units; and the prefects of the warships in the harbor. The air was thick with the smell of wet leather, sweat, and the metallic aftertaste of blood and fear.

"Gentlemen," Vespasian began, his voice rough but firm. "We have held. Against overwhelming odds, we have held. The gods were merciful to us—and our discipline was our shield." He paused, his gaze sweeping over the exhausted faces. "The

XXX. THE BREAKING POINT

loss reports are in." He nodded to a scribe, who handed him a wax tablet. Vespasian scanned the figures. "They are… more bearable than feared, yet still painful."

He looked up. "We have lost nearly three hundred men, fallen in battle or succumbed to their wounds." A murmur of relief went through the room. Given the ferocity of the attack, many had expected far worse. "Another one hundred and fifty are wounded, some severely. Our *medici* work without pause." He sighed softly. "Every loss is one too many, but we have held. The enemy, however…" He smiled grimly. "Our scouts, who observed their withdrawal, report thousands of dead and wounded on the Celtic side. Their first wave was practically shredded by the *tribuli*. The assault on the walls was a bloodbath, and the fire broke their elite unit and their morale. Caratacus paid a high price for his attack today."

"Will he try again, Legate?" Longinus asked.

Vespasian shook his head. "I think not. Not immediately, not tonight. His army is battered, demoralized. He must withdraw, lick his wounds, regroup his forces. We have bought time." He looked around the room. "But we must not become complacent. The alert remains at the highest level. The guards remain doubled. Sleep will be in full gear."

"The forges continue work on the caltrops, Legate," Brutus interjected, his voice still thick with pain. "We already have a considerable quantity. I suggest we use the darkness to lay more fields before the walls, especially to the west and north."

"An excellent idea, Brutus," Vespasian agreed. "Organize it. Small squads, well-secured. Scatter them widely, but discreetly. Should Caratacus attempt a surprise night attack after all, let him find a nasty surprise." Brutus nodded.

"However, there is a weak point, Legate," Brutus continued,

his gaze turning serious. "The west gate. It withstood the assault, but the rams damaged it severely. The hinges are loose, the bolts bent. Another concentrated attack… and it could give way."

Vespasian frowned. "The engineers are working on it, but a complete repair under these circumstances is difficult."

"I propose we barricade it," Brutus said directly, "completely, from the inside, with earth, stones, anything we can find. Make it part of the wall."

A murmur went through the officers. Blocking the main gate was a drastic measure.

"That would mean we can make no more sorties from there," Longinus objected. "We would deny ourselves an important option."

"What option, Longinus?" Brutus asked sharply. "A sortie against fifteen thousand Celts? That would be suicide. Right now, this gate is a danger, not an option. If Caratacus gathers his forces and attacks again, he will aim here. We must eliminate this weak point."

"But what if Sabinus arrives?" another officer asked. "Should the Fourteenth Legion find a barred gate?"

"Sabinus won't be here before dawn the day after tomorrow, perhaps even later," Vespasian said thoughtfully. "Until then, the gate must hold. Brutus is right; the risk is too great." He made the decision. "Barricade the west gate, immediately! Use all available materials. Make it as strong as the wall itself."

"Yes, Legate!" several Centurions said in unison.

"Good," Vespasian said. "That settles the immediate defensive measures. Rest, gentlemen, but remain vigilant. The night is still long." He gestured dismissal.

The officers saluted and left the *praetorium* to implement

XXX. THE BREAKING POINT

the orders. Only Brutus remained behind for a moment.

"Legate," he began hesitantly, "what… what about Flaccus?"

Vespasian sighed, rubbing his tired eyes. "Flaccus is… a problem for later, Brutus. I have sent scouts to try and pick up his trail, but I doubt we'll find him in this chaos. Right now, we must focus on Caratacus. If we survive this battle, I will personally deal with Tribune Flaccus. You have my word on that."

Brutus nodded slowly. It wasn't a satisfying answer, but he understood the priorities. "And Sabinus? Is there news from Camulodunum?"

"The messenger who brought news of Sabinus's departure was the last to arrive," Vespasian said, a rare warmth in his voice. "Likely no one can get past Caratacus's army now."

"Sabinus… will he make it in time?"

"That now rests in the hands of the gods… and the endurance of the Fourteenth Legion," Vespasian replied gravely. "We can only hope and hold."

He clapped Brutus on the shoulder. "Go now, Centurion. You need rest too, even if you won't admit it."

Brutus saluted and left the *praetorium*. The night air was cool and damp, but the rain had stopped. Stars began to appear between shreds of cloud. The camp was filled with muted activity. Men worked on the walls, reinforced the west gate, carried wounded, tossed more caltrops over the parapet into the darkness beyond. The deafening noise of battle had yielded to a tense but industrious silence.

Brutus walked slowly towards the hospital tent. He wanted to check on his men, ensure the wounded were being cared for. He thought of the coming days: the waiting, the uncertainty, the next attack. Would they hold? Would Sabinus arrive in time? Would he see Maximus again? Would he see Anwen again?

So many questions, so few answers. He looked up at the sky, at the distant, cold stars. They were silent witnesses to this bloody drama on a remote island at the edge of the known world. He was just a small part of it, a Centurion trying to do his duty, protect his men, and maybe, just maybe, get out alive. He took a deep breath, inhaling the cold night air. Tomorrow, a new day of waiting would begin. The unit's breaking point had only just begun to be tested.

XXXI. Between Mistrust and Unity

The darkness over the vast Celtic camp before Rutupiae was heavy, filled with a depressed mood, starkly contrasting the fierce determination of the previous day. Countless fires still burned, but triumphant roars and war chants had given way to muffled murmurs, the groans of the many wounded, and the ominous sound of smiths' hammers hastily repairing damaged weapons and shields. Blood, smoke, and death hung heavy in the air, a bitter perfume of defeat—or at least of a painful setback.

In the center of the camp, Caratacus sat at the head of a crudely built table inside the largest tent, serving as a provisional war council. Candles and oil lamps cast flickering light on the grim, often angry or despairing faces of the assembled tribal leaders and chieftains. The air was thick with unspoken accusations, mistrust, and the naked fear of what might come. The unity Caratacus had painstakingly forged threatened to shatter under the weight of yesterday's losses and the failed assault.

Outwardly, Caratacus appeared calm, his royal composure unbroken, but inwardly, a storm raged. The sight of his army dashed against the Roman walls, the heaps of dead, the futility of the sacrifice—it gnawed at him. He had underestimated

Roman resistance: their discipline, their lethal efficiency, the diabolical effect of their war machines and those cursed caltrops. He had paid the price for haste, driving his men into a poorly prepared attack. He feared the escaped Roman officers might raise the alarm in time, and now knew they had succeeded. Scouts reported the departure of the Fourteenth Legion from Camulodunum. Time was running out; his army was battered, its morale low.

"We have lost thousands!" cried Cadan, his voice trembling with suppressed emotion, slamming his fist on the table. "Thousands of our best warriors, sacrificed on the walls of this cursed Roman fortress! And for what, Caratacus? For what? We achieved nothing!"

"Nothing achieved?" snarled Cadeyrn, the young cavalry leader, his face dark with anger and wounded pride. His riders had also suffered heavy losses in the frontal assault. "We showed them we are not afraid! We made them bleed! The gate was about to break! If only we had…"

"If only we had, what, Cadeyrn?" Branwen interrupted coolly, her gaze sweeping soberly over those present. "Sent more men to their deaths? Waited until the last of us lay before these walls? Cadan is right; the attack was a mistake. A costly mistake."

An angry murmur went through the assembled chieftains. Some nodded in agreement, others shook their heads, their faces reflecting the alliance's fractured state.

"It was not a mistake!" Caratacus retorted, his voice now loud and firm, needing to assert his authority. "It was a necessary blow! We had to try to take Rutupiae before the other legion arrived! Yes, we suffered losses, heavy losses." Pain crossed his face. "Every fallen warrior is a brother, a son,

XXXI. BETWEEN MISTRUST AND UNITY

a father. But their deaths were not senseless! They died for Britannia! For our freedom!"

"Freedom is worth little to a dead man!" shouted a burly chieftain of the Durotriges, his arm in a bloody sling. "My men didn't come here to bleed out uselessly against Roman palisades! We fought bravely, but we cannot storm this fortress! We should withdraw, protect our villages!"

"Withdraw?" Caratacus asked icily. "And then what? Wait for the Romans to hunt us down one by one? Wait for the Fourteenth Legion to arrive and unite with Vespasian? Then all is lost! Here, before Rutupiae, we still have a chance! Here we can face them, here we might defeat them!"

"Defeat them?" another chieftain scoffed. "We tried, Caratacus! And we failed! The Roman walls are too strong, their weapons too deadly. And their leader, Vespasian, he is no fool."

"Vespasian is just one man," Caratacus countered. "And his men are tired, just like ours. Their losses may have been fewer, but they are battered too. And they are trapped. We have them surrounded."

"A trap we are stuck in ourselves!" Cadan cried out. "We cannot breach the walls, and soon the other legion will be here! We must leave, Caratacus! While we still can!"

The discussion grew heated; old tribal rivalries resurfaced. The Durotriges accused the Catuvellauni of leading them into a hopeless fight. Smaller tribes from the west feared for their unprotected villages. Cadeyrn continued to argue for another assault. Branwen tried to reason with cool logic, suggesting maintaining the siege but halting the attacks, trying instead to completely cut off Roman supply lines.

Caratacus listened, letting the storm of opinions washes

over him. He understood their fears, their anger, their doubts. He felt the unity he had so painstakingly built beginning to crumble. He had to act, unite them again, give them new hope, a new plan. But what plan?

He looked at the map, at the outlines of Rutupiae, the marked positions of his own troops and the suspected Roman dispositions. His mind worked feverishly. Another frontal assault was indeed futile; the day had proven that. A long siege? They lacked the time, and likely the discipline and logistics. Retreat? That would be admitting defeat, the beginning of the end.

Then his gaze fell on the harbor, on the Roman warships anchored there, and on the narrow strip of land connecting the fortress to the sea—the only side not enclosed by his army.

An idea began to form. Risky, unorthodox, but perhaps... perhaps their only chance.

He raised his hand, commanding silence. The arguing chieftains slowly quieted, their gazes turning towards him.

"Listen to me!" Caratacus began, his voice calm again but filled with a new intensity. "You are right. Another assault on the walls would be senseless. We would only lose more men." Murmurs of agreement. "But retreat is also not an option. We would give up everything we have fought for." He paused. "There is another way. A way the Romans do not expect."

All eyes were now fixed on him, expectant, suspicious.

"The Romans expect us to attack their walls," he continued. "They focus their defense there. But their weak point... lies not on land, but on the water." He pointed towards the harbor. "Rutupiae is a port. Its strength is also its weakness. If we control the harbor, if we destroy or capture their ships, we cut them off completely from supply. Then they cannot hold out

XXXI. BETWEEN MISTRUST AND UNITY

long, even behind the strongest walls. And Sabinus's arrival would be meaningless."

A surprised silence followed his words. Then Cadan spoke up. "Attack the harbor? Caratacus, we are land warriors! We have no ships, no experience in sea combat! The Romans have warships there, Liburnians, armed with ballistae!"

"We don't need large ships, Cadan," Caratacus replied. "We need only courage, cunning, and darkness." He unfolded his plan. "We will use small, fast boats—fishing boats, skiffs, anything we can find. Under cover of night, we will infiltrate the harbor. Small groups of elite warriors will board the Roman ships, overpower the crews, set the ships ablaze or, if possible, capture them. Simultaneously, other groups will attack the harbor facilities, the storehouses, the docks. We sow chaos and destruction at the heart of their supply."

"And meanwhile?" Branwen asked. "What does the rest of the army do?"

"The rest of the army," Caratacus said, a cold smile on his lips, "does exactly what the Romans expect. We feign another major assault on the walls. We make noise, shoot arrows, advance with ladders. We tie down their forces on land while our true attackers take the harbor."

An excited murmur went through the ranks. The plan was bold, dangerous, but possessed a compelling logic. It played on Roman expectations, exploited their focus on land defenses.

"It is risky," Cadan said, still hesitant, "very risky."

"All war is risky, old friend," Caratacus replied gently. "But this plan gives us a chance, a better chance than blindly charging their walls." He looked around the circle, meeting the gaze of each chieftain. "Who is with me? Who is willing to dare this final, bold act? For Britannia?"

Cadeyrn was the first to draw his sword. "I am with you, Caratacus! My riders will storm the docks!"

Branwen nodded slowly. "It is a daring plan, but it could work."

After a brief hesitation, Cadan also agreed. "May the gods aid us."

One by one, the other chieftains joined in, their doubts yielding to a new, albeit tense, resolve. Unity was restored, bound by a new, dangerous plan.

"Good," Caratacus said, relief mixing with tension. "Then let us waste no time. Gather the boats. Select the best, quietest warriors for the harbor assault. The rest prepare for the feint attack." He glanced towards the tent entrance, where the first rays of dawn peeked through the gap. "Tomorrow night. Tomorrow night we strike. Tomorrow night, the fate of Rutupiae will be decided."

The chieftains left the tent to relay the orders. Caratacus remained alone, bending over the map again, his finger tracing the outlines of the harbor, the Roman ships. It was a desperate plan, he knew, but it was his plan. And he would see it through to the end. His anger had yielded to cold, calculating determination.

XXXII. In Uneasy Anticipation

The day after the repelled battle passed in an agonizing, tense silence, almost more unbearable than the noise of combat. A gray, impenetrable sky arched over Rutupiae. Cold drizzle fell incessantly, turning the muddy paths within the fortress into an ankle-deep mire. A damp, clammy veil lay over everything. The air was filled with the smell of wet wood, cold ash, the stench of latrines, and the groans of the wounded in the overcrowded hospital tent.

On the ramparts and towers, the legionaries stood guard, their gazes fixed on the empty, corpse-strewn field before them where the Celts had withdrawn. The enemy was hidden in the fog and forests, but their menacing presence was palpable. Everyone knew this was just a lull, the calm before the next storm. When would Caratacus attack again? And how? The uncertainty gnawed at the defenders' nerves.

Brutus couldn't bear to stay in the hospital tent or his quarters. His injured shoulder had been freshly dressed by the *medici*, but the forced inactivity drove him mad. With his arm in a sling, he restlessly paced the camp, inspecting the repaired sections of the wall, talking to the men on the ramparts, trying to boost their morale even though his own was clouded by worry and anger.

He saw the exhaustion in their eyes, the tension in their faces. They had fought heroically and held, but the price was high. Many comrades were missing. The news that Legate Sabinus and the reinforcements were still at least two days away spread like wildfire, worsening the mood. They were still on their own, a small garrison against a huge army.

"Will we hold out, Centurion?" a young legionary from his century asked him, fear written plainly on his face despite his efforts.

"We are Romans, soldier," Brutus answered harshly, though he didn't entirely feel the hardness. "We always hold. Let the barbarians come. They will break against our shields." He clapped the boy on the shoulder, projecting more confidence than he possessed.

Brutus spoke with the engineers tirelessly working to barricade the shattered west gate, turning it into an impassable obstacle with earth, stones, and heavy timbers. He spoke with the smiths, who continued to churn out multitudes of caltrops, their hammers beating a defiant rhythm against the silence. He spoke with the archers and *ballistarii* on the towers, reminding them to keep their weapons clean and ammunition ready.

Everywhere he saw the scars of battle, felt the tense anticipation. But nowhere did he see Tribune Flaccus. Brutus's anger at the man boiled anew at the thought. Traitor, coward. He had abandoned them, caused Decimus's death, and now lied brazenly to save his skin. Vespasian might hesitate to hold him accountable for political reasons, but Brutus swore to himself that Flaccus would not escape unpunished.

"By Jupiter, Greatest and Best, that disgusting patrician will pay for what he did to us," he muttered. He needed to speak

XXXII. IN UNEASY ANTICIPATION

with Longinus, the Centurion who had accompanied Flaccus, who had also witnessed the retreat. Vespasian trusted him, had used him as his eyes and ears. But could Brutus trust him? Had Longinus merely followed orders, or was he part of Flaccus's betrayal? The uncertainty tormented Brutus.

He finally found Longinus on the walkway near the east gate, supervising his men reinforcing the palisades. Longinus, the lean, nondescript Centurion with watchful eyes, turned as Brutus approached, his expression unreadable as always.

"Centurion Longinus," Brutus said directly, without preamble. They were alone, only a few legionaries working out of earshot. "I need to speak with you. About the ambush. About Tribune Flaccus's retreat."

Longinus's gaze flickered almost imperceptibly. He nodded slowly. "I expected such a question, Brutus."

"Then speak," Brutus demanded, his voice rough. "Why did you abandon us? Why did you allow Flaccus to order the retreat while we were surrounded, fighting for our lives?"

Longinus sighed softly, his gaze briefly drifting out towards the gray sea. "It was… a difficult situation, Centurion." He looked directly at Brutus again. "Tribune Flaccus received reports from scouts—his own, not ours—that another, even larger Celtic force was approaching to cut off our retreat. Simultaneously, he saw your position at the head being overrun. He said… he said he saw you and Tribune Maximus fall."

Brutus stared at him incredulously. "Fall? That's a damned lie! We were fighting! We could have held the position if you had supported us!"

"That may be, Centurion," Longinus replied calmly. "But Tribune Flaccus invoked Tribune Maximus's last order, which

I also heard: 'Retreat upon heavy enemy contact.' He argued that holding further was pointless, that saving the rest of the cohort was now the priority. He gave the order for an orderly withdrawal." Longinus's expression remained impassive, but Brutus thought he saw a flicker of regret or doubt in his eyes.

"And you… you obeyed that order?" Brutus asked, his voice trembling with suppressed rage. "You just left us behind? Decimus… my men… they died because you fled!"

"I followed orders, Centurion," Longinus said firmly, his gaze hard again. "Tribune Flaccus held diplomatic command; Tribune Maximus held military command. When Maximus fell—or when Flaccus claimed he fell—command passed to Flaccus. His order to retreat was valid. My duty was to execute that order and bring back as many men as possible safely." He paused. "Believe me, Centurion, it was not an easy decision. But in that chaos… under enemy fire… I had to act."

Brutus stared at Longinus for a long time, trying to find the truth in his eyes. Was the man lying? Covering for Flaccus? Or was he genuinely just a soldier obeying orders, caught in an impossible situation, deceived by an unscrupulous Tribune? Longinus's gaze was steady, his posture correct. He didn't seem like a liar. But Brutus's mistrust ran deep.

"I believe you… for now, Longinus," Brutus finally said slowly. "But I will find out the truth. If I learn you were part of this betrayal…"

"I have nothing to hide, Centurion," Longinus replied calmly. "I did my duty as best I could. As for Tribune Flaccus… " He hesitated. "…let others judge him."

Brutus nodded curtly. The conversation hadn't brought him final clarity, but it had eased some of his anger towards Longinus specifically. The real culprit was Flaccus. And

XXXII. IN UNEASY ANTICIPATION

perhaps Adminius, but both had vanished as if swallowed by the earth.

"We must remain vigilant," Brutus said. "Flaccus is dangerous."

"I know that, Centurion," Longinus said. "Legate Vespasian has also given me… instructions."

A silent understanding passed between the two experienced Centurions. They might walk different paths, but their loyalty lay with Rome and their men, not the political machinations of individual Tribunes.

Brutus left Longinus with a curt nod and continued his way along the walkway. The conversation hadn't brought final certainty, but it had at least partially dispelled his suspicion of Longinus as a person. The man seemed to have done his duty, trapped by the orders of a treacherous superior. The true enemy within was Flaccus. But that enemy was irrelevant for now. The real enemy lay encamped out there, in the darkness, preparing its next blow.

He found Vespasian near the *praetorium*. The Legate stood with arms crossed, also gazing westward, his face showing focused tension, torches casting deep shadows beneath his eyes.

"Still no movement, Legate?" Brutus asked, stepping beside him.

Vespasian slowly shook his head. "Nothing. Our scouts report only the usual camp activities. Fires, guards, the sound of thousands of men. But no signs of forming up for attack. No movement towards us." He rubbed his tired eyes. "It's… strange."

"Strange?" Brutus repeated. "After what happened yesterday? After he sacrificed his elite?"

"Precisely because of that," Vespasian said, turning to Brutus. "Caratacus is no fool, Brutus. He's a capable strategist, even if he is a barbarian. Yesterday, he put everything on the line, tried to storm the west gate before his losses became too great and his morale broke. He committed his personal bodyguard."

"And he failed," Brutus stated. "Thanks to your oil and fire."

"Yes. He failed," Vespasian agreed. "And that's exactly what makes me suspicious. Why isn't he attacking again today? He knows Sabinus is on the way. He knows his time is running out. Every day he waits gives us more time to prepare and brings Sabinus closer."

Brutus frowned. "Perhaps his losses were higher than we thought? Maybe he needs time to reorganize his army, restore morale?"

"Possible," Vespasian conceded. "The caltrops and fire certainly took their toll. But fifteen thousand men... even if he lost a third, which I doubt, he still has overwhelming superiority." He looked out into the darkness again. "No, I don't think it's just about regrouping."

"What then, Legate?" Brutus asked. "What could he be planning?"

"That's the question that kept me awake all night," Vespasian replied. "Is he playing for time, hoping we make a mistake? Risk an ill-advised sortie? Or is he preparing something else? A ruse? An attack from an unexpected direction?" His gaze drifted towards the harbor. "The seaside... it's our Achilles' heel. The walls there are lower, the defenses weaker."

"But he has no ships," Brutus objected.

"Not that we know of," Vespasian corrected him. "But the coast is rugged, full of small coves and river mouths. He could have gathered fishing boats, skiffs, enough for a surprise night

XXXII. IN UNEASY ANTICIPATION

attack on the harbor." He shook his head. "I've reinforced the guards there; the warships are on high alert. But it remains a risk."

They both fell silent, listening to the howl of the wind and the distant murmur from the Celtic camp. The uncertainty was almost as grueling as the fight itself.

"Or," Brutus said quietly after a while, "or he isn't waiting to attack us at all."

Vespasian looked at him questioningly.

"Perhaps he's waiting for Sabinus," Brutus continued. "Perhaps he intends to intercept the Fourteenth Legion before it reaches us, lure them into an ambush, right here, just short of Rutupiae, when they are tired from the march and expecting our rescue."

Vespasian drew a sharp breath. The possibility was terrifying. An entire Roman legion, annihilated in an ambush just miles from its destination. It would be a catastrophe of unimaginable proportions. "I have sent messengers to Sabinus, warning him to exercise extreme caution," he said, but his voice sounded less confident than before. "But if Caratacus plans that…"

"Then we sit here trapped, unable to do anything while our brothers are slaughtered," Brutus finished the sentence bitterly.

Silence fell again between the two men. They were trapped in a fortress, surrounded by an overwhelming enemy whose intentions they didn't know, while another Roman legion marched towards them, possibly straight into a trap.

"We can only wait, Brutus," Vespasian finally said resignedly. "Wait, remain vigilant, and pray that Sabinus is cautious and that Caratacus makes the mistake of attacking us here first."

He clapped Brutus on the good shoulder. "Go, get some rest. Ensure the men are ready. The night is still long, and tomorrow… tomorrow fate will decide."

Brutus nodded silently. He left the Legate and returned to his post on the walkway. He looked out at the sea of hostile fires. What was Caratacus really planning? Why this hesitation? Was it weakness, or the calm before an even more terrible storm? He didn't know. He only knew the night was filled with ill foreboding, and the morning must bring an answer—one bloody way or another.

As evening dusk fell and torches were lit on the walls, Brutus stood again on the walkway of the north gate, looking out at the now silent, dark field where the dead lay. The rain had stopped; the wind had died down. An eerie calm lay over the land—the calm before the storm. He didn't know what tomorrow would bring: victory or defeat, life or death? But he was ready. He was a Roman Centurion, and he would do his duty, to the end.

XXXIII. Night and Fog

The night over Rutupiae was a deceptive shroud of silence and darkness, stretched taut like a bowstring just before release. The wind had died down, the rain paused, but the sky remained an impenetrable black, swallowing the stars. Only the restless flicker of torches on the Roman walls and the distant, menacing glow of countless Celtic campfires broke the gloom. The air was clammy, smelling of saltwater, damp earth, and the underlying tension of thousands of men waiting for the inevitable.

Brutus stood on the walkway of the north gate, wrapped in his thick woolen cloak, protectively pressing his splinted left arm against his body. The wound throbbed dully with his heartbeat, a constant reminder of life's fragility in this brutal war. Brutus stared out into the darkness, trying to penetrate the blackness, his ears straining for any suspicious sound. The enemy's silence was louder than any war horn, the stillness of a beast poised to strike.

Brutus knew they would come. Caratacus was not a man to give up after one setback. He was wounded, humiliated, but not beaten. He would return, with all the force he could muster, before Sabinus and the Fourteenth Legion arrived. The only question was when and where the blow would fall.

The surrounding men were equally tense, veterans of the Second Augusta, battle-hardened but weary. Their faces in the torchlight were hard, angular masks, eyes watching vigilantly into the night. They stood shoulder to shoulder, *scuta* leaning ready against the palisade, *pila* stuck in the ground beside them. They spoke little, only occasional low murmurs, a curse, a nervous clearing of the throat. They waited. That was the worst part of war: waiting for the enemy.

Hours passed, marked only by the calls of the changing guard. Cold crept through cloaks, making the men shiver. Fatigue gnawed at them, trying to weigh down their eyelids. Discipline kept them awake: the soldier's instinct, the sense of lurking danger, and the harsh penalties for dereliction of duty.

Shortly after midnight, in the deepest hour, when vigilance slackened and the world sank into heavy sleep, something shattered the silence.

It began not with the expected roar of drums or the shrill blast of war horns, but more subtly, more insidiously. Soft rustling in the tall, wet grass directly below the walls, barely audible above the sigh of the sea. From the direction of the harbor came muffled splashing, as if something had slipped into the water. Where the ditches were deep, the faint but unmistakable clink of metal on stone could be heard.

A scream! Loud, sharp, full of panic. A Roman sentry on the western section of the wall, near the barricaded gate, yelled, "Alarm! In the ditch! They're in the ditch! Movement!"

Almost simultaneously, another cry pierced the night from the harbor, followed by splintering wood, clashing blades, and the choked calls of overwhelmed men.

The trap had sprung. Caratacus was attacking. Not with

XXXIII. NIGHT AND FOG

a frontal assault like the day before, but with a coordinated, nighttime infiltration attempt at multiple points simultaneously, under cover of darkness, just as Brutus and Vespasian had feared.

Brutus roared, "Trumpeter, sound the alarm!" His voice cracked with urgency. Adrenaline banished fatigue and pain. He ripped his *gladius* from its sheath. "All men to the walls! Spread out! Archers, fire arrows! Light up the fore field! Scorpions, load incendiary bolts! Aim for the ditches!"

The shrill, panicked notes of Roman signal trumpets ripped the camp from its slumber. Everywhere, legionaries stumbled from their tents, groping in the dark for weapons, helmets, shields, running towards the walls. Confused shouts, commands, and the clang of equipment filled the night. Torches were hastily lit, their light dancing across the scene, revealing the extent of the attack.

From the walkway of the north gate, Brutus saw dozens, then hundreds, of dark figures emerge from the gloom. They didn't charge blindly at the walls as before but moved low, skillfully using the darkness and terrain. Some carried short ladders of wood or rope with grappling hooks. Others seemed to be using tools to undermine or breach the palisades. The caltrops laid during the night seemed to be carefully avoided by many attackers.

Simultaneously, an even more menacing scenario unfolded at the harbor. Small, flat fishing boats and skiffs, whose existence Vespasian had feared, had indeed silently entered the harbor basin. Celtic warriors, clad in black, faces smeared with soot, climbed like shadows up the mooring ropes of the docked Roman ships. Brutus heard the muffled sounds of fighting from there—the clash of blades, choked cries, the crash of splintered doors. Then the first flames erupted. A supply ship suddenly burst into bright flames, casting an eerie red glow over the water, revealing the full scale of the chaos. More fires followed on other ships, including one of the precious Liburnians.

"By Jupiter's balls!" Brutus cursed. Caratacus's plan was devilishly clever: a diversionary attack on the main walls while the real blow struck the vulnerable harbor. "Damn it!" Brutus swore again, louder this time, filled with rage and worry. "They're attacking the fleet! They want to destroy our ships!" He knew what that meant. Without the ships, supply from Gaul was impossible. Rutupiae would be completely isolated.

"Longinus!" he bellowed across the din towards the Centurion commanding the adjacent section of wall. He had hoped Longinus would react on his own, but the man seemed to be waiting for orders. "Take your damned century and get down to the harbor! Now! Defend the ships! Put out the fires! Vespasian needs every man there, do you hear?!"

Longinus, his face unreadable in the torchlight, gave a curt salute. "Yes, Centurion!" He barked sharp commands, and his men disengaged methodically from the defensive line on the walkway, hurrying down the ramp towards the burning harbor.

Brutus watched them go, an uneasy feeling in his stomach. He sent one of his best men to inform Vespasian at the *praetorium*, though he suspected the Legate was long since alerted. Now the defense of the north wall was weakened. Was this part of Caratacus's plan? To split their forces?

The assault on the walls now intensified. The Celts charged with renewed fury. Ladders were placed; grappling hooks

XXXIII. NIGHT AND FOG

flew over the palisades. The fight for the walkway began.

It was brutal, merciless close combat in the flickering, unreliable light of torches and the burning ships in the harbor. The darkness was an additional enemy, making it hard to distinguish friend from foe, turning every shadow into a potential threat.

Brutus fought like a man possessed, his *gladius* an extension of his will. He stood at the most threatened section near the barricaded west gate, where attackers repeatedly tried to get over the walls. He parried a spear thrust, kicked the attacker back, stabbed another climbing over the parapet deep in the chest. Blood sprayed his face, warm and sticky. He didn't wipe it away.

Around him, his men fought with the same desperate determination. They knew a breakthrough here meant the end. They formed small, mobile shield walls, repelled attacks, thrust, threw the dead or wounded Celts back into the darkness. They cursed, shouted, groaned with pain and exertion. The walkway floor grew slick with blood and rain.

Again and again, individual Celts gained the walkway. Chaotic melee erupted: man against man, axe against sword, fist against shield. The Romans were better armed and trained, but the Celts fought with the wild strength of desperation and hate. Brutus saw a huge Celt in a bearskin helmet overwhelm his veteran Piso, felling him with a brutal club blow. Brutus lunged at the bearskin-wearer, his *gladius* finding a gap in his defense, sinking deep. The giant roared, sinking to his knees before Brutus finished him with a swift cut to the throat.

Instantly, two more attackers were there. Brutus fought them off, aided by a young legionary who bravely jumped to his side. An arrow grazed his thigh, causing a burning pain he ignored.

The crash of weapons, the screams of the wounded, the throb of drums, the howl of the wind, and the crackle of flames in the harbor created a deafening cacophony. It was the symphony of hell.

Brutus glanced towards the harbor. The fires seemed to have spread. Several ships were now fully ablaze, black smoke billowing skyward. Roman soldiers fought on the decks, forming bucket brigades to draw water from the harbor basin. Apparently, Longinus and his men had arrived and were putting up fierce resistance.

A glimmer of hope. But the fight here on the walls was far from decided. The Celts attacked relentlessly, wave after wave, their numbers seeming endless. Brutus felt his own strength waning. His shoulder ached unbearably, his thigh burned, his breath came shallow. How much longer could they hold?

"Hold!" he roared again, more to himself than his men. "Don't let the bastards through!"

The Celts now seemed to concentrate their attacks on the barricaded west gate. Though the gate itself was impassable, the damaged wall beside it offered a weak point. They tried to tear down the palisades there, climbed over each other, formed human pyramids.

"Ballistae! Fire on the west gate! Smash them!" Brutus yelled towards the towers.

The heavy *ballistae* thundered again, their bolts slamming into the dense mass at the west gate, causing horrific casualties. But the Celts didn't fall back. Driven by Caratacus, whom Brutus could now see again in the melee, personally urging his men on, they attacked with the fury of desperation.

Suddenly, a loud crash from the west gate. Part of the makeshift barricade gave way. Celts streamed through the gap.

"Alarm! They're through! West gate!" the sentries screamed.

Panic threatened to erupt. If the Celts got inside the walls…

"Second Century! To me!" Brutus roared, gathering the men still standing on his section. "We push them back! Follow me!"

With a final, desperate effort, Brutus charged down the ramp with his handful of remaining men, into the chaos at the west gate. They met the invading Celts head-on; a last, brutal melee erupted in the narrow alley behind the gate.

Brutus fought like a wounded bear. He saw Caratacus, just paces away, leading his warriors. Their gazes met for a moment over the fray—an expression of mutual hatred and grudging respect.

Then a blow from the side struck him, knocking him to the ground. He saw stars, felt a sharp pain in his chest. A Celtic warrior stood over him, long sword raised for the death blow. Brutus closed his eyes, bracing for the end.

But the blow never came. Instead, he heard a cry, a dull thud. He opened his eyes. The Celt lay dead beside him, a Roman *pilum* protruding from his back. Above him stood Vespasian, sword blood-smeared, his face a mask of grime and grim determination.

"Up, Centurion!" the Legate said curtly. "The fight isn't over yet!" He offered Brutus a hand and pulled him up.

Brutus looked around, confused. The noise seemed to be lessening. The Celtic attacks were weakening. He saw Roman reinforcements—Vespasian with his bodyguard—supporting the handful of legionaries pushing the Celts back through the small breach, closing the gap again.

And he saw Caratacus, slowly, reluctantly withdrawing with the remnants of his bodyguard, his face a mask of fury and bitter defeat.

The attack was repulsed. Again.

Brutus leaned panting against the blood-splattered palisade. He had survived. Vespasian had survived. Rutupiae had held. But the price was immeasurable. Dead and wounded lay everywhere. "Shit, that was close!" Brutus said, breathing heavily, to himself. The fortress was a slaughterhouse. And Sabinus still wasn't here. Victory was won, but it tasted like ashes.

XXXIV. The Aftermath

The first pale light of dawn fought through the smoke and haze still lingering over Rutupiae, revealing the full extent of the previous night's destruction and suffering. The Roman fortress had held, but the price was staggeringly high.

The field before the walls presented a horrific tableau of death. Hundreds of Celtic bodies lay where they had fallen: scattered among treacherous caltrops, piled in the ditches, smashed beneath the palisades. The ground was stained dark red with clotted blood mixed with mud and ash. Ravens and other carrion birds circled greedily overhead.

Inside the walls, the picture was scarcely less grim. The main assault had been repulsed, but the scars of battle were everywhere. Sections of the palisade were damaged, the west gate a shattered, barricaded ruin. In the harbor, the wrecks of three Roman ships—two large supply transports and one of the nimble Liburnians—still smoldered, their black, oily smoke rising skyward, obscuring the morning sun. The smell of burnt wood and tar mingled with the omnipresent stench of death and decay.

The hospital tent overflowed with wounded. *Medici* and their assistants worked tirelessly, faces pale with exhaustion, hands bloodstained. The groans and whimpers of the injured formed a low but constant chorus of suffering.

In the *praetorium*, the mood was somber but focused. The Legate sat at the large wooden table, maps pushed aside, replaced by wax tablets listing casualties. Vespasian rubbed his tired eyes. Throughout the night, he had issued orders, coordinated the defense, and appeared himself at the most critical points—like Brutus at the west gate—to bolster morale. His key commanders were gathered around him: Brutus, his left arm splinted and in a sling; Centurion Longinus, his armor bearing the marks of fierce combat; the tribunes of the auxiliary units; and the prefects of the warships in the harbor. The air was thick with the smell of wet leather, sweat, and the metallic aftertaste of blood and fear.

"Gentlemen," Vespasian began, his voice rough but firm. "We have held. Against overwhelming odds, we have held. The gods were merciful to us—and our discipline was our shield." He paused, his gaze sweeping over the exhausted faces. "The casualty reports are in." He nodded to a scribe, who handed him another tablet. Vespasian scanned the figures. "They are… more bearable than feared, yet still painful."

He looked up. "We have lost four hundred and twelve men, fallen in battle or succumbed to their wounds." A murmur of relief went through the room; given the ferocity of the attack, many had expected far worse. "Over one hundred and fifty more are wounded, many severely. Our *medici* work without pause." He sighed softly. "Every loss is one too many, but we held. The enemy, on the other hand…" He smiled grimly. "Our scouts, observing their withdrawal, report thousands of dead and wounded on the Celtic side. Their first wave was practically shredded by the *tribuli*. The assault on the walls

XXXIV. THE AFTERMATH

was a bloodbath, and the fire broke their elite unit and their morale. Caratacus paid a high price for his attack today."

"Do you think he will try again, Legate?" Longinus asked.

Vespasian shook his head. "I think not. Not immediately, not tonight. His army is battered, demoralized. He must withdraw, lick his wounds, regroup his forces. We have bought time." He looked around the room. "But we must not become complacent. The alert remains at the highest level. The guards remain doubled. Sleep will be in full gear."

"The forges continue work on the caltrops, Legate," Brutus interjected, his voice still thick with pain. "We already have a considerable quantity. I suggest we use the darkness to lay more fields before the walls, especially to the west and north."

"An excellent idea, Brutus," Vespasian agreed. "Organize it. Small squads, well-secured. Scatter them widely, but discreetly. Should Caratacus attempt a surprise night attack after all, let him find a nasty surprise." Brutus nodded.

"However, there is a weak point, Legate," Brutus continued, his gaze turning serious. "The west gate. It withstood the assault, but the rams damaged it severely. The hinges are loose, the bolts bent. Another concentrated attack… and it could give way."

Vespasian frowned. "The engineers are working on it, but a complete repair under these circumstances is difficult."

"I propose we barricade it," Brutus said directly, "completely, from the inside, with earth, stones, anything we can find. Make it part of the wall."

A murmur went through the officers. Blocking the main gate was a drastic measure.

"That would mean we can make no more sorties from there," Longinus objected. "We would deny ourselves an important option."

"What option, Longinus?" Brutus asked sharply. "A sortie against fifteen thousand Celts? That would be suicide. Right now, this gate is a danger, not an option. If Caratacus gathers his forces and attacks again, he will aim here. We must eliminate this weak point."

"But what if Sabinus arrives?" another officer asked. "Should the Fourteenth Legion find a barred gate?"

"Sabinus won't be here before dawn the day after tomorrow, perhaps even later," Vespasian said thoughtfully. "Until then, the gate must hold. Brutus is right; the risk is too great." He made the decision. "Barricade the west gate, immediately! Use all available materials. Make it as strong as the wall itself."

"Yes, Legate!" several Centurions said in unison.

"Good," Vespasian said. "That settles the immediate defensive measures. Rest, gentlemen, but remain vigilant. The night is still long." He gestured dismissal.

The officers saluted and left the *praetorium* to implement the orders. Only Brutus remained behind for a moment.

"Legate," he began hesitantly, "what... what about Flaccus?"

Vespasian sighed, rubbing his tired eyes. "Flaccus is... a problem for later, Brutus. I have sent scouts to try and pick up his trail, but I doubt we'll find him in this chaos. Right now, we must focus on Caratacus. If we survive this battle, I will personally deal with Tribune Flaccus. You have my word on that."

Brutus nodded slowly. It wasn't a satisfying answer, but he understood the priorities. "And Sabinus? Is there news from Camulodunum?"

"The messenger who brought news of Sabinus's departure was the last to arrive," Vespasian said, a rare warmth in his

XXXIV. THE AFTERMATH

voice. "Likely no one can get past Caratacus's army now."

"Sabinus… will he make it in time?"

"That now rests in the hands of the gods… and the endurance of the Fourteenth Legion," Vespasian replied gravely. "We can only hope and hold." He clapped Brutus on the shoulder. "Go now, Centurion. You need rest too, even if you won't admit it."

Brutus saluted and left the *praetorium*. The morning light was gray. Cleanup was in full swing. The dead were being recovered, the wounded carried to the hospital tent, debris cleared away. But the scars of the night were omnipresent. He took a deep breath, ignoring the pain in his shoulder. Vespasian was right. They had to hold the city. They had to wait. And they had to hope that Maximus and Sabinus arrived in time. He went to his tent. Once there, he could barely remember how he got there. He lay down just as he was and fell asleep immediately.

XXXV. Caratacus's Gamble

The mood in Caratacus's large tent was icy. Smoke from the central fire rose slowly towards the opening in the roof but couldn't dispel the bitter smell of burnt wood, sweat, and defeat. Caratacus sat on a crudely carved chair, his face a mask of suppressed rage and deep frustration.

Before him stood or sat his key chieftains and advisors: Branwen, Cadan, the impulsive Cadeyrn, and the leaders of the Durotriges and other allied tribes. Their faces reflected exhaustion, mutual recrimination, and the grim realization that their bold plan had failed.

"Almost!" growled a bearded Durotrigan chieftain, slamming his fist on the table. "We almost had them! The west gate was breached! Why didn't we press the attack? Why did we retreat?"

"Because our men failed at the harbor!" Cadeyrn retorted heatedly. "We had too few boats! We couldn't ferry enough warriors across quickly enough to overwhelm the Roman ships and set the storehouses ablaze! The Romans there were prepared!"

"Prepared, or warned?" Branwen asked quietly, her gaze resting on Caratacus.

XXXV. CARATACUS'S GAMBLE

Caratacus felt the unspoken accusation. The escape of Maximus and Brutus. Could he have prevented it? Should he have had them killed immediately instead of hoping for information? Doubts gnawed at him, but he showed no weakness.

"We were repulsed," he said in a hard voice, cutting off any further discussion of blame. "The Romans held. Their walls were stronger, their discipline more unyielding than expected. And their Legate Vespasian… he is no fool." He thought of the oil and fire that had devastated his elite warriors at the west gate. A devilish weapon.

"What now, Caratacus?" Cadan asked, his voice weary. "We have suffered heavy losses. The men's morale is shattered. Many speak of returning home."

"How heavy are the losses?" Caratacus asked, though he dreaded the answer.

A captain stepped forward. "We estimate… about three thousand fallen, Caratacus. At least. And another two thousand are too badly wounded to fight."

A horrified silence followed the report. Five thousand men lost. A third of his entire force, sacrificed in two failed assaults. Caratacus felt a chill seep into him.

"Ten thousand remain," he said after a moment, forcing calm. "Ten thousand battle-hardened warriors. Enough to still take this fortress."

"But the other legion is on its way!" cried the Durotrigan chieftain. "Our scouts have sighted them! They march fast! They are only a few hours away!"

"How many hours?" Caratacus asked sharply.

The scout stepped forward. "They broke their last marching camp this morning. They are disciplined, holding formation.

We estimate… four, maybe five hours until their vanguard arrives here."

Four to five hours. Time was running out. If Sabinus's legion arrived and united with Vespasian, their numerical superiority wouldn't vanish, but they would be caught between hammer and anvil.

"We can wait no longer," Cadeyrn urged. "Let us attack now! One last desperate assault before the other legion arrives!"

"And have even more men slaughtered?" Cadan asked bitterly. "No! We must retreat while we still can!"

The chieftains began arguing again, unity threatening to collapse completely.

"Silence!" Caratacus thundered, his voice silencing everyone. He rose, his gaze sweeping over his men's faces. He saw their fear, their exhaustion, but also the spark of hope still glimmering in their eyes.

"Retreat is not an option," he said firmly. "We would be hunted down and destroyed. But another blind assault on these walls is not an option either." He paused, then announced his new plan. "We divide our forces."

Surprised murmurs.

"Two thousand men," Caratacus continued, "the lightest, fastest warriors, remain here, under Branwen's command." He nodded to the warrior woman. "Choose someone; their task is to pin down the Romans in Rutupiae. Avoid open battle. Buy us time."

Branwen nodded gravely. "Understood, Caratacus. I will have one of my most experienced captains take charge."

"The rest of us," Caratacus looked around the circle, his eyes burning with determination, "eight thousand men, we break camp immediately. We march to meet Sabinus and his

XXXV. CARATACUS'S GAMBLE

legion!"

Renewed murmurs, louder this time, tinged with disbelief.

"We face them on open ground!" Caratacus cried, his voice swelling. "Where their walls are useless! Where our courage and numbers will make the difference! We will surprise them, intercept them on their march, destroy them before they can reach Rutupiae!"

He saw hesitation in some faces, but also dawning hope, fierce battle lust in others, especially Cadeyrn.

"It is our last chance!" he shouted. "An open field battle! Man against man! As our ancestors did! We will smash Sabinus, destroy his legion, and then return to take Rutupiae! Let us show Rome the worth of Britannic steel!"

He drew his sword. "Who is with me? Who fights for Britannia?"

Cadeyrn let out a wild cry and drew his sword as well. One by one, the other chieftains followed, their doubts swept away by Caratacus's infectious resolve and the prospect of an honorable battle.

"Good!" Caratacus said, relief mingling with tension. "Then let us waste no time! Gather the men! We depart immediately! May the gods grant us victory!"

XXXVI. Locked Out

The night after the repulsed major assault had been one of uneasy waiting, yet the expected further Celtic onslaught never came. Instead, as the first pale light of dawn emerged, Roman sentries on the walls of Rutupiae observed a surprising and initially inexplicable movement in the vast enemy camp.

"They… they're pulling out!" cried an Optio from the north tower, his voice filled with disbelief.

Brutus, who despite his aching shoulder and Vespasian's instructions had only slept for two hours, hurried to the edge of the palisade. He squinted, staring through the slowly lifting morning fog. The Optio was right. A large part of the Celtic army was on the move, not towards Rutupiae, but away from it, north and west, back inland. Long columns of warriors on foot and horseback were detaching from the camp, marching off in disciplined fashion.

"What in Hades is happening?" Brutus muttered to himself. Was Caratacus giving up? Retreating after his defeat? That didn't fit the man he had encountered, didn't fit his determination.

But not the entire army was leaving. A considerable portion, perhaps two thousand men by Brutus's rough estimate,

XXXVI. LOCKED OUT

remained behind. They reformed, establishing a loose siege line around the landward side of the fortress, lighting new fires. They weren't retreating; they were maintaining the siege—but with significantly reduced strength.

"Legate Vespasian must be informed immediately!" Brutus ordered the Optio.

A short time later, another hastily convened council of war took place in the *praetorium*. Vespasian stood before the large map, his officers—Brutus, Longinus, the auxiliary tribunes, the *nauarchi*—gathered around him. The mood was a mixture of relief and confusion.

"Our scouts confirm it," Vespasian said after hearing the reports. "Caratacus has withdrawn the bulk of his army, an estimated eight, perhaps ten thousand men. They are marching northwest." He tapped the map. "They are moving fast. Too fast for an orderly retreat after a defeat."

"But why?" Longinus asked. "Why leave us here? Why give up the siege when Sabinus isn't even in sight?"

"He isn't giving it up," Brutus contradicted. "He left two thousand men behind. Enough to pin us down here, block us, but not enough to seriously threaten the walls." His mind worked feverishly, trying to decipher Caratacus's strategy. "He wants to tie us down here, while with his main force…" His gaze met Vespasian's.

"Sabinus," Vespasian finished the thought, his expression grave. "Caratacus marches to meet Sabinus and the Fourteenth Legion. He wants to face them on open ground before they can reach us."

A shocked silence filled the tent. The plan was bold, desperate, but logical from Caratacus's perspective. If he could defeat Sabinus, Rutupiae was doomed, even with its strong walls.

"We must warn Sabinus!" cried one of the tribunes.

"I have sent riders," Vespasian said calmly. "Our fastest riders, but whether they make it or are intercepted by Caratacus's scouts, we don't know. No, Sabinus is on his own." He paused. "But he is not alone. He has the Fourteenth Legion. One of Rome's best."

"But against such superior numbers, Legate?" Longinus objected. "Ten thousand or more against five thousand? On open ground?"

"The odds are not good, that is true," Vespasian admitted. "But we cannot remain idle." His gaze became resolute. "We cannot warn Sabinus directly, but we can help him. We can attack Caratacus from the rear, catch him in a pincer!"

"A sortie, Legate?" Brutus asked skeptically. "With our remaining forces? Against the two thousand men besieging us, and with Caratacus's main army nearby?"

"Not with our entire garrison," Vespasian explained. "But we have the auxiliary cavalry." He turned to the prefect of the mounted auxiliary troops, a weather-beaten Batavian. "Prefect Rufus, how many cavalrymen do you have combat-ready?"

"About three hundred, Legate," Rufus replied. "We've suffered losses, but the men are ready."

"Three hundred cavalry," Vespasian murmured. "Too few to seriously threaten Caratacus, but enough to harass his rearguard, force him to detach troops, buy Sabinus time." He considered. "Yes. Prefect Rufus, you will break out with your *ala*. Bypass the besiegers under cover of night or fog, then push towards Sabinus. Support him, scout for him, hit Caratacus's flank wherever possible."

XXXVI. LOCKED OUT

"Sir!" Rufus said with a grim look that betrayed no enthusiasm.

"But there is a problem, Sir," Brutus interjected before the plan could be finalized, thinking of the smiths' work, his own idea. "The caltrops."

Vespasian looked at him questioningly.

"We scattered the entire forefield before the walls with caltrops, especially to the west and north," Brutus explained. "Thousands of them. They served us well last night, but now they are also a danger to our own men, especially the cavalry. A sortie through that field would be suicidal; the horses would break their legs."

Vespasian frowned, having forgotten this in the heat of the moment. "Damn it! You're right, Centurion. That makes a land sortie impossible, at least for now." He slammed his fist on the table. "So are we condemned to inaction after all? Must we watch as Sabinus fights and dies?"

A tense silence followed. The officers looked at each other helplessly.

Then one of the *nauarchi*, the commander of the small naval fleet in the harbor, an experienced man named Vitulus, cleared his throat. "Legate… there might be another way."

All eyes turned to him.

"The ships, Legate," Vitulus continued. "We still have several Liburnians and some faster transports that are seaworthy. The sea is rough, yes, but not impassable for experienced sailors." He pointed to the map. "The coast curves north here. If we sail along the coast, a few miles north, we can land troops behind Caratacus's siege line. From there, they could fall upon his rear while he engages Sabinus, or they could march inland and link up with Sabinus's army."

Vespasian's eyes lit up. "A landing behind enemy lines… bold, Nauarchus. Very bold. But also dangerous."

"Indeed, Legate," Vitulus agreed. "The sea is unpredictable, especially with fully laden ships. And landing on an unsecured coast carries risks. But," he shrugged, "it is a possibility. A way to support Sabinus and surprise Caratacus."

Vespasian thought quickly. The plan was daring, but it offered a chance to regain the initiative. "How many men can we transport on the available ships?"

Vitulus calculated briefly. "If we pack them tightly… perhaps a thousand men, Legate. No more."

"A thousand men," Vespasian repeated. "Not much against Caratacus's main force, but enough to cause significant disruption, sow confusion." He made a decision. "Good, we do it." He looked around the room. "Longinus, you will lead this force. Select a thousand of your best, fittest men from the Third and the other cohorts remaining here. Plus ten cavalrymen with their horses as scouts, even though getting them onto the ships will be difficult. Nauarchus Vitulus will provide the ships. You depart as soon as tide and darkness permit. Sail north, land at a suitable spot behind Caratacus's presumed position. From there, you decide based on the situation: either you fall on Caratacus's rear, or you attempt to link up with Sabinus. Primary objective: support Sabinus, thwart Caratacus's plan."

"Yes, Legate!" Longinus and Vitulus said simultaneously, their faces showing a mixture of tension and determination.

Brutus felt a pang of disappointment, but also relief. Finally, something was happening! He wanted to be part of this operation himself, wanted to finally fight again, get out of this damned fortress. He stepped forward. "Legate, I request

XXXVI. LOCKED OUT

permission to accompany Centurion Longinus."

Vespasian turned to him, his gaze serious, but also fatherly. "No, Brutus."

"But Legate…!"

"No buts, Centurion," Vespasian said firmly, but without harshness. "Your shoulder. You are not yet fully fit. A landing behind enemy lines, a swift march, a hard fight—that is no place for a man with only one good arm. Your courage does you credit, but I need you here."

He stepped closer to Brutus. "I myself will participate in this operation, Brutus. I will accompany Longinus and the men."

Brutus stared at him incredulously. "You, Legate? But… the command here?"

"I entrust it to you, Brutus," Vespasian said calmly. "You are the senior and most experienced Centurion here. You have proven you can hold this fortress. Continue to hold it. Secure the city. Take care of the men. Wait for Sabinus. And," his gaze intensified, "should we… fail… should Caratacus catch us at sea or on land… then it falls to you to hold Rutupiae at all costs until Sabinus arrives. Understood?"

Brutus swallowed. The weight of responsibility was enormous. Command of the entire fortress, Rome's last bastion in the south, now rested on his shoulders. But he also understood Vespasian's decision. The Legate wanted to personally ensure this risky operation succeeded, that Sabinus received the support he needed. And he trusted Brutus to defend his rear.

"I understand, Legate," Brutus finally said, his voice firm. "I will hold Rutupiae, to the last man."

"I know you will." Vespasian nodded. "May the gods be

with us."

He turned away and began planning the details of the operation with Longinus and Vitulus. Brutus remained behind, a whirlwind of conflicting emotions in his chest—disappointment at not being able to fight himself, but also pride in the command entrusted to him and the heavy burden of responsibility. He knew the coming days would be decisive, not just for Rutupiae, but for the fate of Rome in Britannia.

XXXVII. Hours of Decision

The fourth day of the march south dawned, and a palpable change was in the air. The incessant rain of previous days had yielded to a sun peeking tiredly through the gray clouds. Though the ground remained muddy, visibility was better, and the prospect of reaching Rutupiae that same evening had noticeably lifted the morale of the exhausted legionaries of the Fourteenth Gemina. They marched faster, their steps sounding firmer, discipline unbroken. The hope of finding their comrades of the Second Augusta alive and fighting drove them onward.

Maximus rode beside Legate Sabinus, feeling the same mixture of hope and gnawing uncertainty. The doubts Sabinus had sown a few days earlier—the possibility of a ruse by Caratacus, the question of the true threat—had haunted him through the nights. But the proximity to Rutupiae, the prospect of clarification, of battle, pushed those doubts into the background for now. His focus was now on the goal, on uniting with Vespasian and Brutus, on the impending confrontation with Caratacus. He thought of Brutus's injured shoulder, of the faces of the men sacrificed in Bryn's camp. Lust for revenge mingled with concern for the living.

They had been marching for about four hours since breaking their last fortified camp at dawn. The landscape gradually flattened, opened up, dense forests giving way to scattered groves and wide meadows laced with wisps of fog. They were approaching the coastal strip; Rutupiae could not be far now.

"We're making good time, Legate," Maximus remarked, his voice sounding more confident than the day before. "If we maintain this pace, we'll reach the fortress before nightfall."

Sabinus gave a curt nod, but his gaze was tense, fixed on the scouts riding ahead, appearing and disappearing like small dots on the horizon. "Let us hope we do not find only rubble and ashes there," he muttered darkly. "Caratacus had a head start. Enough time for a determined leader to storm a fortress if the defenders are caught by surprise."

"Vespasian is not easily surprised, Legate," Maximus countered. "And Brutus... Brutus fights to the last breath." He spoke the words with more conviction than perhaps he felt.

At that moment, they saw one of the scouts galloping towards them at full speed, his horse throwing up clumps of mud. It was the Decurio of the auxiliary cavalry leading the reconnaissance. He pulled his horse up so sharply before Sabinus and Maximus that the animal nearly reared. The Decurio was pale, his breath coming in ragged gasps.

"Legate! Tribune!" he panted. "Enemy sighted! Massive force! Directly ahead!"

Sabinus's expression darkened. "Report, Decurio! Clear and concise!"

"Caratacus's main army, Legate!" the Decurio blurted out. "They are marching directly towards us! They are... perhaps two hours away! At least ten thousand men, probably more!"

Two hours. The news struck like a hammer blow. Caratacus hadn't waited for them. He was coming to meet them. He wanted the battle here, on open ground, before they could reach Rutupiae.

"And Rutupiae?" Maximus asked immediately, his heart clenching. "Did you see smoke? Signs of fighting? Has the city fallen?"

The Decurio shook his head. "No, Tribune. We could see the fortress from a rise. No excessive smoke, no visible signs of a major assault or destruction. But," he hesitated, "we were too far to be certain. Caratacus's army blocked our path as they emerged from the woods."

So they didn't know if Rutupiae still stood. They only knew that a superior force of at least ten, perhaps fifteen, thousand Celts marched towards them, while they themselves numbered just under five thousand and were weary from the march.

"Damn," Sabinus cursed softly, but with an intensity that betrayed his control. He looked around, rapidly assessing the surroundings. "He means to face us here. Here, where we have no walls to protect us."

"What do we do, Legate?" Maximus asked, his voice tense. "Turn back? Try to evade him? Lure him into an ambush?"

Sabinus rubbed his chin thoughtfully, his gaze sweeping the landscape before them—open, rolling meadows, crossed by small streams and scattered groves, bordered by a larger section of woods directly ahead. "Turning back is not an option," he said decisively. "He would hunt us down and destroy us. Play cat and mouse?" He shook his head. "We are too slow for that, too cumbersome. And he likely has cavalry that could outflank us." He looked directly at Maximus. "No, Tribune. Only one possibility remains: We make our stand."

"Here? On open ground? Against such superior numbers?"

Maximus asked incredulously.

"Not here," Sabinus said, "but not in retreat either." His gaze sharpened again. "We choose our battlefield. We force our terms upon him." He turned back to the Decurio. "What is the terrain like behind that patch of woods ahead?"

The Decurio nodded. "Beyond the woods, it opens up again. There's a slight rise, elongated, with relatively clear views west and north. The ground is firmer there, less marshy. The flanks are protected by the edge of the woods and a steeper slope down to a stream."

Maximus listened intently. A rise. Firm ground. Protected flanks. It sounded familiar. He had crossed this area on his desperate ride to Camulodunum. "Legate," he interjected, "I know that rise! It's perfect for a defensive position! We'll have the height advantage, clear fields of fire for our archers and ballistae. The woods protect our left flank, the stream the right. The Celts would have to attack uphill, frontally, on a relatively narrow front!"

Sabinus looked at him searchingly, then at the Decurio. "Is that correct, Decurio? Does this position offer the advantages the Tribune describes?"

The Decurio nodded eagerly. "Yes, Legate. Absolutely. It's the best defensive position for miles around."

Sabinus made his decision instantly. "Good! That is our battlefield!" He immediately gave orders. "Signal halt! All Centurions and Tribunes to me at once! Decurio, send your fastest riders out to closely observe Caratacus's advance and report any change in direction! The rest of your men form a vanguard and secure the path through the woods to the rise! Move!"

The officers hurried over, their faces full of questions.

XXXVII. HOURS OF DECISION

Sabinus briefly, concisely explained the situation and his plan. "We withdraw to the rise behind the woods. There, we await the enemy. There, we fight."

Some officers looked relieved, others concerned.

"Legate," said the *Primus Pilus* of the Fourteenth, an experienced veteran named Cilo, "shouldn't we try to reach Rutupiae? Perhaps Vespasian still holds out? Uniting our forces…"

"Impossible, Cilo," Sabinus interrupted firmly. "Caratacus stands between us and the city, and even if we got through, we would be too exhausted to be of any help. No, our fate is decided here, on this rise." He looked around the circle, his voice hardening. "We lure Caratacus into a trap. We let him charge a prepared position. We use our discipline, our ranged weapons, and the advantage of terrain to break his superior numbers. We fight on our terms."

He saw agreement growing in his officers' eyes. The plan was risky, but it was logical; it offered a chance.

"The formation," Sabinus continued, spreading a makeshift map on a table. "We form a triple line (*acies triplex*), staggered up the slope. The first line takes the main assault; the second and third serve as reserves and for flank security. We position the auxiliary archers and slingers on the elevated flanks, protected by the woods and the stream. They are to subject the charging Celts to crossfire." He looked at his artillery prefect. "And the *ballistae*!"

"Yes, Legate?"

"I am glad we did not leave them behind in Camulodunum," Sabinus said with a hint of grim satisfaction. "They are our trump card. As soon as we reach the position, I want them immediately positioned on the highest points of the rise, ready for action, but still concealed! They are to break up the Celtic formations before they even reach us! That is your most important task!"

"Sir!" the prefect replied.

"Good," Sabinus said, straightening up. "That is the rough plan. We will finalize the details when we reach the position. Now, we must get there quickly and in order, before Caratacus cuts off our path." He looked into the determined faces of his officers. "Questions?"

There were none.

"Then to your posts! Move the legion! March!"

The *tubae* and *cornua* blew again for an orderly march. The legion set off once more, not aimlessly south this time, but with a clear objective in sight: the rise behind the woods, their chosen battlefield.

Maximus rode beside Sabinus again, but the atmosphere had changed. The paralyzing uncertainty had yielded to a tense but focused determination. Sabinus had voiced his doubts, yes, but he had also presented a clear plan, shown leadership. Maximus felt a renewed surge of respect. This man was more than just Vespasian's older brother; he was a Roman Legate, experienced, rational, resolute. Though his caution sometimes drove Maximus to despair, he now recognized the wisdom behind it. He himself still had much to learn about the burden of command, about weighing risks, about the art of not just leading a legion but preserving it.

XXXVIII. The Eagle Against the Wolf

The march through the final stretch of woods was short but marked by feverish haste. The legionaries of the Fourteenth Gemina moved with new resolve; knowing their objective and having a strategic plan lent them fresh strength. The vanguard of auxiliary cavalry had secured the way. As the main column emerged from the trees, the terrain described by Decurio Aelius and Maximus unfolded before them: a long, gently rising hill, nestling into the landscape like the back of a sleeping giant.

Here the ground was firmer, less boggy than in the valley below. The view to the west and north—the direction from which Caratacus was expected—was wide and open, interrupted only by scattered groves. The dense edge of the forest they had just left protected the hill's left flank. The right flank sloped more steeply down to a stream whose banks were thick with brush, forming a natural obstacle against a broad flanking attack. Maximus had recognized a nearly perfect defensive position.

"Here!" Legate Sabinus called out, his horse dancing restlessly on the highest point of the rise. "Here we await them!" His voice echoed across the field. "Centurions, form up your men! According to plan! Engineers, begin digging ditches and erecting palisades at the weakest points immediately! Ballistarii, get the engines in position! Quickly! We don't have much time!"

Instantly, the disciplined marching column transformed into an organized anthill. Centurions bellowed orders; Optios directed the men. Cohorts deployed, taking their assigned positions on the slope, forming the triple-staggered line, the *acies triplex*. Shields were set up, *pila* driven into the ground. The men of the first line formed an impenetrable wall of wood and steel. Behind them, the second and third lines stood ready to fill gaps, secure the flanks, lead the decisive counter-thrust.

The auxiliary archers and slingers took position on the higher flanks, utilizing the cover of the woods and the steep stream bank, ready to subject the charging Celts to crossfire.

With enormous effort, the heavy *ballistae* were lifted from their transport carts and positioned on the most strategic points of the rise. The artillery crews worked feverishly but precisely, tensioning the massive torsion arms, loading the first heavy bolts. Their silent muzzles now pointed menacingly towards the plain from which the enemy must come.

Within hours, the rise had transformed into a fortified position, a Roman bulwark ready to withstand the Celtic onslaught. The men stood at their posts, the initial haste giving way to a tense, focused calm. They waited.

Maximus stood beside Sabinus on the highest point, from where they could survey the entire battlefield. He had checked his own armor, sharpened his sword. The headache had subsided, replaced by a cold clarity. Fear was still there, a low thrum beneath the skin, but overlaid by the determination,

XXXVIII. THE EAGLE AGAINST THE WOLF

the concentration of a soldier before battle. He looked down at the ranks of men, the disciplined lines, the steel helmets, the gleaming spear points. He felt a surge of pride. They were ready.

"A good position, Legate," he said appreciatively. "And well taken."

Sabinus gave a curt nod, his gaze still fixed on the western horizon. "We have done what we could, Tribune. The rest now lies in the hands of the gods—and the courage of our men." He turned to Maximus, a rare expression of camaraderie in his eyes. "You led us here. Your knowledge of the terrain was crucial."

"I was fortunate to know the area, Legate," Maximus replied.

"'Fortune favors the prepared,' they say," Sabinus remarked. "But do not forget what I told you about Caratacus's cunning. Stay vigilant. Distrust the obvious."

"I will not forget, Legate," Maximus assured him. Doubts about his friends in Rutupiae still plagued him, but the immediate danger and the necessity of battle left no room for dwelling on them.

Sabinus nodded again. Then he straightened and drew his sword. "It is time, Tribune. The men await." He signaled his staff officers. *Tubae* and *cornua* blew a signal, echoing across the field, drawing the attention of every legionary to the highest point of the hill.

Sabinus stepped forward, his figure silhouetted clearly against the gray sky. He raised his sword. Absolute silence fell over the Roman ranks. Even the wind seemed to hold its breath. Then Sabinus began to speak, his voice calm at first, but swelling into a thunderous call that reached every single man, penetrating their hearts.

"Soldiers of the Fourteenth Gemina! Men of Rome!" His gaze swept over the thousands of faces looking up at him. "Hear me! Today is the day we fight not just for our lives! Today we fight for the honor of Rome! We fight for our brothers trapped in Rutupiae, waiting for us! We fight an enemy superior in number, yes! An enemy that is savage, barbaric, filled with blind hatred!"

He paused, letting the silence work. "They may be more numerous! But are they stronger?"

"NO!" the answer roared back from thousands of throats, a single, immense cry.

"Are they more disciplined?"

"NO!"

"Do they have Roman steel in their hearts? Do they have the Eagle on their side?"

"NO!"

"We are Romans!" Sabinus cried, his voice vibrating with passion. "We are heirs to a glorious history! We have overthrown kings, conquered empires, subdued barbarians! We have brought civilization to the darkest corners of the world! We are the wall that defends order against chaos!"

He pointed west with his sword. "There comes Caratacus! He comes with his hordes! He thinks he can slaughter us here, tired from the march, far from any help! He is mistaken!"

"YES!" came the roar again.

"We are not tired! We are ready! We are not alone! We are the Fourteenth Gemina! A legion that has never yielded, never been broken! We fought on the battlefields of Germania; we have vanquished Rome's enemies everywhere! And we will vanquish them here too!"

"We will hold this rise!" he thundered. "We will make it our

XXXVIII. THE EAGLE AGAINST THE WOLF

shield! We will defend it with our bodies! Let the barbarians charge! Let them break upon our steel! Let them burn in the fire of our *ballistae*! Let them be impaled upon our *pila*!"

"Each one of you," his gaze swept the ranks again, "is a hero! Each of you bears responsibility for the man beside you! Hold the line! Protect your brother! Show no doubt! Show no fear! Show them only your wrath! Your courage! Your indomitable Roman soul!"

He raised his sword higher. "Swear to me, soldiers! Swear by Jupiter Optimus Maximus! Swear by Mars Ultor! Swear by the spirits of your ancestors! That today you will fight as never before! That you will hold to the last man! That you will cover the name of the Fourteenth Gemina with glory! Swear it!"

A deafening cry erupted from the ranks, a single, immense oath of resistance that made the hills tremble. "WE SWEAR IT!" Men beat their swords against their shields, a thundering, rhythmic sound filling the air.

Sabinus slowly lowered his sword, an expression of grim satisfaction on his face. He had reached them. Fear had yielded to fury, doubt to determination. They were ready.

He turned briefly to Maximus, a short, understanding nod. Then he looked west again.

And then they saw them.

First, just a dark line on the horizon, a smudge detaching itself from the woods. Then the line widened, thickened, transforming into a surging mass moving inexorably across the plain towards them: Caratacus's army.

Maximus felt his heart plummet. Even from this distance, the sheer size of the force was terrifying. Not just thousands, it seemed an endless sea of warriors, flanked by cavalry, their spear points glinting in the pale sunlight. The ground began to vibrate faintly under the tramp of thousands of feet. A deep, menacing rumble, the Celtic battle cry, carried towards them on the wind, growing louder as they drew nearer.

An involuntary murmur of apprehension went through the Roman ranks, despite Sabinus's speech, despite their own determination. The sight was overwhelming, intimidating. Even the most seasoned veterans felt a cold touch of fear.

Maximus forced himself to be calm, took a deep breath. He looked at the disciplined ranks of his men, the ready *ballistae*, the protected flanks. Sabinus was right. They had the better position. They had the better equipment. They had discipline. They just had to hold.

"They come, Legate," he said to Sabinus, his voice steady.

"Let them come, Tribune," Sabinus replied just as steadily, pulling his helmet lower onto his face. "We are ready."

The Celtic army rolled closer, an unstoppable tsunami of wild determination. The Roman legion waited on the hill, a steel rock in the raging sea. The hour of decision had arrived.

XXXIX. The Eagle on the Hill

The sight made Caratacus instinctively rein in his warhorse. Sitting upright in the saddle, his eyes narrowed as he assessed the scene. The drizzle had stopped, and the low afternoon sun broke through a gap in the clouds, bathing the landscape in a cold, golden light that revealed with unsettling clarity what his scouts had already reported:

There stood the Fourteenth Legion Gemina, arrayed on the elongated rise that dominated the plain like a sleeping guardian. No longer marching, neither surprised nor unprepared, but drawn up in perfect, triple-staggered battle formation. A steel wall of shields, helmets, and menacing spear points ascended the slope. The Roman eagle of the legionary standard gleamed defiantly in the pale sunlight at the highest point, flanked by the banners of the individual cohorts.

Caratacus cursed softly. The Roman commander—Sabinus, Vespasian's brother—was no fool. He had recognized the trap or at least anticipated the danger, avoiding open battle on the plain and choosing this ground instead. Reluctantly, Caratacus had to admit: the position was excellent.

The rise gave the Romans a clear height advantage. Their

archers and slingers had an open field of fire onto his men should they attack, positioned on the flanks, protected by the dense forest edge and the steep stream bank. His cavalry under Cadeyrn would be severely hampered on the ascending, likely muddy, terrain. They would have to attack frontally, uphill, against a disciplined, well-entrenched Roman line. It was exactly the kind of battle he had wanted to avoid, a grinding contest where Roman discipline and equipment often proved decisive.

Beside him, his key chieftains and advisors gathered, their faces mirroring his own concern, mixed with impatience and the still-burning anger over the losses before Rutupiae.

"They expect us," Branwen stated soberly, her eyes surveying the Roman formation with cool precision. "Their position is strong. A direct assault will be costly."

"Costly? It's madness!" cried Cadan, his voice trembling slightly. "They stand up there like eagles on their aerie! We will bleed our men dry on that slope, just like before Rutupiae! Let us besiege them, Caratacus! Starve them out!"

The young cavalry leader Cadeyrn scoffed impatiently, "Besiege? We have no time for that, old man! Plautius could turn back from the north any day. Reinforcements from Gaul could land. We must strike them now, while we have superior numbers! Let us attack! Immediately! Overwhelm them with our force!"

A heated argument erupted again among the chieftains. Some agreed with Cadan, fearing another massacre and pleading for caution, perhaps even a tactical withdrawal to lure the Romans from their position. Others, especially the younger, more war-hungry leaders like Cadeyrn, pushed for an immediate, massive assault, convinced their sheer numbers

XXXIX. THE EAGLE ON THE HILL

and courage could break Roman discipline.

Caratacus listened, his gaze shifting between his arguing chieftains and the unmoving Roman line on the hill. He understood both sides. Cadan was right: the Roman position was strong; a frontal assault would be costly. But Cadeyrn and Branwen were also right—time was against them. Every day they waited increased the risk of Plautius seeing through the deception, of reinforcements arriving from Gaul. The chance to defeat the Roman legions separately diminished with every hour.

Added to this was the morale of his army. They had suffered a heavy blow before Rutupiae. Another setback, hesitation now, could finally shatter their fragile unity. He had promised them swift victory, led them here with vows of vengeance and glory. He couldn't back down now.

He had to attack. Now. While his men's will was still unbroken, while they still believed they could win.

He raised his hand, commanding silence. His authority, reinforced by royal blood and proven leadership, eventually prevailed. The chieftains fell silent, their gazes fixed on him.

"We will attack," Caratacus said, his voice calm but filled with an iron resolve that brooked no dissent. "Cadan, your caution does you credit, but a siege is not an option. We have no time. Cadeyrn, your courage honors you as well, but blind fury is not strategy." He looked around the circle. "We attack, but we do it wisely. We use our superior numbers, but we do not charge blindly onto their spears."

He gestured towards the Roman formation. "Their strength is their discipline, their staggered line. But that is also their weakness. They are less flexible. We will attack them at multiple points simultaneously, attempt to roll up their flanks, sow chaos in their ranks." He turned to Cadeyrn. "Your cavalry will attack the right flank, where the stream lies. It's difficult terrain, but if you break through, you can fall upon their rear."

Cadeyrn nodded grimly, his eyes gleaming.

"The Durotriges and the men from the west," he looked at the respective chieftains, "you form the main wave. Attack the center and the left flank. Break their first line! Pin down their reserves!"

The chieftains nodded resolutely.

"Branwen," he turned to the tactician, "your warriors and my *Teulu* form the second wave, the reserve. You push forward wherever a gap opens. You will decide the battle."

Branwen gave a curt nod, her gaze focused.

"Deploy the army!" Caratacus commanded. "Form the lines here, just outside the range of their slingers and archers." He glanced at the sky. The sun was already low. "We do not attack immediately. We let them wait. We let darkness become our ally. Shortly before sunset, when the light grows deceptive, then we strike!"

He noticed the Druids gathering at the edge of the host, their chants growing louder, arms raised to the sky. He felt the power of their rituals inspiring his men, giving them courage. Though he sometimes doubted their bloody demands himself, he needed all the help he could get now, from gods and men.

"Let the Druids complete their prayers," he said to Cadan. "May their blessings grant us strength."

Cadan nodded in agreement.

Caratacus looked again towards the Roman hill. The legion stood up there, unmoving, a steel eagle awaiting its prey. He felt no hatred anymore, only a cold, clear determination. This was the moment of truth. Here, the fate of Britannia would be decided. He, Caratacus, against Sabinus. Celt against Roman. Freedom against Empire.

He drew his sword, his father's heirloom, its blade having tasted blood in many battles. The blade glinted coldly in the last light of the sun. He raised it high, a signal to his army. A tremendous roar answered him, the sound of ten thousand warriors ready to fight and die.

"As soon as the formations are set, and the Druids are ready," he called to his chieftains, putting on his boar-crested helmet, "on my signal! For Britannia!"

XL. The Might of Rome

The silence on the hill was almost unbearable. The sun sank relentlessly towards the western horizon, painting the clouds in hues of blood-red and violet, while the plain below already lay shrouded in twilight. Like figures carved from stone, the Roman legion stood: a triple-staggered wall of dark red shields, gleaming helmets, and armor plates, the menacing points of thousands of *pila* thrusting skyward like a steel forest. Every man stood at his post, breathing shallowly, gripping the hilt of his *gladius* or the shaft of his *pilum*. They waited.

Besides Sabinus on the highest point stood Maximus, his gaze fixed on the vast Celtic army now formed up on the plain below. It was a terrifying sight: a surging, restless mass of tens of thousands of warriors, their colorful shields, animal hides, and the wild patterns of their war paint forming a chaotic but menacing tapestry. The noise from their ranks had become a deep, constant rumble, a mixture of chants, drums, and the occasional shrill blast of a *Carnyx*, echoing through the dusk like the cry of some mythical beast. They were ready. The attack was imminent.

"They wait for the last light," Sabinus said quietly. "They want to attack in the twilight, when visibility is poor and their

XL. THE MIGHT OF ROME

savagery counts most." His voice was calm but tense.

Maximus nodded. "Our discipline will be our advantage. And our ranged weapons." His gaze shifted to the flanks, where the auxiliary archers and slingers crouched behind improvised breastworks of earth and branches, bows drawn, slings ready. He glanced at the strategically placed rises along the front line, where beneath rough tarpaulins camouflaged with leaves and twigs, the heavy *ballistae* lay in wait. Maximus now considered Sabinus's decision to bring them on this forced march, despite slowing the baggage train, an act of strategic foresight.

"Give the signal as soon as their first wave is in range, Maximus," Sabinus ordered. "Not too soon. Let them get close."

Maximus nodded again, his heart hammering against his ribs. He relayed the command to the horn blowers standing beside the legion's standards. A single, clear note would be the signal.

The tension was almost physically palpable. Men licked dry lips, checked the fit of their helmets one last time, loosened swords in their scabbards.

Then, finally, the moment everyone had awaited. A tremendous roar erupted from the Celtic army, thousands of throats uniting in a deafening bellow. The mass surged forward, not as a disorganized mob, but in broad, deep wedges, rushing up the slope with frightening speed. At the forefront ran the elite warriors, Caratacus's *Teulu*, and the fiercest fighters of the Durotriges, their long swords and axes flashing in the last light.

"Hold!" Sabinus roared. "Let them come!"

The Celtic tidal wave rolled closer, the thunder of their feet making the ground tremble. They were now within range of the archers and slingers.

"Auxiliaries! Fire!" Maximus commanded.

A hiss filled the air as hundreds of arrows and sling stones rained down from the flanks into the charging wedges. Men screamed, fell, stumbled, but the mass pressed relentlessly onward, closing the gaps, their roar only growing louder, angrier.

They were now dangerously close to the first Roman line, almost within *pilum* range. They seemed not to have noticed the camouflaged positions on the rises.

"*Ballistarii!*" Maximus called to the horn blowers. "Signal! Uncover!"

The single, clear note of the *tuba* cut through the din. On the rises, legionaries ripped the camouflage tarps from the heavy war machines. For a split second, the charging Celts saw the monstrous wooden structures suddenly appear before them, throwing arms cocked, ready to hurl death. A moment of hesitation, of confusion, flickered through their ranks.

"FIRE!" Sabinus bellowed.

With a deafening crash that shook the ground, the *ballistae* unleashed their deadly cargo. Heavy bolts slammed into the densely packed Celtic wedges with devastating force, shattering shields, armor, and bone, throwing men yards through the air. Solid iron bolts pierced multiple warriors at once, leaving bloody swaths.

The effect was devastating. The spearhead of the Celtic attack waves was literally torn apart, decimated, thrown back. Entire formations dissolved into chaos and screams. Men tried to escape the projectiles, trampling each other. The momentum of the assault was broken before it even properly

XL. THE MIGHT OF ROME

reached the main Roman line.

"Reload! Fire again!" the Roman artillery officers yelled.

While the *ballista* crews worked feverishly, the legionaries of the first line seized their chance.

"*Pila*! Throw!" roared Primus Pilus Cilo.

Thousands of heavy throwing spears rose like a steel forest, flying in high arcs into the confused and depleted Celtic ranks. The sound of impacting *pila* mingled with the screams of the struck. Wood and metal splintered; flesh was pierced. Many *pila* punched through Celtic shields, rendering them useless, their bent iron shanks making them impossible to remove quickly. Others found their mark in chests, bellies, or legs, tearing gaping wounds.

The Celtic wave faltered, wavered. Some warriors turned to flee. Others desperately tried to reform. Still others charged blindly forward, driven by rage or disregard for death.

"*Gladii*! Draw! Hold the line!" Cilo commanded.

The first Roman line drew their short swords. The men now stood shoulder to shoulder, shield to shield, forming an unyielding wall of steel and determination, ready to receive the impact of the remaining attackers.

The Celts who had survived the barrage now reached the Roman line. With a final roar, they crashed against the wall of *scuta*. The impact was heavy, but the Roman line held firm.

Now the brutal melee began. Romans thrust with their *gladii* over or under shield rims—short, swift, lethal stabs aimed at unprotected areas. Celts hacked at Roman shields with long swords and axes, trying to break the formation, find a gap.

Maximus watched the fight from his elevated position, his heart pounding. He saw the legionaries fight, hold, kill. But he also saw the sheer mass of the enemy still there, gathering behind the first wave, ready to advance. The *ballistae* fired again, tearing more gaps, but they couldn't stop everyone.

"Second line, prepare!" he yelled to Cilo, who was already reforming his remaining men.

The fight on the first line raged on, a gruesome struggle for every foot of ground. The Romans fought with the efficiency of a well-oiled machine, but the Celts fought with the fury of a wounded wolf. Slowly, inch by inch, the first Roman line began to give way under the pressure of superior numbers.

"Now!" Sabinus screamed. "Second line, forward! Relieve the First!"

With a thunderous shout, the second line, led by their Centurions, charged partway down the slope, pushed through the gaps in the first line, and met the exhausted but still attacking Celts. Fresh Roman troops clashed with tired warriors. The impact was again fierce.

Maximus watched a Centurion in the front-rank thrust, parry, use his shield as a weapon, ramming it against attackers, throwing them back. His men followed his example, fighting with renewed ferocity.

The Celtic charge stalled. The second Roman line not only held but began to slowly push the Celts back. The third line also moved up, closing ranks, forming an even deeper, more insurmountable wall.

Maximus felt a spark of hope. Sabinus's plan seemed to be working. The layered defense, the use of the *ballistae*, the discipline of the men—it was effective.

He saw Caratacus observing the battle from a slight rise, surely seeing the effect of the Roman resistance, realizing his attack was failing. Would he order the retreat?

XL. THE MIGHT OF ROME

But Caratacus did something unexpected. Instead of sounding the retreat, he raised his sword and gave a new signal. From the woods on the flanks of the Roman position, hundreds of Celtic cavalry suddenly erupted. They had apparently found a way around the protected flanks and now charged towards the less heavily defended sections of the second and third Roman lines, where the auxiliary units stood.

"Flank attack!" Maximus roared. "Auxiliaries, hold them! Third line, wheel out!"

Chaos threatened again. The Roman formation, geared for a frontal assault, was vulnerable on the flanks. The Celtic cavalry hit the surprised auxiliary units with full force. Spears met light shields; horses trampled men underfoot.

Sabinus reacted instantly. "Reserve cohort! To the left flank! Maximus, secure the right! Hold the cavalry! Don't let them break through!"

The battle now shifted, becoming a desperate struggle on three fronts simultaneously. In the center, the Romans pushed back the Celtic infantry, but on the flanks, a wild fight raged against the penetrating cavalry.

Maximus gathered men around him to counter the flank attack. As if in a frenzy, he wielded his *gladius*, a whirling blade of steel and death. Shoulder to shoulder, he stood with the men of the first line, defying the main onslaught of Celtic infantry. The ground beneath his feet was slick with blood and mud. The infernal noise of battle filled the air: the roar of attackers, the screams of the wounded, the crash of shields, the shriek of metal on metal. He parried a wild blow from a huge, bearded Celt, used the man's momentum to thrust under his shield, ramming the blade deep into his unprotected stomach. The Celt made a gurgling sound and collapsed before him.

Instantly, two more warriors replaced him, rushing Maximus with raised axes.

Maximus deflected the first axe blow with his *scutum*, feeling the impact shudder up to his shoulder. He avoided the second blow only with a desperate leap aside. A legionary next to him was less fortunate: the heavy blade struck his helmet with full force, splitting metal and skull. Maximus thrust his *gladius* into the axe-wielder's side while another legionary engaged the second attacker.

It was a brutal battle of attrition. The first Roman line held, but paid a heavy price. Men fell constantly, replaced by soldiers from the second line who, under the command of the experienced Primus Pilus Cilo, relentlessly moved up to fill the gaps. The discipline was admirable, but Maximus saw the exhaustion on their faces, the sheer terror in the eyes of some younger soldiers facing this carnage for the first time.

On the flanks, however, the real nightmare unfolded. Cadeyrn's cavalry seemed to be everywhere, attacking in swift, furious waves, using their speed and agility to bypass the slower Roman infantry, find gaps, and sow chaos. The auxiliary archers and slingers on the flanks put up fierce resistance, their missiles taking a toll on the horsemen, but they couldn't completely stop the onslaught. Again and again, small groups of cavalry broke through, hitting the second and third Roman lines in the side, forcing the legionaries to break formation and defend themselves in chaotic melees.

"Left flank wavering!" screamed a Centurion from the third line, his voice almost cracking. "We need support!"

Sabinus, sitting stoically on his horse in the center, directing his men, heard the call. His face was an impenetrable mask, but worry flickered in his eyes. He had no more reserves

XL. THE MIGHT OF ROME

to send. The third line was already fully engaged, trying to stabilize the flanks.

"Hold the line!" Sabinus roared back, his voice barely carrying over the din. "Form a tighter circle! Protect the flanks! Do not yield a single step!" Messengers rode off to deliver the commands.

Easier said than done. The Celtic cavalry were like hornets, stinging, withdrawing, attacking again. Maximus saw an entire century of the third line collapse under the onslaught, the riders cutting the men down, their screams lost in the tumult. A dangerous gap opened.

"We're losing," Sabinus thought with sudden, cold certainty. *"We can't hold them. They are too many, too fierce."* Sabinus's plan to face Caratacus here had been bold, but he had underestimated the sheer ferocity and determination of the Celts, as well as the effectiveness of their cavalry on this terrain.

Sabinus saw Primus Pilus Cilo desperately trying to hold the first line, now pressed from three sides. He saw the *ballistae* on the rise, firing incessantly, but their heavy projectiles were less effective against the fast cavalry and dispersed infantry formations.

The sun sank lower, casting long shadows across the battlefield, bathing the slaughter in blood-red light. The Roman formation was no longer an orderly wall but a ragged circle, attacked from all sides, relentlessly compressed.

Caratacus, observing the battle from his position, must have sensed victory was near. He urged his men onward with loud cries. Fresh waves of infantry stormed up the slope to deliver the killing blow.

Maximus felt cold sweat trickle down his back. He saw the

exhaustion on his men's faces, the desperation in their eyes. He saw the Celtic lines drawing ever closer, beginning to encircle the Roman position. They were about to be overrun. The Fourteenth Legion fought bravely, but sheer numbers threatened to crush them.

"This can't be the end," he thought desperately. *"Not after everything we've been through."* He looked skyward as if seeking a divine sign, but saw only the gray, indifferent clouds. He looked east, towards Rutupiae. Were Brutus and the others still alive?

Then, just as hope began to fade, as the Roman line threatened to break in several places at once, it happened.

A new sound cut through the deafening roar of battle, clear, blaring, unmistakably Roman: the call of *tubae* and *cornua*. But it wasn't coming from the direction of Rutupiae. It came from behind them, from the woods they themselves had passed through, at the rear of the attacking Celtic army.

Confusion spread like wildfire across the battlefield. Heads turned, Roman and Celt alike. Caratacus, who was driving his men at the base of the hill for a final assault, paused, his gaze snapping backward. His chieftains looked at each other in disbelief.

From the edge of the woods, precisely where the Celtic reserve had been waiting for the breakthrough, a compact, disciplined Roman force erupted. Heavily armored legionaries. At their head rode an officer on a black horse, his purple cloak whipping in the wind—Legate Vespasian. Beside him, a stocky legionary carried the proud standard of the Second Augusta, the silver eagle with wings outstretched. It was the men from Rutupiae, led by their Legate!

"AUGUSTA! AUGUSTA!" Vespasian roared, drawing his

XL. THE MIGHT OF ROME

sword and charging with his fresh troops into the completely surprised Celtic reserve and rearguard.

The psychological effect was devastating. The Celts had thought the Romans nearly defeated. Now, they were suddenly attacked from the rear by a new, unexpected Roman force. Panic spread. Formations dissolved. Warriors looked around, unsure where the greatest danger lay.

"VESPASIAN!" Sabinus yelled, his face reflecting incredulous joy and relief. "By Jupiter, he made it!"

"Now!" Maximus screamed, new hope surging through him. "Legionaries! Reinforcements are here! Push forward! Destroy them!"

The Fourteenth Legion, spurred by the arrival of their comrades and the enemy's evident confusion, gathered their last strength. With a tremendous battle cry, they surged forward again, pushing the now hesitant Celtic lines down the slope.

Caratacus reacted swiftly to the new threat, bellowing orders, trying to reform part of his army to face Vespasian's attack from the rear, ordering his reserve to counter the new threat.

But before this new front line could fully form, before the fight between Vespasian and Caratacus's reserve truly began, another horn signal sounded.

This time it came from the south, from the woods the Fourteenth Legion had traversed that afternoon. And they weren't Roman horns. They were the shrill, wild notes of Celtic *carnyx*.

Maximus and Sabinus froze, their hearts sinking. More Celts? Had Caratacus brought further allies? Was this the final death blow?

But the banners that emerged shortly thereafter from the woods were not those of Caratacus's army. They were the blue boar banners of the Atrebates. At their head rode King Cogidubnus, flanked by a surprising figure in gleaming Roman armor—Tribune Flaccus. And beside Flaccus, on an elegant horse, Prince Adminius. Behind them, an army of about three thousand Atrebate warriors streamed from the woods, falling upon the right flank of Caratacus's army.

"Flaccus? Adminius?" Maximus gasped in disbelief. "What… what are they doing here?"

Sabinus stared at the scene, equally stunned. "By all the gods… they're attacking Caratacus!"

The confusion in the Celtic host was now complete. Sabinus's legion attacked from the front, Vespasian's cohorts from the rear, and now the Atrebates, their own countrymen, assaulted their flank.

Caratacus had just turned to face Vespasian at his rear. He wrenched his horse around, his face showing incredulous rage and horror as he saw the Atrebates attack. At that moment, his scouts reached him, screaming reports of the new threat.

The Britannic king understood instantly. His army, already weakened and demoralized, finally broke under this three-sided assault.

Panic seized the Celtic warriors. There was no stopping them now. Men threw down their weapons, trying to flee, running in all directions, only to be cut down by the pursuing Romans of the Second Augusta and the now equally attacking Atrebates.

The slaughter was complete. The plain transformed into a single, vast charnel house.

Caratacus saw the catastrophe. With a final, desperate cry,

he gathered the remnants of his bodyguard around him, broke through the Atrebate line on the flank, fled northwards, and disappeared into the gathering darkness.

Maximus watched the Celtic king's flight, then looked out over the battlefield. Romans and Atrebates pursued the fleeing Celts, taking prisoners, killing those who resisted. Vespasian's force had linked up with Sabinus's legion. The victory was total, crushing.

He sank to his knees, his sword slipping from his grasp. He gasped for breath, his body trembling with exhaustion and the aftermath of adrenaline. Around him, the sounds of battle slowly died down, replaced by the groans of the wounded and the triumphant shouts of the victors.

Sabinus rode up beside him. "We did it, Tribune. By all the gods, we did it." His face was drawn with exhaustion, but his eyes shone with relief and triumph.

Maximus looked up. He saw Vespasian approaching Longinus, shaking his hand. He saw Cogidubnus sitting proudly on his horse, surrounded by his warriors. And he saw Flaccus and Adminius approaching Sabinus, expressions of feigned relief on their faces.

Victory was won. But the questions remained. What was the King of the Atrebates doing here, and how in Hades had Vespasian gotten behind them?

Maximus didn't know. He only knew they had survived, that Rutupiae was saved, and that the Britannic resistance had suffered a severe blow.

XLI. Council of Victors and Shadows of Doubt

The sun had set, and heavy darkness descended like a wet curtain over the blood-soaked battlefield before the rise. Countless torches, lit by Roman and Atrebate soldiers, pierced the gloom, their light reflecting eerily in puddles and on polished helmets and armor, while also revealing the gruesome details of the slaughter: the contorted bodies of the fallen, broken weapons, and dark stains soaking the ground. The noise of battle subsided, replaced by the groans of the wounded, the crunch of boots in the mud, the curt commands of officers, and the distant, ominous howling of wolves.

Inside the command tent hastily erected by the Fourteenth Legion, the air was thick, heavy with the smell of sweat and wet leather emanating from the armor of those present. Legate Titus Flavius Sabinus sat at the head of the rough-hewn table, his angular face marked by the day's exertion and responsibility, though his eyes radiated a hard satisfaction. Beside him sat his brother, Legate Titus Flavius Vespasian, whose surprise arrival had decided the battle. Vespasian's expression was calmer, more thoughtful, his gaze sweeping over the faces present. Opposite them sat Tribune Maximus

XLI. COUNCIL OF VICTORS AND SHADOWS OF DOUBT

and King Cogidubnus of the Atrebates. Despite his youth, Maximus's exhaustion was evident. Cogidubnus's royal composure formed a stark contrast to the rough surroundings. Standing slightly apart, Tribune Flaccus listened attentively, his armor inexplicably less battle-scarred than the others'. Behind him stood Prince Adminius modestly, his eyes darting nervously between the Roman commanders. The most important Centurions, including Longinus of the Second and Cilo of the Fourteenth, along with Cogidubnus's advisors, stood along the walls.

"Let us begin with the losses," Sabinus opened the meeting, his voice tired but firm. *"Primus Pilus* Cilo?"

Cilo stepped forward, his expression grim. "Legate, the Fourteenth Gemina bled heavily but held. We count one thousand seventy-eight fallen and seven hundred twenty wounded, many severely."

A collective sharp intake of breath filled the room. The numbers were brutal, confirming the ferocity of the battle Sabinus's legion had borne almost alone.

"And the Second Augusta?" Sabinus asked, looking at Vespasian.

"Our losses were… surprisingly light," Vespasian replied, his gaze resting briefly on Longinus. "We hit an already faltering enemy from the rear. Nineteen fallen, about fifty wounded."

"The Atrebates also lost comparatively few men," King Cogidubnus added. "Perhaps thirty dead, twice as many wounded. We attacked an already fleeing flank."

The numbers made the strategic situation clear: Sabinus's legion was heavily damaged, while Vespasian's intervention force and the Atrebates were relatively fresh.

"And the enemy?" Vespasian asked.

"Caratacus's army is shattered but not annihilated," reported the prefect of Sabinus's cavalry. "We estimate their losses at six to seven thousand men, perhaps more. However, scouts report he is retreating northeast with a still considerable force, towards Camulodunum. We estimate five to six thousand warriors."

"So he flees," Sabinus stated. "But he is still dangerous."

"Indeed," Vespasian agreed. "We must not give him time to regroup or rally more tribes."

"One question remains, however," Vespasian said, turning his gaze directly to Flaccus and Adminius. "How do you explain your timely intervention with the Atrebates, Tribune Flaccus? And where were you, Prince Adminius? We had missed you for days." His voice was neutral, but the question hung heavy in the air.

Flaccus stepped forward, his expression showing feigned regret and relief. "Legate Sabinus, Legate Vespasian, it was a chain of fortunate and unfortunate circumstances." He glanced at Adminius.

Adminius seamlessly took over, his voice sounding sincerely concerned. "As you know, I had ridden ahead to scout the Druid path. But instead of a safe route, I found an ambush. My small escort was attacked by an overwhelming force of savage warriors—presumably Durotriges or Bryn's men." His face darkened. "My brave Roman companions were all killed." He beat his chest theatrically. "Only by the grace of the gods and the speed of my horse did I escape. I fled east, into the territory of the Atrebates, knowing King Cogidubnus was our ally."

"I found refuge with King Cogidubnus," he continued, "and informed him of the ambush. I immediately dispatched a messenger—a swift trader I trust—to Rutupiae, requesting aid from Tribune Flaccus."

Flaccus nodded confirmingly. "I received Prince Adminius's message, Legate. I immediately recognized the strategic opportunity." He addressed Sabinus. "It occurred to me that King Cogidubnus, now directly affected by the threat from Caratacus's allies, might be willing to help us—not just in defending Rutupiae, but actively against Caratacus." He sighed dramatically. "I instructed one of my slaves to immediately inform Legate Vespasian in Rutupiae of my plan and departure. Unfortunately," he shook his head, "that duty-shirker seems not to have fulfilled his task. I will find him and have him severely punished for this negligence."

He turned back to Sabinus and Vespasian. "I immediately departed with my escort, met with Prince Adminius, and we rode to King Cogidubnus. Together, we were able to persuade him to mobilize his troops and march towards Rutupiae. We marched and reached the battlefield... just in time, it seems." He finished his report with a self-satisfied smile.

Maximus listened to the story with growing disbelief. It was a masterful lie, artfully woven with half-truths. The ambush, the escape, the messenger, the vanished slave—it sounded plausible but was barely verifiable. And the result spoke for itself: the Atrebates had intervened and decided the battle. He glanced at Vespasian. The Legate listened attentively, his expression impenetrable, but Maximus thought he saw a barely perceptible twitch around his eyes. Vespasian didn't believe him either.

"A remarkable chain of events, Tribune Flaccus, Prince Adminius," Vespasian finally said slowly, his voice neutral. "And a fortunate confluence for us all." He paused. "Rome owes you and King Cogidubnus a deep debt of gratitude."

Cogidubnus nodded regally. Flaccus beamed. Adminius smiled modestly.

"Now, to the future," Vespasian continued, returning to strategic planning. "Caratacus is beaten but fleeing. He still has a dangerous force. We must pursue him and destroy him definitively."

"I agree," Sabinus said. "The Fourteenth will take up the pursuit as soon as the men are cared for and we have recovered the dead. King Cogidubnus, will you support us with your warriors?"

"Of course, Legate Sabinus," the King replied. "Caratacus is now my enemy too."

"I, however," Vespasian said, "will return to Rutupiae with the Second Augusta. The fortress must be secured; the supply line is crucial." He looked around the room. "I will take the wounded from all units who are fit for transport. Rutupiae is not far, and our *medici* there can care for them better than we can here in the field."

It was a logical yet generous offer, acknowledged by the officers of the Fourteenth with grateful murmurs.

"Tribune Flaccus, Prince Adminius," Vespasian continued, "you will accompany Legate Sabinus on the pursuit. Your knowledge of the tribes and terrain in the north could be useful." His gaze was unreadable.

Flaccus and Adminius nodded assent, their true thoughts hidden behind polite masks.

"Then the plan is clear," Sabinus concluded the meeting. "We recover the dead, tend the wounded. Tomorrow, at dawn, the hunt begins. May the gods aid us."

The officers saluted and left the tent to implement the

XLI. COUNCIL OF VICTORS AND SHADOWS OF DOUBT

orders. Maximus lingered for a moment, his gaze meeting Vespasian's. The Legate gave him a barely perceptible nod, a silent message of understanding. The game continued. Today's victory was just one stage in the world of intrigue and war.

XXXXII. Waiting

The silence after the deafening roar of the battle for Rutupiae was deceptive. Though the wild Celtic assaults had been repelled and their main army under Caratacus had withdrawn north, the threat remained. Two thousand Celtic warriors still besieged the fortress, a constant, visible reminder of the Romans' precarious situation. They acted less aggressively than before, staying out of range of Roman artillery, but their mere presence tied down valuable forces and cut Rutupiae off from all land communication and supply.

On the walkway of the north rampart stood Brutus, his gaze shifting restlessly between the Celtic siege ring and the western horizon, from where he expected—or feared—the arrival of Sabinus and the Fourteenth Legion, or the return of Caratacus. His left arm still rested in its sling, the shoulder aching with every careless movement, though the wound was healing well, as the Greek *medicus* had assured him. Far worse were the gnawing uncertainty and the weight of responsibility that now rested upon him. Vespasian had departed by sea with Longinus and a thousand men to support Sabinus, leaving Brutus in command of Rutupiae's remaining garrison. An honor, undoubtedly, but also a burden.

XXXXII. WAITING

The day after the great battle was spent cleaning up and reorganizing. The dead were buried, the wounded tended to, and the damage to the walls crudely repaired. Among the men, there was a strange mixture of relief at having survived, pride in repelling the attack, and deep fatigue. They had performed inhuman feats but knew the war was far from over.

On the morning of the second day after the battle, the sentries noticed a change in the Celtic camp. The two thousand warriors Caratacus had left behind began to break their positions. There were no signs of another attack. Instead, they hastily packed their few belongings, not even extinguishing their fires, and withdrew in small groups to the northwest, disappearing in the same direction as Caratacus's main army.

"They're pulling out!" an Optio excitedly reported to Brutus. "The siege is over!"

Brutus watched the withdrawal with suspicious eyes. "Don't be too hasty, Optio," he warned. "This could be a ruse. Perhaps they want to provoke us into a careless sortie." He thought of the caltrops still littering the fore field. "Keep the men on the walls. Highest vigilance."

But as the morning wore on, it became clear it was no trick. The Celts were indeed withdrawing completely, leaving behind only the traces of their camp and the unburied dead from the battle. A wave of relief washed through Rutupiae. The immediate threat was gone.

Yet, Brutus remained tense. Why were the besiegers withdrawing? Had they received news from Caratacus? Was the battle in the west already decided? And if so, in whose favor?

"We need to clear the fore field!" he ordered. "I want those damned caltrops gone before our own men or horses step on them." His gaze fell on the gruesome field before the walls. "We must bury the dead, the enemy's too. We are Romans, not barbarians." Besides, he wanted to avoid the stench that would soon set in.

He had one of the smaller side gates carefully opened. A well-armed century under an experienced Optio marched out, step by step, yard by yard, covered by archers and *scorpiones* from the walkway. Methodically, they began collecting the treacherous *tribuli*, a tedious and dangerous task. Simultaneously, burial details recovered the dead and dug mass graves. The grim but necessary work took the rest of the day.

Brutus spent most of his time on the walkway, his gaze constantly scanning westward. Every dust cloud on the horizon made his heart beat faster. Was it Sabinus, or Caratacus returning victorious? The uncertainty was almost unbearable. He thought of Maximus. Had the Tribune survived the battle? What was happening at Camulodunum if the Fourteenth Legion fell? The thought that his young friend might have fallen, or that something might happen to Anwen while he waited safely behind walls here, constricted his throat.

Late in the afternoon, as the sun sank low, casting long shadows across the cleared but still scarred fore field, the relieving news finally arrived. A lone auxiliary cavalryman galloped in from the west, having clearly taken a wide detour around the battlefield, his horse utterly exhausted. He was brought immediately to Brutus on the walkway.

"Centurion Brutus!" the rider gasped, giving a fleeting salute. "Message from Legate Vespasian! The battle is won!

XXXXII. WAITING

Caratacus is defeated and fleeing!"

A tremendous cheer erupted from the walls of Rutupiae. Men hugged each other, threw their helmets in the air, thanked the gods. The tension of the past days dissolved in a single, liberating outburst of joy.

"Legate Vespasian? Tribune Maximus?" Brutus asked immediately, his heart pounding.

"Both well, Centurion!" the rider reported, beaming. "Legate Vespasian arrived with reinforcements at the crucial moment and fell upon the enemy's rear! The Atrebates under King Cogidubnus also attacked! Caratacus's army was shattered!"

Brutus closed his eyes for a moment, a profound sense of gratitude and relief washing over him. Maximus was alive. Vespasian was alive. They had won.

"Where is the legion now?" he asked further.

"Regrouping after the pursuit, Centurion," the rider replied. "Legate Vespasian is returning here immediately to Rutupiae with the wounded and the Second Legion. They should arrive this evening. Legate Sabinus himself, with the rest of the Fourteenth and the Atrebates, will take up the pursuit of Caratacus."

"Good," Brutus said. "Excellent." He clapped the rider on the shoulder. "You brought good news, soldier. Go and rest. You've earned it."

The cheering in the camp continued. News of the victory and the impending arrival of Vespasian and the wounded spread like wildfire. The mood was exuberant, almost giddy. Brutus, however, remained thoughtful.

Late in the evening, just before sunset, the first units arrived. It was a long, somber procession. Riding at the front was Vespasian, his face weary but resolute. Behind him followed litters carrying the many wounded of the Fourteenth Legion, escorted by the remnants of the Second Legion under Centurion Longinus. The men were exhausted, their armor bloodstained, but they marched upright, the standard with the eagle carried before them.

Brutus received Vespasian at the gate. The two men looked at each other for a long moment, a silent understanding passing between them.

"Welcome back, Legate," Brutus said, saluting.

"Good to see you well, Centurion," Vespasian replied. "You held the city."

"We held it," Brutus confirmed. He looked around, looking for the arriving ranks. "Where is Tribune Maximus?"

Vespasian smiled faintly. "He's coming. Insisted on securing the rearguard and organizing the recovery of the wounded. A good man. Almost too dutiful."

Brutus nodded, relief washing over him again. Maximus was not only alive but unharmed. He looked up as the last rays of sunlight broke through the clouds, bathing the returning legion in golden light. The storm was over. At least for the moment.

XLIII. Homecoming

The sun had already sunk below the horizon, twilight casting a purple veil over Rutupiae as the last units of the returning force marched through the main gate. Torches were lit, casting a warm, restless light on the scene. Brutus still stood at the gate, though Vespasian had long since dismissed him to rest. He couldn't leave. He watched the men arrive, nodding to familiar faces from his legion, seeing the infinite weariness etched into their features.

They had achieved the unimaginable: defending Rutupiae against overwhelming odds, the surprise seaborne sally under Vespasian, landing behind enemy lines, the hard march, and finally the decisive flank attack that shattered Caratacus's army. They had won, but the price was high. The ranks were thinned; many men wore fresh bandages, others leaned on comrades or were carried in on makeshift litters. The sweet smell of blood and wound ointments mingled with the smoke from the torches.

Brutus felt deep respect for these men, his brothers-in-arms. Despite his rank, despite the burden of command, he was one of them. He knew their fears, hopes, and pains. He knew what this victory had cost them.

Then he saw the rearguard. The men looked even more

exhausted than the others, faces blacker with soot, armor more stained with blood. At their head rode Maximus, upright in his saddle, though visibly straining to maintain posture.

A wave of relief washed over Brutus so strong it nearly buckled his knees. He was back. The Centurion stepped forward as Maximus dismounted, his movements stiff with fatigue. Their gazes met. The arguments of the past days, the tension, the doubts—all vanished, wiped away by shared experience, survived danger, and a deep bond beyond words.

"Maximus," Brutus said roughly, his voice thick. He extended his good hand.

"Brutus," Maximus replied, gripping the Centurion's forearm with a firm, warm pressure. A genuine smile, full of relief, spread across his dirty face. "You're alive, old dog. I was worried."

"Should have worried more about yourself, Sir," Brutus countered with a hint of his old, grim humor. "I heard you gave Sabinus quite a hard time."

Maximus laughed, a hoarse, exhausted sound. "Someone had to. But," his expression turned serious, "we did it, Brutus. We beat them."

"Yes," Brutus said softly. "We did."

At that moment, an excited cry cut through the scene. "Brutus!"

Both men spun around. A figure pushed through the crowd of arriving soldiers, running directly towards Brutus. It was Anwen. Her red hair was tied back in a simple knot, her face overwhelmed with emotion, tears streaming down her cheeks as she reached him.

"Brutus! By the ancestors, you're alive!" she sobbed.

XLIII. HOMECOMING

Brutus was thunderstruck. He hadn't expected to see her here. He opened his mouth to say something, but before a word could escape, she swung her hand and slapped him soundly across the face, the crack echoing over the camp noise.

"You damned, stubborn good-for-nothing!" she yelled at him through tears, her voice trembling with a mixture of anger and relief. "Not a word! Not a single message since we saw each other in Camulodunum! Months! I thought… I thought you were dead! I thought I'd never see you again! How could you?!"

Brutus, completely perplexed by the slap and the emotional outburst, dazedly rubbed his cheek. Maximus beside him struggled to suppress a laugh, as did several nearby legionaries watching the scene with amusement and curiosity.

But Anwen's anger seemed to vanish as quickly as it had come. The next moment, she threw her arms around his neck, hugging him so fiercely that he staggered despite his size. She pressed her face against his chest, her shoulders shaking with suppressed sobs. "I was so scared for you," she whispered, her voice muffled now.

Brutus, still somewhat stunned but his heart pounding wildly, awkwardly put his good arm around her, holding her tight. The familiar scent of herbs, of *her*, filled his senses, driving away the stench of death and battle. He closed his eyes, a feeling of peace and unexpected happiness washing over him, so strong it almost hurt. "Anwen…" he murmured, finding no other words.

She pulled back slightly, looking up at him, tears still glistening in her blue eyes, but now an unmistakable sparkle danced within them. Without another word, she stood on tiptoe, pulled his head down, and kissed him. It wasn't a gentle kiss like the one at the gate before. It was passionate, demanding, full of pent-up longing, fear, and relief. Brutus returned the kiss, forgetting for a moment his wound, the fatigue, the war, everything around him. There was only her, here and now.

When they finally broke apart, both panting, flushed, they heard the amused whistles and cheers of the surrounding legionaries.

"Well, Centurion," Maximus called out with a broad grin, "looks like someone finally learned how to greet a woman! And here I thought your heart was as rusted as your old breastplate!"

Brutus shot Maximus a withering look, but a deep blush rose on his face. Anwen laughed softly, wiping tears from her eyes. "He just needs the right motivation, Tribune." She patted Brutus's cheek.

"I... I must get back," she said, her voice growing serious again as her gaze fell on the many wounded being carried towards the hospital tent. "My patients need me." She looked deeply into Brutus's eyes. "Rest. We'll see each other tomorrow. We have... much to discuss."

"Yes," Brutus said, his voice still rough. "We do."

With one last, long look, Anwen released him and hurried towards the hospital tent, a determined figure amidst the military bustle.

Brutus watched her until she disappeared. A strange, unfamiliar feeling filled him—a mixture of pain, exhaustion, but also a deep, unexpected joy and hope.

"Well, old friend," Maximus said quietly, clapping him on the good shoulder. "Looks like the army isn't your only love

XLIII. HOMECOMING

after all."

Brutus slowly turned, a thoughtful smile on his lips. "Perhaps not." He looked at Maximus, the old camaraderie restored, stronger than before. "We've been through a lot, Maximus. Too much."

"Yes," Maximus agreed. "But we survived. And we won."

"For the moment," Brutus added. "Caratacus is still out there. And Flaccus."

"I know," Maximus said seriously. "The war isn't over. But today… today we won. And you…" He grinned again, "… apparently won too."

Brutus playfully shoved him in the chest. "Shut up, Tribune." But he was smiling. They stood silently for a moment, watching the last soldiers of the rearguard march into camp. The battle was over; the return complete. It was a new beginning—uncertain, dangerous, but also full of new possibilities, both on the battlefield and perhaps… in the heart. For the first time in a long while, Brutus felt something like hope stirring within him.

XLIV. The Shadows of the Past

The morning after the return to Rutupiae was filled with busy, orderly activity, a stark contrast to the chaos of battle and the tension of the siege. The sun shone more clearly, as if the victory over Caratacus had driven away the clouds. The air was fresh, smelling of the sea and the smoke from cook fires where soldiers prepared a hearty breakfast, their relief palpable. It was a sense of respite before the wheels of war inevitably turned again.

Maximus and Brutus sat with several officers of the Second Augusta at an improvised table near the *praetorium*, enjoying a simple meal of warm bread, cheese, and thin wine. Brutus ate with a good appetite, his mood better than before, though he still held his left arm carefully in its sling. The encounter with Anwen the previous evening had clearly revived his spirits. Maximus was quieter, more thoughtful. Relief over the victory was present, yet the events of the past weeks still echoed within him: the betrayal, the captivity, the brutal battle. Furthermore, the secret of his origins, painfully brought back to consciousness by Sabinus's words, weighed on him.

"Slept well, Tribune?" Brutus asked with a slight grin, pulling Maximus from his thoughts.

XLIV. THE SHADOWS OF THE PAST

Maximus managed a faint smile. "I slept like a stone, Brutus, but my dreams were… less sweet." He sighed. "We were lucky. Very lucky."

"Luck and Roman discipline," Brutus corrected him, "and a Legate who was in the right place at the right time." He nodded towards the *praetorium*. "Speaking of the Legate, he has summoned us for a briefing."

They finished their breakfast and went to the *praetorium*. Vespasian, Longinus, the other ranking officers of the Second Augusta, and the commanders of the remaining auxiliary units were already assembled. The mood was serious but imbued with a new confidence.

Vespasian opened the meeting without preamble. "Gentlemen, we have won a great victory. Caratacus's main army is shattered; he himself is fleeing. Sabinus and the Fourteenth, reinforced by the Atrebates, are in pursuit. Rutupiae is secure." He looked around the room. "But the war is not over, and we have paid a high price."

A sober assessment followed. The field hospitals were overflowing. The wounded—both from the Second Augusta's fight for Rutupiae and those of the Fourteenth brought back by Vespasian—needed care. Resources were stretched to the limit.

"We urgently need more *medici* and more dressing materials," the chief *medicus* reported. "I suggest we expand the hospital and utilize the empty storage buildings by the harbor."

"Approved," Vespasian said. "Organize it immediately."

Next, the fortifications were discussed. "The walls held, but they are heavily damaged, especially to the west and north," reported Longinus. "The palisades need extensive repairs, the ramparts reinforcing, and the west gate... it's only crudely barricaded."

"Repair and further strengthening of the fortifications have top priority," Vespasian decided. "We don't know if Caratacus will return or if other tribes will seize the opportunity to attack us. Rutupiae must remain impregnable." He assigned cohorts and centuries to the work.

Then the issue of troop strength arose. "We have suffered heavy losses, both legions," Vespasian said gravely. "We urgently need replacements. I requested recruits from Gaul and other provinces weeks ago. With luck, the first will arrive before winter makes sea travel impossible."

"And the outposts, Legate?" Brutus asked. "Many were abandoned when Caratacus's army approached. They must be reoccupied to secure supply lines and the surrounding territory."

"Correct, Centurion," Vespasian agreed. "As soon as things are somewhat orderly here in Rutupiae and the first reinforcements arrive, we will gradually reoccupy the posts. But caution is necessary. The land is still hostile."

The meeting continued for some time, clarifying logistical details, issuing orders. Finally, when most points were covered, Vespasian said, "That will be all for now, gentlemen. To your duties." The officers saluted and left the tent. "Centurion Brutus, Tribune Maximus—stay a moment longer, please."

When they were alone, Vespasian's expression grew more serious. He motioned for them to sit. "We need to discuss Flaccus."

Brutus's face immediately darkened. "The traitor. What happens to him?"

XLIV. THE SHADOWS OF THE PAST

"That is the question," Vespasian said thoughtfully. "Your report, Brutus, about his retreat and betrayal during the attack, is… troubling. Very troubling. But," he sighed, "we have no proof. Only your word and the disappearance of a man already considered… difficult."

"Difficult? He betrayed us, Legate!" Brutus burst out, his voice trembling with suppressed rage. "He led us into a trap! Decimus and dozens of other men died because of him!"

"I believe you, Brutus," Vespasian said calmly but firmly. "Every word. But belief is no basis for an indictment in Rome, especially not against a man from Flaccus's family. We need proof. Conclusive proof. And complicating matters further, he brought King Cogidumnus with three thousand warriors, saving two legions." He looked from Brutus to Maximus. "Therefore, I ask you both for utmost restraint. Do nothing rash. Do not try to hunt him down or bring him to account yourselves. That would only harm you, ruin your careers, perhaps even cost you your lives. Flaccus has powerful friends in Rome."

"So we are simply to… do nothing?" Brutus asked incredulously.

"No," Vespasian said. "We wait. We observe. We gather information. Men like Flaccus make mistakes. Sooner or later, he will make a mistake that exposes him. And then, Brutus, then we strike. But until then: patience. And caution." He looked intently at Brutus. "I know this is hard for you. But I ask it of you. For your own sake. I sent both of them with Sabinus so he could keep an eye on them, and so you wouldn't do anything foolish with them here."

Brutus pressed his lips together, his jaw working. He wrestled visibly with himself. Finally, he nodded reluctantly. "As you command, Legate." But his eyes burned with suppressed anger.

Maximus had remained silent but nodded agreement with Vespasian. An open confrontation with Flaccus without proof would be suicide and drag him into the spotlight in Rome. They had to proceed more cleverly. "And we will be careful," he said quietly.

"Good." Vespasian seemed relieved. "One more thing. You both have endured inhuman hardships these past weeks. The fighting, the captivity, the battles. You urgently need rest." He glanced at Brutus's splinted arm. "Brutus, you are unfit for duty anyway. And Maximus, even if you won't admit it, you are at the end of your strength." He smiled paternally. "I hereby officially order you both one month's leave. Recover. Tend your wounds. Forget the war for a while, as best you can."

Brutus and Maximus looked at each other, surprised. Leave? In the middle of a campaign?

"But Legate…" Brutus began.

"No arguments, Centurion," Vespasian said firmly. "That is an order. Longinus will temporarily assume your duties. And Tribune Marcellus can handle Maximus's administrative tasks here. You both have earned it. And I need you rested and ready for what is yet to come."

They had to accept. Perhaps it wasn't such a bad idea, Maximus thought. A break from the constant tension, the bloodshed. Time to think, to heal.

"Thank you, Legate," Maximus said.

"Go now," Vespasian said. "Enjoy the quiet." He hesitated a moment. "Brutus, you may go. Maximus, stay a moment longer, please. There is something else I must discuss with

XLIV. THE SHADOWS OF THE PAST

you in private."

Surprised and curious, Brutus looked from Vespasian to Maximus. Then he shrugged, exchanged a military salute, and left the *praetorium*. The door closed behind him.

Maximus now faced Vespasian alone. The Legate indicated he should sit again. He himself remained standing, pacing slowly back and forth, hands clasped behind his back.

"Maximus," he began after a moment of silence, his voice quieter now, more personal. "This matter with Flaccus... it is more complicated than it seems."

Maximus waited tensely.

"His sudden disappearance, his connection to Adminius... that is suspicious, yes," Vespasian continued. "But I wonder if there aren't deeper reasons. Reasons that perhaps have to do with you."

Maximus felt his blood run cold. He tried to keep his expression neutral. "With me, Legate? I don't understand."

Vespasian stopped before him, his gaze direct and penetrating. "I have already told you I knew your grandfather. And your father." He paused. "He was more than just a comrade to me, Maximus. He was a friend. A true friend. He saved my life once, in Germania, risking his own." Vespasian's voice was low, filled with a deep emotion Maximus had never witnessed in him before.

"I swore to him then that I would watch over his family should anything happen to him. Especially over... over you. Over the grandson of Tiberius."

The words were spoken. Openly. Directly. No more hiding. Maximus sat as if turned to stone, unable to speak, unable to move.

"You know that I know your origins, Maximus," Vespasian

continued. "Have known for a long time. Your father confided in me shortly before his death, under the seal of strictest secrecy. He wanted to protect you, allow you a normal life, far from the intrigues and dangers of the imperial court." Vespasian sighed. "A wish I have respected. Until now."

"What... what does this mean, Legate?" Maximus asked hoarsely.

"It means your very existence poses a danger," Vespasian said gravely. "To yourself. To me. And potentially to the stability of Rome. There are men in Rome, powerful men like Narcissus, who tolerate no rivals, no uncontrollable variables with imperial blood." He stepped closer. "I wonder if Flaccus learned of your origins. If Narcissus informed him. If his betrayal, his attempt to eliminate you, was part of a larger, sinister plan directed straight from Rome."

Maximus was stunned. The intrigue was even more far-reaching, more dangerous, than he had suspected.

"What... what are your plans, Maximus?" Vespasian asked after a while, his gaze searching. "What do you intend to do? Do you wish to use your heritage? Do you wish to grasp for the power that might be yours by right?"

Maximus shook his head vehemently. "No, Legate! Never!" His voice was firm, convinced. "I do not want to rule. I want to serve. I am a soldier and son of Rome, just as my father was, just as you are. My loyalty lies with the legion, my men, my friends." He thought of Brutus. "My heritage... it is a curse, not a blessing. I want nothing to do with it."

Vespasian studied him for a long moment, then nodded slowly. "That is what I hoped." A hint of relief was in his voice. "It is probably better this way, for all concerned." He placed a hand on Maximus's shoulder. "Then let us hope Flaccus's betrayal had other causes, that Narcissus suspects nothing yet, and that your secret remains safe." He squeezed Maximus's shoulder. "I swore to your father I would protect you. I will do so. But you must be careful, Maximus. Very careful. Trust no one lightly."

"I understand, Legate," Maximus said. The burden on his shoulders hadn't lightened, but it had changed. It was no longer just the burden of war, but also the burden of his past, his blood.

"Good," Vespasian said, stepping back, his expression professional again. "Go now. Use your leave. Recover. But stay alert."

Maximus saluted, the gesture feeling strangely significant. He left the *praetorium*, stepping out into the bustling camp. The world had irrevocably changed in the last few minutes. He was still Maximus, Tribune of the Second Augusta. But he was also the grandson of Tiberius. A shadow of the past facing an uncertain future.

XLV. Brothers in Spirit

Some days later, an exhausted normality returned to Rutupiae. Repair work on the walls progressed steadily, the wounded received care, and the constant threat from Caratacus seemed, for the moment, banished. Vespasian organized supply lines with his usual efficiency. Sabinus, with the heavily damaged Fourteenth Legion and the Atrebates, took up the pursuit, though the outcome remained uncertain.

For Maximus and Brutus, an unaccustomed period of quiet began—their "leave" ordered by Vespasian. Brutus's shoulder healed well, though his arm still rested in a sling. Maximus's headaches subsided, and physical exhaustion slowly gave way to a deep mental weariness. The conversation with Vespasian about his heritage still echoed within him, a constant, unsettling melody beneath the surface of his thoughts.

That evening, they left the confines of the camp for a few hours. Near the harbor was a simple tavern frequented mainly by sailors, merchants, and less disciplined auxiliary soldiers. Officers of rank did not patronize it, which was precisely its appeal to them: for a short time, they could cease being Tribune and Centurion and simply be Maximus and Brutus.

XLV. BROTHERS IN SPIRIT

Two soldiers who had cheated death, now trying to exorcize the ghosts of battle with cheap wine.

They found a secluded table in a dark corner of the smoke-filled tavern. The noise from the other patrons—loud laughter, dice games, drunken singing in various languages—shielded their conversation. A surly innkeeper brought them a pitcher of harsh red wine, likely from Gaul, tasting of resin but strong and serving its purpose.

They drank the first cup in silence, reviewing the events of the past days and weeks. The battle on the hill, the betrayal, the captivity, the sacrifice, Caratacus's intervention, Bran's help, the escape, the warning, the victory—it felt like a fever dream, an ordeal for body and soul.

"We were damned lucky, Maximus," Brutus finally said quietly, his gaze drifting over the simple clay cup in his hand. "More luck than we deserved."

"Luck and courage," Maximus replied. "Our men… Decimus… they were heroes."

"Aye," Brutus said, his voice rough. "Heroes. And now they're dead." He took a deep drink. "Because of Flaccus. Because of that treacherous patrician worm." His grip tightened on the cup. "I still don't understand it, Maximus. Why? What was his motive? Why lure us into that trap? What did he gain from seeing us die?" The question clearly tormented him; the thought of senseless betrayal was incomprehensible to the straightforward Centurion.

Maximus felt his stomach clench. He knew, or at least suspected, the answer: his heritage, the fear of a potential rival, the intrigues of Narcissus and men like Flaccus in Rome. Should he tell Brutus? Should he draw his friend into this dangerous secret, expose him to the same danger that now hovered over Maximus himself?

He looked at Brutus, saw the honest confusion and anger in his eyes. Brutus deserved the truth. He had risked his life for him, more than once. Their friendship was built on trust, shared experience. A lie, a concealment of this magnitude, would poison that bond.

Events flashed before his mind's eye: their first meeting, the mistrust, the practice bout, the growing respect, the march through Britannia, the battles side-by-side on the Medway and at Camulodunum, the captivity, the shared fear, the shared hope, the moment on the sacrificial altar when Brutus was ready to die. Brutus was more than just his Centurion; he was his brother in spirit, his moral anchor in this vortex of war and intrigue.

"Brutus, I…" Maximus began hesitantly, wrestling with himself. Dare he do it? Share the burden, but also the danger?

"What is it, Maximus?" Brutus's gaze sharpened; he sensed his friend's inner conflict. "You know something, don't you? Something about Flaccus, about this whole betrayal."

Maximus took a deep breath. He opened his mouth to speak, to utter the truth that would change his life, and Brutus's, forever. But then he paused. He saw the weariness in Brutus's face, the still-unhealed wound on his shoulder, the burden he already carried. Could he really impose this on him? The additional danger? The knowledge that powerful men in Rome saw him, Maximus, and anyone close to him, as a threat? Was it fair to drag Brutus into this whirlpool of imperial politics and potential persecution?

No, he decided at that moment. *Not now. Not while the danger is so great. I must protect him. I cannot drag him into this.* It was a painful decision, another lie by omission, but he

XLV. BROTHERS IN SPIRIT

made it out of friendship, out of concern for Brutus.

He slowly shook his head. "No, Brutus. I don't know any more than you do. Flaccus is an ambitious bastard; we both know that. Maybe he had personal reasons. Maybe someone in Rome promised him something. Maybe he was just a coward trying to save his own skin." He shrugged, trying to sound indifferent. "We can't know right now. And Vespasian is right: we must be careful, wait."

Brutus studied him for a long moment, his gaze probing. He seemed to sense Maximus wasn't telling the whole truth, but he didn't press further, respecting his friend's decision even if he didn't understand it. He sighed. "You're probably right. Wait and drink wine." He raised his cup. "To waiting. And to the damned gods, who hopefully stand by us."

Maximus raised his cup as well. "To waiting," he echoed softly. They drank. The wine was rough, but it warmed them from within.

They sat in silence for a while, listening to the tavern's noise, lost in their own thoughts. Then Brutus seemed to collect himself.

"So," he said with a slight grin. "Leave. What does a highborn officer like yourself do with a month of unexpected free time in this Britannic paradise?"

Maximus laughed. "Good question. Probably try not to get washed away by the rain or die of boredom."

"Boredom? Never!" Brutus leaned forward conspiratorially. "I have a plan. We could go fishing. They say there are big fish in the river. A quiet day by the water would do us good."

Maximus grimaced. "Fishing? Brutus, by Neptune's beard, that sounds even more boring than standing guard!"

"Nonsense!" Brutus protested, laughing. "Fishing is an art!

It requires patience, skill, concentration! Just the thing for a hothead like you!"

"I don't know," Maximus said doubtfully. "I was thinking of something more... active." A mischievous glint entered his eyes. "Perhaps a bear hunt? I hear the woods here are full of large, shaggy specimens." He winked pointedly at Brutus, a clear allusion to the hunt where Brutus had been attacked and nearly killed by a bear.

Brutus stared at him incredulously at first, then burst into loud laughter, drawing the attention of some other patrons. "You impudent pup!" he sputtered, clutching his aching shoulder. "Dare you remind me of that? By Jupiter, next time I'll let the beast eat you!" Brutus wiped a tear of laughter from his eye. "No, Maximus. No bear hunt. Definitely not." He took another deep drink of wine, his expression turning slightly more serious, though a warm sparkle remained. "I was thinking... well, since we have this unexpected time..."

"Yes?" Maximus asked curiously.

"I thought I might try to see Anwen more often," Brutus said, a hint of embarrassment in his voice, unusual for the hardened Centurion. "She... she works tirelessly in the hospital, caring for the wounded. But maybe she has a few hours free in the evening? Just to... talk."

Maximus grinned broadly. "Talk, Brutus? Is that all you can think of? After the kiss she gave you at the gate?"

Brutus blushed even deeper but just nudged Maximus good-naturedly in the shoulder. "Shut up, Tribune! It's complicated." He sighed. "She's a Celt. I'm a Roman. What could come of it? But..." He hesitated. "...I want to find out. I want to spend time with her. As much as possible."

"I think that's good, Brutus," Maximus said seriously, setting

XLV. BROTHERS IN SPIRIT

aside the joking. "Very good, in fact. She's a remarkable woman. And you deserve some peace and… normality."

"Normality," Brutus repeated, laughing softly. "What's normal in this war? But yes, maybe you're right." His gaze turned slightly mischievous again. "And you know what? Anwen has a friend here in camp. Also, a Celt, an Iceni. Nice woman, from what I can tell. Her name is Boudicca." He winked at Maximus. "Maybe the four of us could do something together? Dinner, perhaps? So you won't be so lonely while I'm… talking?"

Maximus understood the implication immediately, feeling warmth rise in his face despite his fatigue. "Are you trying to set me up, Centurion?"

"Who, me? Never!" Brutus replied with feigned innocence. "I just thought it might be time for our esteemed Tribune to… knock the dust off his equipment, if you know what I mean." He grinned broadly. "Or would you rather go fishing with me again?"

Maximus laughed out loud, shaking his head. "By all the gods, Brutus, you're impossible!" But the offer, the camaraderie, the awkward but well-intentioned concern from his friend felt good. "Alright," he finally said. "I have no objection to dinner together. But don't expect miracles."

"Miracles happen, Maximus," Brutus said, his gaze turning serious again for a moment as he thought of their rescue. "Sometimes you just have to believe."

They raised their cups again: to leave, to friendship, to women. The uncertain future lay before them.

They continued drinking, joking, telling old stories. For a few precious hours, they forgot the war, the betrayal, and the shadows of the past. At that moment, they were simply

Maximus and Brutus, two friends in the shadow of the eagle, under the sheltering roof of a loud, shabby tavern at the edge of the world.

About the Author

Marc Beuster was born in Northern Germany in 1981, where he still lives today. History has fascinated him since early childhood, particularly the captivating era of ancient Rome. This passion led to his first historical novel, "In the Shadow of the Eagle" – which is also the start of the planned "Eagle Saga — The Sons of Rome".

Marc loves animals, especially dogs and cats, and enjoys spending time in the nature of his North German homeland, together with his wife. As an author, he aims to tell authentic stories that combine historical events with compelling adventures. He places particular value on richly detailed narratives without getting lost in them.

For him, writing is a personal journey, one where he seeks to grow with each book. He looks forward to immersing his readers in the fascinating world of his stories.

Also by Marc Beuster

The Eagle Saga — Sons of Rome

THE SHADOW OF THE EAGLE
Britain, 43 AD: On the wild coast, the mighty legions of Rome make landfall. For the ambitious young Tribune Gaius Julius Maximus, this marks the greatest challenge of his life. Alongside the experienced and relentless Centurion Brutus, he leads his men into unfamiliar territory, ready to fight for glory and honor.

Opposing them stands Caratacus. A charismatic warrior and cunning strategist, he seeks to protect his people from the overwhelming Roman might. A merciless battle ignites where discipline clashes with ferocity, and iron determination meets a boundless will for freedom.

Who will Mars ultimately bless? Who stands in the shadow of the Eagle?

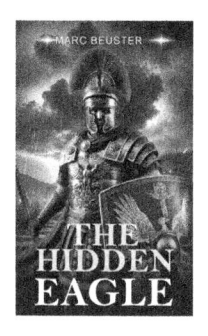

THE HIDDEN EAGLE

Britannia, 43 AD: The Roman eagle has landed, but Britannia remains untamed. The war rages on.

Tribune Maximus and Centurion Brutus struggle to secure the newly conquered territory, battling not only the fierce resistance led by the charismatic Caratacus but also a danger closer to home. For the greatest threat lies within their own ranks.

Sent deep into hostile lands on a treacherous mission, Maximus finds himself surrounded by soldiers of questionable loyalty. When betrayal springs its trap, mere survival becomes a brutal fight against overwhelming odds. And the Britons are gathering for a final, devastating blow—one that could shatter Rome's ambitions in Britannia forever…

Honor is tested, loyalty questioned, and survival uncertain in this dark, thrilling continuation of the Eagle Saga

Printed in Dunstable, United Kingdom